The Time Falling Bodies Take to Light

The Time Falling Bodies Take to Light

MYTHOLOGY, SEXUALITY,
AND THE ORIGINS
OF CULTURE

William Irwin Thompson

St. Martin's Press · New York

Library of Congress Cataloging in Publication Data

Thompson, William Irwin.
  The time falling bodies take to light.

  1. Civilization—Philosophy. 2. Culture—Origin.
3. Myth. 4. Sex and history. I. Title.
CB19.T53   901   80-25467
ISBN 0-312-80512-8

Design by Joyce Cameron Weston

This volume is part of a series
of books to be published by
St. Martin's Press, for the Lindisfarne
Association.

A Lindisfarne
Series Book

Grateful acknowledgment is hereby made to the following publishers for use of material under copyright:

For Figure II from Erich Neumann's *The Great Mother: An Analysis of an Archetype*, trans. Ralph Mannheim, Bollingen Series XLVII, copyright 1955 by Princeton University Press. To Fratelli Alinari, I.D.E.A. S.p.A., Firenze, Italia, for the photograph of Gianlorenzo Bernini's statue, *St. Teresa in Ecstasy*. To Janet and Colin Bord, Pwys, Wales, for the photograph of Bryn-Celli-Ddu. To E. P. Dutton for lines from *The Teachings of Rumi*, trans. E. H. Whinfield, copyright MCMLXXIII by the Octagon Press Ltd, reprinted by permission of the publisher, E. P. Dutton. For eight lines from "Two Songs from a Play," and six lines from "Fragments" by William Butler Yeats, copyright 1933 by Macmillan Publishing Co., Inc., renewed 1961 by Bertha Georgie Yeats. To Yale University Press for material from Thorkild Jacobsen's *Treasures of Darkness: A History of Mesopotamian Religion*, copyright, Yale University Press, 1976. To the University of Chicago Press for material from Samuel Noah Kramer's *The Sumerians: Their History, Character, and Culture*, copyright 1963; and to Samuel Noah Kramer and the American Philosophical Society for material published in the *Proceedings of the American Philosophical Society*. To the University of Chicago Press for material from *The Gilgamesh Epic*, trans. A. Heidel, copyright 1963; and for material from Henri Frankfort's *Kingship and the Gods*, copyright 1948 and 1978. To Harry N. Abrams, Inc., for material from Andre Leroi-Gourhan's *Treasures of Prehistoric Art*, copyright 1967; and for material from Eberhard Otto's *Ancient Egyptian Art: The Cults of Isis and Osiris*, copyright 1967. To Thames and Hudson for the figure of the West Kennet Long Barrow as the squatting Harvest Goddess from Michael Dames, *The Avebury Cycle*, copyright 1977. To Editions D'Art, Lucien Mazenod, Paris for the photographs of the Venus of Laussel, Two Bison from Lascaux, and the Scene from the Pit at Lascaux. To Thames and Hudson for material from Marija Gimbutas's *The Gods and Goddesses of Old Europe*, copyright 1974; and for material from Dragoslav Srejovic's *Europe's First Monumental Sculptures: New Discoveries at Lepenski Vir*, copyright 1972; and for material from Rundle Clark's *Myth and Symbol in Ancient Egypt*, copyright 1959; and for material from James Mellaart's *Catal Hüyük*, copyright 1967. To Harvard University Press for material from E. O. Wilson's *Sociobiology*, copyright 1975; and for material from Sarah Blaffer-Hrdy's *The Langurs of Abu*, copyright 1977; and for material from Kathleen Freeman's *Ancilla to the Presocratics*, copyright 1962. To Alexander Marshack for material from his *Roots of Civilization*, copyright 1972. To Houghton Mifflin Company for material from Jane Van Lawick-Goodall's *In the Shadow of Man*, copyright 1971.

CONTENTS

PART ONE

The Myth Before History

The Time Light Bodies
Took to Fall

Take a photograph of a reflection in a mirror and think of that piece of film, which will in turn reflect an image to the curving surfaces of the eye and the folding surfaces of the brain. Study the events of history as Thucydides did, and the work itself becomes an event of history. Study mythology, and the work itself becomes a piece of mythology, a story in which old gods wear new clothes but live as they did before the fashions became tight and constricting to their ancient, natural movements.

The scientist tries to examine the "real" nature of the photograph; he tries to get away from the psychological configuration, the meaning of the image, to move down to some other, more basic level of patterns of alternating dots of light and dark, a world of elementary particles. And yet what does he find there but another mental configuration, another arrangement of psychological meaning? If he persists in this direction long enough, the mythological dimensions of science will become apparent in his work, as they would have if he had asked himself questions about the meaning of sunlight rather than questions about the behavior of photons.

Science wrought to its uttermost becomes myth. History wrought to its uttermost becomes myth. But what is myth that it returns to mind even when we would most escape it?

Forms of knowledge change as society changes. Sometimes these changes are small and incremental; at other times the changes are transformations of the *structures* of knowledge and not merely the *contents*. From religion to philosophy, from alchemy to chemistry, from legend to history, the social organization of knowledge changes as a new elite comes in to challenge the old authorities. But this movement is not simply a linear and one-

3

directional shift toward increasing rationalization and demystification; when the rational historian has come in to take away authority from the mystical and tribal bard, the artist has returned to create new forms of expression to resacralize, re-enchant, remythologize.

Now that there is very little time left for the twentieth century, a new age seems to have come upon us. The sociologist, Max Weber, characterized the modern period as one of disenchantment; the theologian, Rudolph Bultmann, spoke of demythologizing Christianity; but the artist has taken on his ancient prophetic role to cast spells and share visions. The novels of Doris Lessing have become something more than traditional fiction, prophesy in an extraterrestrial school of theology. The concerts of Karlheinz Stockhausen are no longer exhibitions of an avant-garde school of electronic music; they have become literally oratorios, forms of prayer and moments stolen from the rituals of Sirius.[1]*

As fiction and music are coming close to reorganizing knowledge, scholarship is becoming closer to art. Our culture is changing, and so the genres of literature and history are changing as well. In an agricultural-warrior society, the genre is the epic, an *Iliad*. In an industrial-bourgeois society, the genre is the novel, a *Moll Flanders*. In our electronic, cybernetic society, the genre is *Wissenkunst:* the play of knowledge in a world of serious data-processors. The scholarly fictions of Jorgé Luis Borges, or the reviews of nonexistent books by Stanislaw Lem, are examples of new art forms of a society in which humanity lives, not innocently in nature nor confidently in cities, but apocalyptically in a civilization cracking up to the universe. At such a moment as this the novelist becomes a prophet, the composer a magician, and the historian a bard, a voice recalling ancient identities.

And so I shall begin by recalling that most ancient of all visions of history, one of cycles that, as set out in Vico's *New Science,* is really a fossil from ancient Egypt:

> Two great remnants of Egyptian antiquity have come down to us. One of them is that the Egyptians reduced all preceding world time to three ages; namely, the age of gods, the age of heroes, and the age of men. The other is that during these three ages three languages had been spoken, corresponding in order to the three

*Superior numbers refer to the notes that begin on page 255.

aforesaid ages; namely, the hieroglyphic or sacred language, the symbolic or figurative (which is the heroic) language, and the epistolary or vulgar language of men employing conventional signs for communicating the common needs of their life.[2]

To these three ages Vico added a fourth, the age of chaos, a transitional age in which the line became a spiral and history turned, *corso, ricorso,* up and around to a new age of gods. We moderns are now living in the age of chaos. Our understanding of myth is quite degenerate, but the revelations of the new age of gods have already begun, and our appreciation of myth is deepening. If we set out the four ages in a table, we can see that there are four ways of knowing, four definitions of myth.

THE FOUR LEVELS OF MEANING FOR MYTH

I. The Age of Chaos — Myth is a false statement, an opinion popularly held, but one known by scientists and other experts to be incorrect. An example of this usage would be a statement like, "The notion that the Shah fled Iran with two billion dollars is a myth."

II. The Age of Men — Myth is an imaginative narrative, which, though literally untrue, nevertheless expresses an emotional truth. This level of myth could be associated with Romanticism. Here the culture is no longer religious, but it seeks to hold on to the old sense of the sacred through art. The poetry of Keats expresses the longing for myth as an image of unity in an industrial culture which is, nevertheless, broken and divided against itself.

III. The Age of Heroes — Myth is an answer to the three questions: What are we? Where do we come from? Where are we going? Here myth is a macrohistory giving humanity an answer to the basic riddle of the meaning of existence. Specialized forms of knowledge are not mythic, but if a philosopher or even a scientist attempts to answer these three questions, then the organization of his data into a narrative falls into mythic form. In this sense, Darwinian biology or E. O. Wilson's sociobiology are myths. But to be exact, one should call these pseudomyths, since they are not so much identical to myth in essence and nature, as isomorphic in function. Homer, Dante, Milton, Darwin, Marx, and Freud operate at this level of a heroic attempt to answer the great questions of life.

IV. The Age of Gods

Myth at the level of understanding of the Age of Heroes is symbolic or figurative, but the world is still divided. Level IV is the unitive state of the great mystics; it is a state of being, analogous to music, in which myth is not simply a description, but a performance of the very reality it seeks to describe. Here history becomes the performance of myth, for the experience of recalling *(anamnesis)* enlightens the individual to see that myth is the history of the soul. The ego is locked into a narrow time frame (Plato's cave), and so experiences from the other dimensions of the soul are recast into the forms and imagery of the ordinary world, but in the experience of illumination the ego realizes that the narratives that seem to be saying one thing are saying much more.

In these parables and *koans* of spiritual enlightenment, there are certain root structures or archetypes of order that derive from principles of cosmic order. These principles are not so much *symbols* of being as they are crystalline seeds, or programs, for the unfolding of being. At this level, we have moved beyond the symbolic or figurative level of consciousness to the hieroglyphic. The hieroglyphs are really the nonverbal forms of the languages of gods or angels (the Celestial Intelligences of the Iranian Sufi tradition), for the bottom levels of angelic intelligence overlap with the highest levels of the human. Thus an initiate like Plato can think in the hieroglyphic language of archetypes when he is in an exalted state of consciousness. These hieroglyphic forms and figures of geometry correspond to Plato's world of Forms. There are times, however, when the ordinary individual, whether in dream or work of art, can unconsciously express himself in

archetypal imagery. The uninitiated cannot
remember, and therefore the dimensions of
the soul are reflected down into time in the
imagery of this world. Most mystical schools
of education, whether Quabbalah, Sufi, Yoga,
Zen, or Christian Theosophy, seek to help the
individual move beyond dream or symbolism
through meditation, for in meditation the
individual can move out of ordinary mind to
think in the hieroglyphic modes of gods and
angels.

Because our culture is in a transitional stage there now exists a
great polarization between the mystics and the mechanists. One
section of the culture is caught up in visions of total control, in
space colonies and genetic engineering; the other is caught up in
the spiritual visions of a Doris Lessing, a Karlheinz Stockhausen, a
David Spangler.[3] The age of chaos and the new age of gods
overlap; the artists of our era are not so much describing the
world as creating a new one.

We are all on edge. Human beings feel safe and secure when
they can stand confidently in the center of things, either in the
center of an age or in the center of a class of people with a
common world-view, but when they come to an edge, they feel
nervous and unsettled. There at the edge we see familiar things
end and something else begin, something which makes us try to
recall another state of being. We rummage about in our minds in
search of a feeling that was there before the first fact was
deposited. But searching for facts won't help, for it is not so much
a matter of what we think, but what thinks us. In the interval
between each thought, in the interval between each heartbeat, in
the place where there is no breath, we recall what we always knew.
The world of time-space is recognized to be a projection. Science,
history, or art were always exciting dramas of our own creation
that became just crazy enough at the end to make us laugh and
realize that we were dreaming.

Anything can deliver us from our loss of memory of the soul:
science, history, art, or the sunlight on the grass *taitami* mats in the
Zendo. And anything can enslave us: science, history, art, or the
militarism of a Zen monastery. But if we are lost in time and
suffering from a racial amnesia, then we need something to startle

us into recollection. If history is the sentence of our imprisonment, then history, recoded, can become the password of our release.

Historical scholarship is an image of the movement of events, a photograph of a reflection on a pond. The blue of the sky is reflected on the surface of the pond, but the blue is not a place but a relationship between the light of the sun and the atmosphere of the earth; thus, the surface of the pond becomes another little atmosphere suspended between the mud and the air. The blueness of the sky is a relationship between two different worlds; similarly, history is a relationship between the infinity of consciousness and the ground of a society's local identity. To read a work of history should, therefore, become a lifting of one's eyes to the horizon.

II

EDGES ARE IMPORTANT because they define a limitation in order to deliver us from it. When we come to an edge we come to a frontier that tells us that we are now about to become more than we have been before. As long as one operates in the middle of things, one can never really know the nature of the medium in which one moves. Like a mind moving on a Möbius strip of events, one's consciousness goes over the same territory again and again without ever becoming aware of the nature of awareness. In universities historians are taught to stay away from edges, to deal only with things that can be quantified, measured, and verified by other researchers. As these trained historians go round and round on the Möbius strip of specialized research, their sense of adequacy grows until it knows no bounds.

The professional way to begin a study of the origins of human culture is to begin at the beginning with a discussion of hominization. But as one discovers unconscious mythologies expressed in the narratives of human evolution and Kipling-like *Just-So Stories* hiding in the explanations of sociobiology, the conviction grows that it would be better to deal with human origins less mythologically by dealing with the myths of human origins.

The edge of history is myth. If we study myth in a scientific way, we miss the experience of moving into a mythopoeic mode of consciousness. A line of events has a beginning and an end, but the matrix out of which events arise does not appear to be an event at all.

> Humpty Dumpty sat on a wall,
> Humpty Dumpty had a great fall,
> And all the King's horses,
> And all the King's men
> Couldn't put Humpty together again.

Humpty Dumpty is the cosmic egg, the wall, the edge between transcendence and existence. As nothing breaks up into the world of things, the movement toward entropy becomes irreversible. Humpty Dumpty is the immortal soul before its Fall into time, and neither God's animals nor His angels can put him back into the world beyond time. The human condition is the fallen condition of time and fragmentation.

The nursery rhyme is a memory of the soul, a piece of an old cosmology from a lost culture lingering on in the rational world of science as a trivial piece of children's verse. When clairvoyants see the aura of light and energy around the human body, they describe it as egg-shaped.[4] The human egg of Humpty Dumpty is an image of ourselves and our complete history, a history that takes us beyond what this society will accept into the world of the immortal soul.

In Vedic cosmology, as well as in the cosmology of the Dogon of West Africa, the universe is an egg that shatters as it expands to begin its career of unfoldment in time. As an archetypal image of primordial unity, the cosmic egg suggests that there is unity and fragmentation, eternity and time. The Fall into time is not so much an event itself as the conditioning of time-space out of which all events arise. The Fall exists prior to the world of events, both logically and temporally, and so it seems as if it must be The Event, the single action which echoes down throughout all ancient mythologies, children's nursery rhymes, and modern stories: the Fall of the One into the many, the emergence of the physical universe out of a transcendent God, the Fall of the soul into time, the entrapment of an angelic soul into the body of Australopithecus afrarensis, or the Fall of an unconditioned consciousness beyond subject and object into the syntax of thought pounded into form by each heartbeat. The Fall is not only once and long ago; it is recapitulated in each instant of consciousness. The unfallen world beyond time remains as a background to the figured beats of the heart in our world of serial progression. Like the white page that surrounds the darkness of each letter you are reading here, eternity surrounds each heartbeat, and as the contemplative watches his breath, he can move out of time through the doorway which opens in the interval between each heartbeat. Each open space is a spiritualization, each beat a materialization; and both are sacred, for in one is the spiritualization of matter; in the other, the materialization of spirit.

As the ground out of which all events arise, the Fall is the archetype that stands over our understanding of time. The Fall of Adam and Eve in the Old Testament, the Fall of Satan in Milton's *Paradise Lost,* the Fall of Tim Finnegan in the Irish folk song and in Joyce's *Finnegan's Wake,* or the more recent expressions of the Fall in the films *Kaspar Hauser* and *The Man Who Fell to Earth* are, from the point of view of the soul outside time, all going on at once, like the voices in a fugue. The soul is, like Humpty Dumpty on the wall, above time, seeing past, present, and future at once. From the point of view of the ego, down in time, everything is linear: the past is behind and the future is up ahead.

The ego is like an actor in a movie set. The director shouts, "Cut!" and the actor walks out of his role to the edge of the set to see the boards holding up the artificial scene. If we zoom up to another level we can see Atilla marching on Rome, Napoleon in Russia, and John Wayne standing off the Indians, all going on at once. The consciousness of time for the ego is *diachronic,* but the consciousness of time for the soul is *synchronic.*[5] When the director, the soul, shouts, "Cut!" the ego stops, either in biological death or in yogic meditation, and the edges of the set are experienced as time is gathered up into a single space of consciousness.

The scholarly equivalent of this spatialization of time is expressed in the structural anthropology of Lévi-Strauss. In his classic essay, "The Structural Study of Myth," Lévi-Strauss argues for a point of view in which all the variants of a myth are brought together in a single imaginary space without a concern for their historical context.

Thus, our method eliminates a problem which has been so far one of the main obstacles to the progress of mythological studies, namely, the quest for the *true* version, or the *earlier* one. On the contrary, we define the myth as consisting of all its versions; to put it otherwise: a myth remains the same as long as it is felt as such. A striking example is offered by the fact that our interpretation may take into account, and is certainly applicable to, the Freudian use of the Oedipus myth. Although the Freudian problem has ceased to be that of autochthony *versus* bisexual reproduction, it is still the problem of understanding how *one* can be born from *two:* how is it that we do not have only one procreator, but a mother plus a father? Therefore, not only Sophocles, but Freud himself, should be included among the recorded versions of the Oedipus myth on a par with earlier or seemingly more "authentic" versions.[6]

The structural anthropologist urges us to ignore the orthodox who labor so patiently trying to eliminate the apocryphal variants from the one true text. The priests of the temple of Solomon worked to construct the canon of Biblical literature, and in this work the dubious folktales of the peasantry were dismissed, but for us a legend or a *midrash* (a folktale variation on Biblical stories) may be a greater opening to the archetypal world than the overly refined redactions of the urban priestly intelligentsia.

Once we are freed from the quest for the one true version of a myth, we are also freed from the concern for determining the exact provenance of the variant. How can one tell where a myth comes from? A *midrash* from the Middle Ages may go back as an oral tradition into the darkness of time.[7] Where do children's rhymes come from? What ancient motif is simply reclothed in a modern story or a children's skip-rope song? Can one really claim that the date of the singing is the date of the song? The poet W. B. Yeats understood the difficulty.

> Where got I that truth?
> Out of a medium's mouth,
> Out of nothing it came,
> Out of the forest loam,
> Out of the dark night where lay
> The crowns of Nineveh.[8]

Libraries have been burnt and whole religious movements wiped out because their beliefs and myths have been considered to be of dubious origin by the upholders of orthodoxy; yet it is sometimes precisely the heretical myth that opens a doorway into the archetypal world. The power of myth is so strong in challenging our racial amnesia that priests respond with exaggerated fury, and the myth is pushed out of religion into fairy tales, children's songs, and the work of heretical artists. To resurrect the body of the myth, we have to wander like Isis piecing together the dismembered remains of Osiris.

> It cannot be too strongly emphasized that all available variants should be taken into account. If Freudian comments on the Oedipus myth are part of the Oedipus myth, then questions such as whether Cushing's version of the Zuni origin myth should be retained or discarded become irrelevant. There is no one true version of which all the others are but copies or distortions. Every version belongs to the myth.[9]

But there are also other reasons why all the versions of a myth must be considered, and these reasons have to do with the applicability of information theory to the study of myth as noted by the anthropologist, Edmund Leach.[10] Every message goes from a Sender to a Receiver through a transmitting medium, but every medium of transmission inevitably distorts the message, and so along the way the signal picks up noise. What the Receiver must get is a mixture of noise and information. If there is only one message, then the Receiver has no way of sorting out the noise from the information; but if the message is sent over and over again in many different ways, then the Receiver can line all the versions up in a single imaginary space, see the common structure, and sift the information from the noise. For a structuralist like Edmund Leach, the structure *is* the meaning. Genesis, for example, is about incest taboos; all the rest is noise and mystification. But one man's noise is another man's information, and so the material that Leach would throw out as merely semantic camouflage for the true deep-structure is of intense interest to me.

Every new school of thought teaches us something and adds a new tool to the scholar's kit, but in the process every new school of thought overgeneralizes its contribution and ends up by trying to shape all information with its peculiar monkey wrench. Whether we are dealing with Marxists, Freudians, Jungians, or Structuralists, we are dealing with scholars who end up by reducing everything to their own schemes. The structuralists throw out the semantic and poetic dimensions of Genesis and reduce the meaning to the structure. Since anthropologists spend decades studying kinship structures and therein translating the sexual lives of "savages" into algebraic notation, it is not surprising that Edmund Leach would look at Genesis and see nothing but a mystification of an incest taboo, where Marx would see nothing but alienation and the division of labor after the Fall, and Jung would see an archetype of the process of individuation and the dawn of consciousness.

Luckily, the problem does not reduce to a matter of either/or, for they are all correct. A myth can reflect light from many facets, so I feel no constraint to join any scholarly sect to analyze myth from only a Marxist, Freudian, Jungian, or Structuralist point of view. Lévi-Strauss claims that all the variants of a myth must be considered; I agree but also feel that all the modern schools of thought are the equivalents of variations of a myth, and all must be taken into account. Graduate students are taught by their professors to accept the one true faith and sneer at other schools of thought, but this sectarianism is simply the reincarnation in secular form of the theological battles of another age. And like the battles fought over baptism by sprinkling as opposed to total immersion, these modern-day disputations can be tedious. I would prefer to avoid the tedium of a foolish consistency and take what is interesting from all of them without committing myself to any of them.

III

BY APPROACHING the familiar from a different angle, we see the shape of the subject change dramatically. I would like to begin our consideration of the Fall by approaching the familiar account in the Old Testament, not through Genesis, but through the *midrash* on Genesis.

> Now, although the canonical books were regarded as written by divine inspiration and the least taint of polytheism had therefore to be exorcized from them, the apocryphal books were treated more

leniently. Many suppressed myths were also allowed to re-emerge in the unquestionably orthodox context of the post-Biblical midrashim. For example in Exodus we read that Pharoah's horses, chariots and horsemen pursued the Children of Israel into the midst of the sea (Exodus XIV.23). According to one midrash (Mekhitla di R. Shimon 51, 54; Mid. Wayosha 52) God assumed the shape of a mare and decoyed the ruttish Egyptian stallions into the water. If the mare-headed Goddess, Demeter had been described as drowning King Pelop's chariotry in the river Alpheus by such a ruse, this would have been acceptable Greek myth; but to the pious reader of the midrash it was no more than a fanciful metaphor of the lengths to which God could go in protecting His Chosen People.[11]

According to the story in the *midrashim,* when God made Adam, He asked the angels to bow down and honor His latest creation. One of the highest archangels, Samael or Satan, refused by saying: "You created us from the splendor of your Glory. Shall we then adore a being formed from dust?"[12] God answered that although Adam had been made from dust he surpassed Samael in wisdom and understanding. Incensed at this slight, Samael insisted that God test him against Adam. God accepted Samael's offer and said that, since He had created beasts, birds, and creeping things, Samael should go down, set them all in line, and name them as He would have them named. If Samael succeeded, God promised that Adam would reverence his wisdom, but if he failed, then Samael must revere Adam's superior understanding.

When the animals passed before Samael, however, he could say nothing. "God then planted understanding in Adam's heart and spoke in such a manner that the first letter of each question pointed to the beast's name." And so Adam was able to take God's hint and name the creature. When Samael saw that God had enlightened Adam, he yelled indignantly.

"Do you yell?" asked God.

"How should I not," replied Samael, "when you have created me from your Glory, and afterwards bestow understanding on a creature formed from dust?" The angel that cannot master language can only yell in vain in the face of God.

In Hebrew, the word "Adam" means from dust. The *midrash,* rather than being an unimportant folktale, actually presents a clearer explanation of the uniqueness of man than does the canonical Bible. Perhaps underground streams from the Cabbala (the Judaic esoteric tradition) flow into this story, for in it God is clearly imparting a letter-magic to Adam. To know the secrets of the Cabbala is to know the signature of all things, to know the forms by which the molecules are strung together and the stars held in space; it is not simply a case of knowing the name of a thing, but of knowing the vibratory signature of a being's very existence. The angels had been created from light; man had been created from matter. Matter, the dust of Adam, is seemingly the thing furthest away from the divine emanation, and yet we are led to conclude from the contest of Adam and Samael that the spiral of time has turned and that matter now contains a mystery close to the heart of God. Matter expresses the finitude of time-space; in this world of limitation a new way of knowing becomes possible, and this way is language. Language is the articulation of the limited to express the unlimited; it is the ultimate mystery which is the image of God, for in breaking up infinity to create finite beings, God has found a way to let the limited being yet be a reflection of His unlimited Being. All beings are words in the language of God; therefore, those who are initiates in the mystery of sacred language, the Cabbala, are initiates in the wisdom and understanding of existence itself.

The world of the angelic hierarchy was an evolutionary stream of light in a steady-state, but the creation of Adam from matter disturbs that primordial steady-state; it generates the creative disequilibrium necessary for change, transformation, and evolution. Nothing is more awe-inspiring than an angel, nothing more seemingly unimpressive than a human being, and yet contained in that handful of dust is the signature for the entire universe of space-time. God is up to something, and not even the proud angels who will defy Him can fathom what will become the ultimate Cabbala, the Logos, the Christos to come. Time, rather than being remote from Divinity, now begins to be a most favored and intimate expression of Godhead. With the creation of Adam, history itself becomes a mystery school for the elect of God.

But the creation of man destroys the old angelic steady-state, and so there is war in heaven. Samael falls, but he takes with him nearly half the heavenly host. Unity is lost and existence becomes more intensely polarized. Now separations become important, and one must choose sides. The whole universe shifts and everything is on the move. What Whitehead has called "the creative advance of the universe through novelty"[13] has begun, and things will never be the same again. The Fall of the angels is thus the prelude to the Fall of man. Since language is what has made man great, Samael determines to seek his revenge by turning man's unique excellence *(areté)* into his tragic flaw *(hammartia)*. It is through language that Samael will seek to tempt God's favored ones.

Other *midrashim* tell of Adam's life in paradise. It seems that for all his superiority in language, Adam was not happy, for he could see that the animals in the Garden lived in pairs and coupled, but he was alone. Adam tried coupling with the beasts of the field but was unsatisfied and cried out: "Every creature but I has a proper mate!" God heard Adam's lament and was moved to create a mate for him. Since God had made Adam from dust, He made Lilith from filth and sediment. When God presented Lilith to Adam, Adam was overjoyed and enthusiastically set her on the ground and tried to mount her after the fashion of the animals; but Lilith protested and said: "Why should I be on the bottom and you on the top?" Priapic Adam was in no mood to explain the natural order of things (from his point of view) and so he simply tried to compel her obedience by force. In a rage, Lilith uttered the magic name of God, rose into the air, and left him.

It would seem that Adam's knowledge of the Cabbala was shared by Lilith and that God imparted to her the same human excellence that had amazed Samael. Samael had tried to dominate Adam and was defeated by language; Adam tried to dominate Lilith, and he was in turn defeated by language. But there are deeper mysteries present here.

The brain at the top of the spinal column gives Adam mastery of language, and his tongue is an organ of matter which has mastery over the element of air; but this top-heavy mastery is incomplete and unmatched below. At the base of the spinal column, Adam does not have mastery, for he feels lonely and sexually incomplete. "As above, so below" is an axiom from Hermetic mysticism, and in this Hermetic vision of physiology the tongue is connected through the spinal column to the penis. One organ is the master of the "logos spermaticos," the other, the master of the seed of life. In the higher regions of spirit, the spermatic word is master of the elements of fire and air; in the lower regions of matter, the sperm is master of the elements of earth and water. In Lilith the symmetry of "as above, so below" is completed, for she has the female lips of the mouth which can pronounce the magic name of God, and the female lips of the vulva below which can receive the semen of Adam. The tongue and penis are the polarities mediated by the spinal column for the male; and lips and labia majora, the polarities for the female.

The revolt of Lilith therefore expresses the rising up from below of all that would be denied by the rational, male consciousness. Like the ouroboric serpent which bites its own tail, the spinal column brings the mysteries of language and sexuality, mouth and genitals together. What the *midrash* describes is not simply the division of labor in a patriarchal society, but the structure of consciousness as it is revealed in the architecture of the human body.

This relationship between language and sexuality, oral and genital, has been elaborated in recent research in neurophysiology.

> When the animal is viewed in the ordinary elongated position, the oral and anogenital regions appear to be at opposite poles. A corresponding relation is maintained in the topographical representation of the body in the post-central gyrus of the neo-cortex. In the organization of the lower mammalian brain, however, Nature apparently found it necessary to bend the limbic lobe upon itself in order to afford the olfactory sense close participation in both oral and anogenital functions. . . .
>
> In other words, excitation in a region involved in oral mechanisms readily spills over into others concerned with genital function.
>
> This close relationship helps in understanding the intimate interplay of behavior in the oral and sexual spheres.[14]

Language and sexuality are what distinguish humanity from the angels, and language and sexuality are what come together in myth and physiology. The brain's limbic ring curves, overlapping the oral-genital areas, and the spinal column curves, bringing together the oral and genital areas. The "higher" consciousness of language thus has to be crossed with the "lower" consciousness of sexuality.

In the unconscious, cerebral is genital. The word *cerebral* is from the same root as Ceres, goddess of cereals, of growth and fertility; the same root as *cresco,* to grow, and *creo,* to create. Onians, archaeologist of language, who uncovers lost worlds of meaning, buried meanings, has dug up a prehistoric image of the body, according to which head and genital intercommunicate via the spinal column: the gray matter of the brain, the spinal marrow, and the seminal fluid are all one identical substance, on tap in the genital and stored in the head. The soul-substance is the seminal substance: the genius is the genital in the head. We would then all be carrying our seed in our head, like flowers.[15]

When God created the world He divided the waters which were under the firmament from the waters which were above the firmament. The human body is a recapitulation of this principle of order, for the body itself is the firmament which divides the waters of the brain from the waters of the genitals. Because of the sacred numinosity of the waters, all the fluids of the human body—saliva, sweat, semen, and blood—are sacred and mysterious substances. If Onians has dug up an ancient image of the body in which head and genitals intercommunicate through the spinal column, we do not have to wonder what such a system of meaning could have been like, for that ancient physiology still survives in Tantra yoga.

In Tantric practice the yogi silently intones a special *mantram* while he focuses his attention upon his "third eye." After several years of this practice, the yogi reaches a state in meditation where the vibration in his brain *reverberates* (note the literal meaning of this as a vibrating word) in his spinal column and begins to stimulate a sympathetic resonance at the base of his spine. The spinal column then begins to feel like a rod in which there are two strong magnetic poles at the extreme ends. As the vibration at the base of the spine responds to the vibration intoned with the mantram in the brain, the genitals become flooded with another feeling of vibration, the penis becomes erect, and the vibration within the brain becomes light, intensely energetic, and ecstatic.[16] In Tantra, the Fall into the body is reversed and human consciousness is able to escape its entrapment in matter. In the religious traditions of Tantra, "loss of semen is loss of soul," and so the yogi is counseled to keep himself free of women so that the seminal flow may reverse itself to move up into the brain in the awakening of *kundalini.* In the ancient Jewish tradition, the seminal flow of men was also emphasized. In other stories of the *midrashim,* Adam, in penance for his fall, abstains from sexuality for 130 years, but he is not able to control his nocturnal emissions; in his dream state female spirits, the succubae, come and have intercourse with him, and with Adam's seed they give birth to demons.[17] The succubus lying on top of the man in his sleep and stealing his semen away is, of course, another image of Lilith, the female being who refuses to stay in her "proper place."

The physiology of Tantra yoga focuses on the magical numinosity of the male semen, but the experience of the awakening of *kundalini* is not an exclusively male phenomenon. With women, however, it is the menstrual blood which is seen as the sacred carrier of power, and it is the womb which is its sacred vessel.[18] The spinal polarity in women is not between the genitals and the brain, but between the heart and the womb. In the intense religious practices of yoginis or nuns, the menstrual period can stop altogether. When the energy *(prana)* associated with lunar menstruation is stopped, time stops and the woman is taken up into eternity. She gives birth to herself. By withdrawing into celibacy, the woman no longer generates *karma* (relatedness and relatives in time); instead she gives birth to the divine child. At this stage the nun may have visions of the baby Jesus nursing at her own breast. Now, whereas the experience of the awakening of *kundalini* in man floods the genitals and causes spontaneous erection in meditation, the equivalent experience in the woman causes an ecstatic rapture that can be described as "an orgasm in the heart," or "giving birth in the heart." The sudden opening of the heart, *chakra,* causes an ecstatic experience of illumination; the heart of the woman becomes at the heart of the universe. The Sufi image of this experience is the winged heart. It is for good reason that the sculptor Bernini pictured St. Teresa in ecstasy (see Figure 1) as a woman in orgasm with an angel opening her heart with an arrow.

In the etheric body of a yogini in meditation, the polarity is, therefore, not between the brain and the genitals, the second and sixth *chakras,* but between the inner sexuality of the womb and the heart. Some Marxist feminists who have never practiced yoga become exercised at what they imagine is a sexist doctrine that locates man's consciousness in his brain, but woman's con-

Figure 1. Gianlorenzo Bernini, 1645-52, The Ecstasy of St. Teresa.

sciousness in her heart. In fact, consciousness is not, as Whitehead would say, "simply located" in the brain; the consciousness is suffused throughout the subtle bodies, and after a yogi has opened certain centers in the brain, he is counseled to center his being in the heart, not the head. Thus the place where yogi and yogini alike end up on the path of Illumination is the heart, to experience *"l'amor che move il sole e l'altre stelle"* (the love that moves the sun and other stars).

When the metaphors used in the terminology and imagery of esoteric traditions are taken out of the context of meditational practice and used by people filled with rage, hatred, and lust for power, you do not find the wisdom or understanding of the tradition. When esoteric imagery is used as an apology for the power of men over women, you have a political distortion of a spiritual practice. Lilith is the shadow side of Shakti (the divine feminine as Cosmic Energy); she represents the distortional psychic energy that occurs when man seeks to experience the spiritual while still maintaining control through his ego. When the ego tries to stay on top to force the universal feminine to remain below, it does not experience illumination. When man does not

Figure 2. Vajrasattva in union with the Supreme Wisdom, Tibetan bronze, sixteenth century.

face the instinctive and the unconscious, when his consciousness is split between the daylight of his waking state and the nighttime of his unconscious dreams, then he projects his desires and gives birth to hallucinations in his psyche. In other words, the succubae climb on top of him and use his power to give birth to demons. In Tantric intercourse, or *maithuna,* neither the man nor the woman is on the bottom in the sense of inferiority, but both sit in equality, face to face (see Figure 2).

The uninitiated man of ancient and medieval times feared the succubus, for she was the unnatural demoness who violated the proper order of things by straddling him in sleep or sucking his soul away. But for modern man, art has opened the way for what Freud called "the return of the repressed" and allowed the forbidden to bear its luscious fruit. In Kinsey's original studies of American sexual behavior in the nineteen fifties, he found that in general the working classes did not indulge in oral intercourse, but that the intelligentsia revelled in it. The more conscious and intellectual the individual, the more the face literally confronted the genitals in a mysteriously compelling act that seemed to touch the very foundations of consciousness. Artists such as James Joyce understood this before the scientists. More recently the novelist John Updike has expressed the mystique in his novel *Couples*.

> Mouths, it came to Piet, are noble. They move in the brain's court. We set our genitals mating down below like peasants, but when the mouth condescends, mind and body marry. To eat another is sacred. *I love thee, Elizabeth, thy petaled rankness, thy priceless casket of nothing lined with slippery buds.* Thus on the Sunday morning, beneath the hanging clangor of bells.[19]

Tongue and penis, lips and labia, fellatio and cunnilingus: "as above, so below." Cunnilingus and cunieform: even the ancient form of writing on clay tablets was an archetypal act that externalized the relationship between sexuality and language. The wedge-shaped character was the triangle, the archaic Paleolithic sign of the vulva; the pubic triangle was at the end of the phallic stylus. It impressed into the soft, submissive clay with hard erectile strength the image of the vulva. In the mystery of the writing of language, the two had become the one; the stylus of the scribe was like the older Neolithic statues of the Great Mother carved on the phallus.[20] The instrument of writing became the androgynous insignium for the sacred wedding of sexuality and language. Thus when poets, as initiates of language, celebrate oral sexuality in the face of the shame and indignation of the shopkeepers and their censors, they express a mystique in which the word of the female is joined to the seed of the male, and the word of the male is placed in the womb.

But the artist is only the initiate of the outer mysteries; he is the one who looks in and reports to the outside world. In the inner sanctum of the sacrum, the yogi reverberates the *mantram* and, in the experience of the awakening of *kundalini,* knows quite a different relationship between language and sexuality. The artist tries to remember the forgotten mysteries through the actions of the body; the yogi acts out these relationships not with the physical body, but with the esoteric subtle bodies. For the yogi, sexual intercourse is a "misplaced concreteness" which blocks out one's sensitivities to the energies of the subtle bodies. (The artist, of course, would have his own defense, and I will let God, and not the priests or the censors, decide what is sacrament, and what is sacrilege.)

The strong unconscious drive to make the one become two touches another ancient myth, the myth of the androgynous dawn man. Once again, the *midrashim* are a rich repository of archaic material. In one story, the original Adam is androgynous, with a male facing in one direction and a female in the other. To make sexual intercourse possible, it was necessary that God split the one into two so that they, in the first human revolution, could turn, face one another, and come together in sexual intercourse.

Still other *midrashim* tell of God's attempt to create a proper mate for Adam after the misfortune of Lilith. The God of the *midrash* is more like an Archon of Gnostic religion, for He does not create perfection with a single stroke but labors toward perfection through time. Undismayed by the failure of His first attempt, God tries again. This time Adam stands over God's shoulder and watches as God makes woman from blood, guts, bones, and clumps of hair. The brute anatomical reality of the female body is, however, more than Adam can stomach; he is revolted, and no matter how beautiful the woman appears at the end of the process, Adam cannot forget the gory details of her construction. The *midrash* seems to be commenting on masculine sexuality that requires illusion and ignorance to stimulate its desire. Adam requires a touch of feminine lace and a whisper of diaphanous silk, not a direct vision of the gaping maw of the human vulva. The terror of the female body overcomes him utterly.

Undaunted by two consecutive failures, God tries again. In the marvelous folk humor of the *midrashim* God appears to be something of a congenial Jewish tailor trying to fashion a suit for a difficult customer. When Adam does not like the fit of his mate, He dutifully tries again.

In Adam's desire for sexuality there is a fall long before the Fall. Adam was one but was unhappy in his oneness, or he was androgynous but was unhappy with his life of one as two and wished to become two as one. In the division into sexuality in Hebrew mythology, a great theme of division is being announced which will echo on down throughout history. To be asexual means to be immortal. The amoeba divides and no one can say where the original half has gone; it splits *ad infinitum* and there is no particular death for the entity as a whole. But for the organism that reproduces itself sexually, there is death. First, there is the half-death in which the gamete must throw half its genetic endowment away in passing on only one allele of its paired chromosomes. On the other side of the ecstatic sexual act, the climax which the French call *le petit mort,* the organism reproduces itself and moves that much closer in time to its own dissolution, to *le grand mort* which is to come. In choosing sexuality as a mode of existence, Adam is unconsciously moving toward a world of limitation and death, and it is no accident that the mate he asks for is destined to become the agent for his expulsion from Eden.

Hebrew mythology, for all its apparent folkish simplicity, gives us a rather sophisticated philosophy. Man is a creature made from matter, and sexuality and language are the major characteristics of his limited, material existence. Archangels like Samael do not seem to have genital sexuality or a linguistic consciousness. Creatures of light, they are more intimate expressions of Godhead and emanate directly from His divine will. Why then should God create Adam?

To attempt to answer this question, I need to compose my own *midrash.* Imagine God in Heaven surrounded by the choirs of adoring angels singing hosannahs unendingly. Upon His throne, God ponders the mysteries of Creation, of static perfection versus dynamic evolution toward perfection. "If I create a perfect world, I know how it will turn out. In its absolute perfection, it will revolve like a perfect machine, never deviating from My absolute will." Since God's imagination is perfect, there is no need for Him to create such a universe: it is enough for Him to imagine it to see it in all its details. Such a universe would not be very interesting to man or God, so we can assume that the Divinity continued His meditations. "But what if I create a universe that is free, free even of Me? What if I veil My Divinity so that the creatures are free to pursue their individual lives without being overwhelmed by My overpowering Presence? Will the creatures love Me? Can I be loved by creatures whom I have not programmed to adore Me forever? Can love arise out of freedom? My angels love Me unceasingly, but they can see Me at all times. What if I create beings in My own image as a Creator, beings who are free? But if I introduce freedom into this universe, I take the risk of introducing Evil into it as well, for if they are free, then they are free to deviate from My will. Hmmm. But what if I continue to interact with this dynamic universe, what if I and the creatures become the creators together of a great cosmic play? What if out of every occasion of evil, I respond with an unimaginable good, a good that over-whelms evil by springing right out of the very attempts of evil to deny the Good? Will these new creatures of freedom then love Me, will they join with Me in creating Good out of evil, novelty out of freedom? What if I join with them in the world of limitation and form, the world of suffering and evil? Ahh, in a truly free universe, even I do not know how it will turn out. Do even I dare to take that risk for love? Now it all begins to be truly interest-ing . . ."

We may imagine that since we exist, God chose to create the dynamic, free universe, the one in which God and man, angels and demons, play a complex game, a game of which all others are copies. The angelic steady-state was broken, man was created, and a creative disequilibrium was introduced in the form of Time. For those closest to the Old Order, this was a whole new universe, a revolution. Small wonder the angels are said not to like us, for when man was created, all hell broke loose in Heaven.

IV

THE COUPLING of language and sexuality in human nature and the numerous attempts at the creation of humanity are not unique to the mythological vision of the Hebrews. If we cross the world to move to the American Southwest, another people of the desert present a similar vision. According to Frank Water's and White Bear Fredericks' redaction of Hopi myths, the creation is as follows:

> The First People of the First World did not answer her; they could not speak. Something had to be done. Since Spider Woman received her power from Sotuknang, she had to call him and ask him what to do. So she called Palongwhoya and said, "Call your uncle. We need him at once."
> Palongwhoya, the echo twin, sent out his call along the world axis to the vibratory centers of the earth, which resounded his message throughout the universe. "Sotuknang, our Uncle, come at once. We need you!"

All at once, with the sound as of a mighty wind, Sotuknang appeared in front of them. "I am here. Why do you need me so urgently?"

Spider Woman explained. "As you commanded me, I have created these First People. They are fully and firmly formed; they are properly colored; they have life; they have movement. But they cannot talk. That is the proper thing they lack. So I want you to give them speech. Also the wisdom and the power to reproduce, so that they may enjoy life and give thanks to the creator.[21]

In the world-view of the Hopi there is a homology between the human body and the earth. Between the two poles of the earth, there runs a spinal axis which contains vibratory centers (or *chakras*) which can send out sounds into different dimensions to summon the gods. Along the spinal column of the human, there are also vibratory centers. At the opposite ends of this spinal column are the organs of the twin mysteries, sexuality and speech. Since the First People cannot speak, it is not surprising that they therefore cannot reproduce. Both the seed and the word are forms of information; the seed is the word in water and the word is the seed in air.

The organ which holds these two forms of generated information together is the spine. The central nervous system is the instrument of duality; it is there to separate the organism from oneness with infinity, to keep out the million signals a second so that a restricted consciousness can focus on *this* and *that* in the *here* and *now*. The infinite is broken down into a serial progression of thoughts, sensations, and words. Within the finite world of space-time, limited creatures can reproduce their bodies through sexuality, their thoughts through language.

The world of manifestation is a world of limitation and of opposites—good and evil, light and dark, male and female, life and death. Out of sexuality comes death, but out of death comes the decay to fertilize new life.

Since the opposites are not the static poles of a universe at rest, but the polarities of an oscillating field, it is not surprising that the *midrash* and the Hopi cosmology present the creation of humanity in a dynamic pattern of failure and renewed attempt. For the ancient Hebrews, God had to make several attempts at creating woman, but man was acceptable from the start. However, the imperfections of woman eventually lead to the fall of the presumably perfect man, Adam. For the Hopi, the universe evolves; it is not created perfect from the start. A world-order is created and it grows until its full nature, with all its inherent limitations and internal contradictions, has expressed itself; then a great world destruction overtakes it. The gods, like gardeners ploughing under a field, take the best of the old as seeds for the new, and then they destroy the old world-order completely. After the destruction has cleared, they plant the seeds of the new, and an entirely new world-order begins its temporary life. This view of world succeeding world in destruction after destruction is shared by the Maya of Mesoamerica. The Mayan gods labor to create humanity, but time after time their efforts are met with failure.

> For this reason another attempt had to be made to create and make men by the Creator, the Maker, and the Forefathers.
> "Let us try again! Already the dawn draws near; let us make him who shall nourish and sustain us! What shall we do to be invoked, in order to be remembered on earth? We have already tried our first creations, our first creatures; but we could not make them praise and venerate us. So, then, let us try to make obedient, respectful beings who will nourish and sustain us." Thus they spoke.
> Then was the creation and the formation. Of earth, of mud, they made man's flesh. But they saw that it was not good. It melted away, it was soft, did not move, had no strength, it fell down, it was limp, it could not move its head, its face fell to one side, its sight was blurred, it could not look behind. At first it spoke, but had no mind. Quickly it soaked in the water and could not stand.
> And the Creator and Maker said: "Let us try again because our creatures will not be able to walk nor multiply."[22]

The world-view of the Hopi and the Maya is an evolutionary one; each world establishes an ecological niche for a species, and then a catastrophe eliminates that niche. A few survivors are able to make the transition into the new conditions, but they move in terror as the landscape of the planet dramatically alters. With mountains rising and continents sinking after the fashion of Plato's Atlantis, humanity enters a new world to begin a new cycle of evolution. In dealing with the early abortive attempts at the creation of humanity, the mythology represents some species as not quite making it to hominization. It is as if there were enshrined in these

legends a racial memory of the Australopithicines who came close
but never did make it to full humanity.

V

THE COSMOGONIES of the Hopi and Maya bear striking similarities
to the creation myths of the Near Eastern Gnostic religion. In the
myths of the heretical Christians and Jews of the second and third
centuries A.D., humanity is not created by God Almighty, but by a
group of archangels, the Archons or the Elohim. In their first
attempts to create mankind, the Archons fail rather miserably.
Here is one version quoted in the orthodox Bishop Iraeneus's
attack on the Gnostics.

> In the Unutterable Depth were two Great Lights, the First Man, or
> Father, and his Son, the Second Man; and also the Holy Spirit, the
> First Woman, or Mother of all Living. Below this triad was a
> sluggish mass composed of the four great "elements," called Water,
> Darkness, Abyss, and Chaos. The *Universal* Mother brooded over
> the Waters; enamoured of her beauty, the First and Second Man
> produced from her the third Great Light, the Christ; and He,
> ascending above, formed with the First and Second Man, the Holy
> Church. This was the right-hand birth of the Great Mother. But a
> Drop of Light fell downwards to the left hand into chaotic matter;
> this was called Sophia, or Wisdom, the *World*-Mother. The Waters
> of the Aether were thus set in motion, and formed a body for
> Sophia (the Light-Aeon), viz., the Heavenly-sphere. And she,
> freeing herself, left her body behind, and ascended to the Middle
> Region below her Mother (the *Universal* Mother), who formed the
> boundary of the Ideal Universe.
>
> By her mere contact with the Space-Waters she had already
> generated a son, the chief Creative Power of the Sensible World,
> who retained some of the Light-fluid; this son was Ialdabaoth (said
> by some to mean the Child of Chaos), who in his turn produced a
> son, and he another, until there were seven in all, the great
> Formative Powers of the Sensible Universe. And they were "fight-
> ers," and quarrelled much with their fathers. And by means of this
> interplay of forces on matter came forth the "mind," which was
> "serpent-formed," and "spirit," and "soul," and all things in the
> world.
>
> And Ialdabaoth was boastful and arrogant, and exclaimed: "I am
> Father and God, and beyond me is none other." But Sophia hearing
> this cried out to her son: "Lie not, Ialdabaoth, for above thee is the

Father of All, the First Man, and Man the Son of Man." And all the Powers were astonished at the word; but Ialdabaoth, to call off their attention, cried out: "Let us make 'man' after our image." So they made "man," and he lay like a worm on the ground, until they brought him to Ialdabaoth, who breathed into him the "breath of life," that is to say the Light-fluid he had received from Sophia, and so emptied himself of his Light. And "man" receiving it, immediately gave thanks to the First Man and disregarded his fabricators (the Elohim).

Whereupon Ialdabaoth (Yahweh) was jealous and planned to deprive Adam of the Light-spark by forming "Woman." And the six creative powers were enamoured of Eve, and by her generated sons, namely the angels. And so Adam again fell under the power of Ialdabaoth and the Elohim; then Sophia or Wisdom sent the "serpent" (mind) into the paradise of Ialdabaoth, and Adam and Eve listened to its wise councils, and so once more "man" was freed from the dominion of the Creative Power, and transgressed the ordinance of ignorance of any power higher than himself imposed by Ialdabaoth. Whereupon Ialdabaoth drove them out of his Paradise, and together with them the "serpent" or "mind"; but Sophia would not permit the Light-spark to descend, and so withdrew it to avoid profanation. And "mind," (the lower mind), the serpent-formed, the first product of Ialdabaoth, brought forth six sons, and these are the "daemonial" powers, which plague man because their father was cast down for their sake.

Now Adam and Eve before the fall had spiritual bodies, like the angels born of this Eve; but after their fall down from the Paradise of Ialdabaoth, their bodies grew more dense, and more and more languid, and became "coats of skin," till finally Sophia in compassion restored to them the sweet odour of the Light, and they knew that they carried death about with them. And so a recollection of their former state came back to them, and they were patient, knowing that the body was put on for a time.[23]

For contemporary humanity this bizarre narrative seems almost incomprehensible, like the ravings of a lunatic; but if one stops to realize that this is the story of the evolution of the solar system told in anthropomorphic imagery, then some of the narrative begins to make sense. The Seven Formative Powers of the Sensible Universe are the planets of archaic astronomy; in their early stages, before they have become distinct orbs, they are "fighters" with one another, as they swirl in their dust cloud. Ialdabaoth, the sun, claims to be the entire universe, but the gods are not God, and beyond the solar system is the immensity of the Chain of Being. Man is created by the Elohim but is rescued from their tyranny by Sophia. As in the Maya *Popul Vuh,* the first man cannot stand but sinks to the ground like a worm. For the followers of the Gnostic religion, Jahweh is not the universal Godhead and Almighty Creator of Perfection; he is simply a local deity who attempts to mask his provincialism by lording it over man with absurd delusions of cosmic grandeur. Hebrew mythology, cast into the mirror of Gnosticism, comes out reversed: Jahweh is the Devil, and the serpent in the garden is the Saviour.

Gnosticism has been regarded as a forgotten faith, but although this religion went underground because of persecution by orthodox Christianity,[24] it nevertheless lived in Europe as an underground stream which kept feeding the cisterns of the occult. Twentieth-century mediums without the benefit of education in classical languages or of scholarly research seem to connect with these subterranean streams when they go into trance or take up automatic writing, for Gnostic ideas issue forth from their supposedly new religions. Edgar Cayce, a trance-medium from Kentucky, who achieved posthumous fame in the sixties, has described a prehistory of earth in which certain souls were hovering in the ether, observing with fascination the evolution of life on earth. As an expression of their fascination, they projected themselves into the bodies of the animals, and after repeated projections, they became caught in these animal bodies and could not escape.[25] For Cayce, the legends of the minotaurs and centaurs are not children's fairytales but racial memories of the true prehistory of earth.

For another trance-medium, Randall-Stevens, the prehistory of earth is a chapter in the career of the Devil.[26] According to his automatic writings, Satan, a great god, created the human body and asked "Arbal-Jesus," his name for Adam, to project his being into it for a few móments. Arbal-Jesus complied with this seemingly innocent request, but once he was in the body, he was trapped and could not get out. Although Arbal-Jesus screamed in agony, Satan only laughed in triumph; then he began to mock his captive by committing "unspeakable sexual acts" with him in sacriligious violation and contempt. But in those ancient days, souls were not simply single, but "twin rays"; Arbal-Jesus's other half, his feminine polarity, hovered over him and longed to be reunited. But the feminine half of his soul was unable to descend into the dense vibrations of the body; she could only spiritually accompany him beyond his physical awareness to begin the long search through space and time for her lost and fallen half. Contained in this contemporary automatic writing is a modern variation of the ancient Egyptian myth of Isis and Osiris, which I will discuss at greater length later in this book.

Randall-Stevens's concept of the twin-soul is not a modern invention but the reemergence of one of the critical points of Gnostic doctrine. This feature of the Gnostic vision has been explained by Professor Hans Jonas.

> In our narrative the garment has become this figure itself and acts like a person. It symbolizes the heavenly or eternal self of the person, his original idea, a kind of double or *alter ego* preserved in the upper world while he labors down below . . . Applied to the messenger or savior as it is here and elsewhere, the conception leads to the interesting theological idea of a twin brother or eternal original of the savior remaining in the upper world during his terrestrial mission.[27]

Another contemporary scholar of Gnosticism, C. G. Jung, has taken this notion of the twin ray and applied it to his own model of the contrasexual nature of the self. In the Jungian model of the psyche, the male has an internalized female counterpart, the *anima;* while the female has an internalized masculine counterpart, the *animus.* The subterranean streams of Gnosticism thus do not only flow into the regions of the occult; they also feed the wellsprings of psychoanalysis.

Rudolph Steiner is a twentieth-century mystic whose work seems to bridge the world of academic scholarship and the demimonde of cult and occult. Having written his doctoral dissertation on the scientific writings of Goethe, Steiner experienced a dramatic midlife change and began to have religious experiences. In this transformation, the scholar became a clairvoyant and claimed to have the ability to read "the Akashic Record," the imprint in the ether of space-time of all events of history and prehistory. Steiner's work on the contrasexual nature of the self antedates Jung's by more than a decade, and like Jung's work it seems to draw on the subterranean streams of Gnostic mythology. In his *Cosmic Memory*, Steiner wrote:

> The external formation of earth resulted in that the body assumed a one-sided form. The male body has taken a form which is conditioned by the element of will; the female body on the other hand, bears the stamp of imagination. Thus it comes about that the two-sexed, male-female soul inhabits a single-sexed, male or female body. In the course of development the body has taken a form determined by the external terrestrial forces, so that it was no longer possible for the soul to pour its whole inner energy into this body. The soul had to retain something of this energy within itself and could let only part of it flow into the body. . . .
>
> When this difference had not yet appeared, every human being could produce another human being out of himself. Impregnation was not an external process, but was something which took place inside the human body itself. . . .
>
> Here an important point in the development of mankind appears. Previously that which is called spirit, the faculty of thought, could not find a place in man. For this faculty would have found no organs for exercising its functions. The soul had employed all its energy toward the exterior, in order to build up the body. But now the energy of the soul, which finds no external employment, can become associated with the spiritual energy, and through this association those organs are developed in the body which later make of a man a thinking being. Thus man could use a portion of the energy which previously he employed for the production of beings like himself, in order to perfect his own nature. *The force by which mankind forms a thinking brain for itself is the same by which man impregnated himself in ancient times. The price of thought is single-sexedness.* [My emphasis.] By no longer impregnating themselves, but rather impregnating each other, human beings can turn a part of their productive energy within, and so become thinking creatures. Thus the male and female body each represent an imperfect external embodiement of the soul, but thereby they become more perfect inwardly. . . .
>
> Upon the male soul in woman the action of the spirit is female, and thus renders it male-female; upon the female soul in man the action of the spirit is male, and thus renders it male-female also. . . .
>
> The human soul had to wait until a brain existed which became the mediator with the spirit. Without this detour, *this* soul would have remained spiritless. It would have remained arrested at the stage of dreamlike consciousness . . . This detour is called the descent of the human soul into matter, or popularly, "the fall of man."[28]

From Steiner's visionary point of view, the evolution of the human body takes place on an etheric plane long before an externalized physical body takes its place in the outer world. If one were to look back at the prehistory of the world with physical eyes, one would see nothing, but, according to Steiner, if one were to look at the oceans with clairvoyant vision, one would see the etheric bodies of the beings who would evolve to become what we know as human beings. Presumably, it is the etheric body which is androgynous and is destined to evolve into the single-sexed physical body of conventional prehistory.

Steiner's vision of the androgynous dawn man is a variant of the androgynous Adam in the *midrashim,* but the idea is even more ancient. In fact, the sculptures from the Upper Paleolithic era found in Europe are figures of the Great Mother Goddess carved on phallic-shaped bones or rocks. The Great Mother Goddess in phallic form is an icon that continues from the Paleolithic through the Neolithic right up to the proto-urban period in Mesopotamia. As the archaeologist Marija Gimbutas has noted concerning "the Great Goddess of Life, Death, and Regeneration," "throughout the Neolithic period her head is phallus-shaped, suggesting her androgynous nature, and its derivation from Paleolithic times."[29]

Steiner's notion that "the price of thought is single-sexedness" seems to fit in well with those theories of Tantra yoga that urge the initiate to try to reverse the fall into the body by reversing the seminal flow from the genitals through the spinal column into the brain. As the male feels as if the semen were traveling up the spine, he feels as if the spinal column were a vagina, and the brain a womb where he is becoming reborn. The yogi is in this way the androgyne of prehistory reachieved.

According to Gnosticism, the mind is "serpent-formed"; the elevation of the snake of *kundalini* in Tantra yoga is the reversal of the Fall and the ascent back into the realms of spirit. Onians traces this doctrine in philosophies of archaic Europe; I will argue in this work that this doctrine is also the meaning of the iniatic practices of the religion of Isis and Osiris. What few people realize, however, is that this esoteric process of initiation is also part of the religion of Jesus. In John, 3:5-6,14, we read:

> Verily, verily, I say unto thee, Except a man be born of water and of the Spirit, he cannot enter into the kingdom of God. That which is

born of the flesh is flesh; and that which is born of the Spirit is spirit. Marvel not that I said unto thee, Ye must be born again.

And as Moses lifted up the serpent in the wilderness, even so must the Son of man be lifted up: That whosoever believeth in him should not perish, but have everlasting life.

For the initiate, Exodus is an allegory of the process of initiation. When Moses raises up the bronze serpent onto a rod where all may see it and be cured of the fiery serpents that are consuming them, he is presenting a figure that represents the midbrain, limbic ring and the spinal column. When the energies of *kundalini* are misdirected, the *chela* feels as if he were being consumed by a burning fire coursing up his spine, but when the elevation is not crooked but rather is straight up through the center of the spine (the yogic *sushumna*), (In Isaiah, 3, we read, "Make straight in the desert a highway for our god"),[30] then the healthy illumination of the mind takes place, and the desert of the body is transformed back into a garden.

VI

FROM THE OLD TESTAMENT to the Gnostics and up into the Theosophy of Rudolph Steiner and the psychoanalytic theories of C. G. Jung and Norman O. Brown, the Western esoteric stream flows unceasingly underground and nourishes widely separated schools of thought and artistic movements. Nor is Jung the end of it, the last survivor of the Hermetic and arcane into the modern technological society. The latest expression of this Gnostic tradition has appeared in the world of the contemporary film.

In Nicholas Roeg's film *The Man Who Fell to Earth*, Gnosticism appears in the guise of science fiction. The film opens with an image of life on another planet, a landscape of desert and isolation. We see a single family, a woman holding a small child, and a man, and we overhear his promises to return after he has secured the water of life from another planet. It seems as if this family is the only young thing left on this ancient and exhausted world. Bidding farewell to his wife and child, the young man enters some sort of projection device that hurtles him through space and time to earth. In the next scene we see him falling out of the sky and crashing down into a pool by an old deserted mine in the American Southwest. As he wakes up on earth he puts on his coat of skin, and some version of contact lenses to make his eyes appear human; then he walks out from the country into a small-town shop to begin his magical encounter with the economic reality of earth.

This creature from a higher world has not forgotten all that he knew before; he retains his unworldly talents and supreme intelligence. Slowly he applies his knowledge of science to patent a whole series of inventions and create a new multinational corporation. He becomes a billionaire. The secret purpose for his accumulation of all this wealth is to set up the economic base with which to bring back the water of life to his dying planet, but the whole process of his amassing a fortune is one of increasing incorporation. The *corporation* becomes the central metaphor for the entrapment of the soul from another world in a body. Everything in the cinematic technique of the film plays upon the theme of entrapment in grossness, in vulgarity, in the noise and squalor of a world constructed of the passion for money. As the hero makes his way through our economic reality, there are occasional flashbacks to his home planet in which we see haunting visions of the wife and child who remain above, waiting for his return. Like the feminine twin ray in Gnostic mythology, the wife hovers above her mate who is caught in the body and fallen to earth.

Hans Jonas has identified the major themes of Gnosticism as "fall, sinking, and capture." Roeg's film explicitly plays out these major themes. As the hero becomes a success on earth and does indeed create the kind of Howard Hughes empire large enough to finance his esoteric mission of planetary rescue, the very mass of his enterprise begins to capture him, to entrap him in the gross matter of our capitalistic world. The conflict between a spiritual world based upon love, yet lacking the seminal water of life that could give body to its love, and a world that is based upon nothing but matter and money, a world that lacks even a clue about the higher world of the spirit, becomes extreme. The process of incorporation continues until the hero is finally caught and cannot get back. The feminine twin soul is cut off and forgotten in her higher, arid world. In the last scene we see the hero reduced to alcoholism and falling asleep in a drunken stupor over his drink in a café. There are even esoteric dimensions to the condition of his alcoholism: our word "whiskey" comes from the Gaelic *uiskebaugh*, which means "the water of life." The man who fell to earth came in search of the water of life for his world; he ends finding not its substance, but its shadow.

The vision of Roeg's film is clearly religious. The intensity with which his cinematic technique psychically assaults our senses, with its loud and irritating sound track and gross imagery, comes from the fact that this moralist wishes to push our faces into our disgusting capitalistic world until we begin to see it for what it is: a world of money and lust in which objects and people are equally consumed. A Gnostic from the second century in Alexandria could not have presented a more intense denunciation of the sophisticated world of international culture.

Gnostic mythology is also presented in disguised form in Werner Herzog's film *Kaspar Hauser*. Herzog has taken up the true story of a sixteen-year-old foundling who was discovered in a village street in Germany early one morning in the eighteenth century. It is almost as if the foundling too had fallen out of the sky, because, having been raised in a tower where he was never allowed to see a human face, he knows hardly anything of normal human life. Herzog allows us to see the tormentor who keeps the boy in the tower, but we are never permitted to understand the motivation behind his incomprehensible schemes. We see him leave food for the boy, take him out of his prison cell to teach him how to walk, and finally take him to the village square where he abandons him at dawn, leaving only a note in the boy's hand.

As we watch the foundling's keeper handle the boy like a puppet and kick his feet to make him walk, it begins to become visually clear that the archetype for what we are seeing is the Archon, the cruel archangel of the creation of man. The keeper always stays behind the boy's back, and so the foundling is never able to see him. A flower cannot turns its head to see its stem; the human brain cannot turn to see what is outside its tiny frame of perception; and so angels and devils are always out of sight. The boy can never see his creator and tormentor, and knowing no other reality he must accept whatever comes his way. The foundling's keeper in the dark tower is Ialdabaoth, the devil who keeps him in prison for his own purposes, then takes him out, teaches him to stand and walk, and abandons him. When the boy has finally made his way in the world, the keeper returns and stabs him in the chest while he is sitting on the toilet in an outhouse. In a moment of the most corporeal of functions, the angel returns, and the being who was the artificer of the physical body proves himself also to be the creator of death. For no apparent reason, the keeper returns and kills Kaspar Hauser.

In the interval between the time of his arrival into human society and his murder by his keeper, we watch the foundling descend deeper and deeper into the absurdities of human society. At one point, Kaspar looks back to his days of solitude and imprisonment with fondness and nostalgia and remarks to one of his companions: "Well, it seems to me my coming into the world was a terrible fall."

Much that is incomprehensible to the ordinary viewer of *Kaspar Hauser* or *The Man Who Fell to Earth* becomes clear and full of meaning when it is understood to be, consciously or unconsciously, Gnostic mythology. That Herzog, like Nicholas Roeg, is a man of religious sensibility becomes even more obvious in his later film, *Heart of Glass*. There the shamanistic director puts all his actors into a hypnotic trance to present his vision of the other great religious theme, the end of the world. Here the central character is not a foundling in an alien world, but a prophet who must live at the edge of human society, for like the artist, he is cursed and blessed with knowledge beyond society's and can see the future. From the Fall to the Apocalypse, the vision of this young German film maker is unmistakably mythological, and although *The New York Times*'s film critic found *Heart of Glass* to be "intolerably obscure," that is only because in our sophisticated world most critics know nothing about the true history of the soul and have never understood the basic documents of human culture, the great myths.

For those sophisticated souls who are closed to religious imagery but have a strong faith in science and technology, a new way has been opened to the old truths of myth, and that is the way of science fiction. The Gnostic vision that the soul has fallen but still carries with it some of the powers of its previous existence was transformed by the novelist Zenna Henderson into a story of a space ship that crashed on earth and marooned "The People" on our strange and primitive planet in her book, *Pilgrimage: The Book of the People.*[31] Gifted with spiritual powers, the People try to hide their extrasensory talents and pass unnoticed among the normal inhabitants. Zenna Henderson's stories are sensitive studies of the problem of being a "stranger in a strange land," and of having spiritual gifts that only alienate the soul from society.

VII

IF WE SPREAD OUT all these different versions of the myth of the Fall before our mind's eye, we can begin to see a great architectonic pattern. From the trances of Cayce, Randall-Stevens, and Steiner to the cosmogonies of the Hebrew, Hopi, and Maya people; from the scholarly analyses of Gnostic texts by Jonas and Mead to the science fiction of Zenna Henderson and the films of Nicholas Roeg and Werner Herzog, the message is repeated over and over again and sent out through enormously different media of transmission. Each separate message in its particular medium has its own ratio of noise to information, but even in the most distorted forms the message still stands out.

The experience of seeing the myths of the world spread out before us in a new planetary culture should lead to a *metanoia,* a conversion experience, or else we have not truly seen; we have only looked. When Rainer Maria Rilke saw the archaic statue of Apollo, he knew that he had to completely make over his life. In effect, the statue spoke to him and said: *"Du musst Dein Leben ändern."* So it is with myth. The materialist sees myth as superstitious gibberish from the old days before we had science and technology; the idolator takes the myth literally. The problem is that both are interested in power. The materialist wants to dominate nature with his culture, and to dominate feeling with reason, for he is interested in control. The idolator is also interested in control, but he wants to dominate the psychic with his ego; he wants a genie in a bottle to grant him his every wish; he wants a world of magic powers. The materialist and the psychic mechanist are, therefore, not that far apart.

The third way, which is the way of neither materialistic science nor psychic idolatry, is to realize that the myth of legend is a translation of experiences from other dimensions into the imagery of this world. Consciousness is universal and precedes even the formation of our solar system. The myths of the past tell the story of the evolution of the solar system, not because astronauts in flying saucers told our ancestors stories about the universe, but because when we move out of "little mind" into "Big Mind" in dream, trance, meditation, or the telling of myths, we remember because we were there. The trick is to know what is meant by "we."

If you stay in the physical body and the consciousness of the ego and look out on the world with two eyes, then the evolution of humanity is seen in one way. If you become a practitioner of yoga to look out through the third eye, then the evolution of humanity is seen to be far more complicated. The way in which the ego in a physical body recalls the more complex history of consciousness is expressed and compressed in myth.

A biological understanding of evolution is only available to initiates who have gone through a long and demanding process of scientific education; similarly, a spiritual understanding of the evolution of consciousness is only available to initiates who have gone through a long and demanding process of contemplative education. There is no good reason why these two traditions of education must be separate, even though in our culture they most definitely are. This split in our culture is not a healthy separation but a fracture, for our science tends to be reductionist, and our spirituality mindlessly undiscriminating and occult. In the future I hope we will have an integral culture that affirms that there are two different paths up the mountain, each provided with beautiful but quite different scenery, but each coming to the same summit of human understanding. Certainly the great physicist Niels Bohr prepared his colleagues for such an appreciation when he said: "The opposite of a correct statement is a false statement. But the opposite of a profound truth may well be another profound truth." [32]

The narratives of evolution and the narratives of the Fall are both true. In the monkey trial of the evolutionist versus the fundamentalist, there is a marvelous irony in which both sides are simultaneously right and both sides simultaneously ignorant and dogmatic. When you cross natural history with myth, the two superimposed patterns generate a third, a moiré pattern. By superimposing history onto myth in this book, I am hoping that you will see a moiré pattern, one that is neither simply scientific fact nor religious dogma, but something more akin to art: *Wissenkunst* and not *Wissenschaft*.

With this vision of the Fall as the prehistory of consciousness before the revolution of the solar system, I would now like to descend from the regions of myth onto the ground of natural history and science to see what the fields of sociobiology and ethology have to say about the origins of sexuality and human culture. If I am right that even a scientific narrative of how human sexuality came into being can be a myth, then perhaps this descent into the matter of science will not be a Fall but simply an incarnation.

PART TWO

The Transformations of Prehistory

CHAPTER ONE

Hominization

THE SCIENTIST is like an explorer climbing a mountain: giddy from the heights and thin atmosphere, he feels a premature elation and thinks that he can reach out and grab the stars. And then he climbs to the top and sees that even higher peaks await him in the distance and that the stars are so far beyond his grasp that they will never become light under the nails of his Heaven-scraping fingers.

In every century since its birth, science has proclaimed itself capable of explaining everything in one complete and grand synthesis, but inevitably human culture has reversed itself, and each period of scientific inflation has been followed by a period of depression over rather painful evidence of just how far off the premature claim of totality really was. But the depressions too are only temporary; after a generation has humbly explored the valleys, a new group takes to the heights again with visions that this time, surely, the summit will be conquered.

The latest scientific explorer to carry on in the tradition of the positivism of Auguste Comte is E. O. Wilson. In his *Sociobiology: The New Synthesis,* Wilson has made a global map that brings the continents of population genetics, ethology, and anthropology into one perspective.

> It may not be too much to say that sociobiology and the other social sciences, as well as the humanities, are the last branches of biology waiting to be included in the Modern Synthesis. . . .
> In this macroscopic view the humanities and social sciences shrink to specialized branches of biology; history, biography, and fiction are the research protocols of human ethology; and anthropology and sociology together constitute the sociobiology of a single primate species. . . .

Scientists and humanists should consider together the possibility
that the time has come for ethics to be removed temporarily from
the hands of the philosophers and biologicized. . . .
The study of moral development is only a more complicated and
less tractable version of the genetic variance problem. With the
accretion of data the two approaches can be expected to merge to
form a recognizable exercise in behavioral genetics.[1]

Perhaps such overly confident and inflated feelings of power and
importance are expressions of the ambition and emotional motivation a scientist needs to maintain himself in a long and arduous
work, for the petty annoyances of tedious research are made light
when mitigated by the belief that one is a heroic Darwin about to
be granted apotheosis for a lifelong labor. Professor Wilson's new
synthesis does seem heroic, a grand heroic myth that tells us who
we are, where we come from, and even where we are going, as in
our future human culture, philosophy and ethics become "biologicized."

To appreciate just how mythopoeic are the root structures of
Wilson's thought, we need to look not just at his descriptions
of the importance of his own work, but at some of the propositions
of sociobiology itself. Since sociobiology claims to subsume most of
behavior under genetics, it makes sense to begin with the subject
of sexual reproduction.

Sexual reproduction is in every sense a consuming biological
activity. Reproductive organs tend to be elaborate in structure,
courtship activities lengthy and energetically expensive, and genetic
sex-determination mechanisms finely tuned and easily disturbed.
Furthermore, an organism reproducing by sex cuts its genetic
investment in each gamete by one-half. If an egg develops parthenogenetically, all of the genes in the resulting offspring will be
identical with those of the parent. In sexual reproduction only half
are identical; the organism, in other words, has thrown away half its
investment. There is no intrinsic reason why gametes cannot
develop into organisms parthenogenetically instead of sexually and
save all of the investment. Why, then, has sex evolved?
It has always been accepted by biologists that the advantage of
sexual reproduction lies in the much greater speed with which new
genotypes are assembled. During the first meiotic division, homolo-
gous chromosones typically engage in crossover, during which
segments of DNA are exchanged and new genotypic combinations
created. The division is concluded by the separation of the homolo-

gous chromosones into different haploid cells, creating still more genetic diversification. When the resulting gamete is fused with a sex cell from another organism, the result is a new diploid organism even more different than the gamete from the original gametic precursor. Each step peculiar to the process of gametogenesis and syngamy serves to increase genetic diversity. To diversify is to adapt; sexually reproducing populations are more likely than asexual ones to create new genetic combinations better adjusted to changed conditions in the environment. Asexual forms are permanently committed to their particular combinations and are more likely to become extinct when the environment fluctuates. Their departure leaves the field clear for their sexual counterparts, so that sexual reproduction becomes increasingly the mode.

The precise means by which this adaptability is rewarded is less certain. Two hypotheses have been proposed, called by Maynard Smith the long-term and the short-term explanations respectively. The long-term explanation first took form in the writings of August Weismann, R. A. Fisher, and H. J. Muller, and was given quantitative expression by Crow and Kimura (1965). *In essence it says that entire populations evolve faster when they reproduce by sex* [my emphasis], and as a result they will prevail over otherwise comparable asexual populations.[2]

The surface structure of a scientific narrative can be rational and even quantitative, but the deep structure of the exposition can often have more to do with modes of thought that are more connected to the unconscious. The surface structure of population genetics says that entire populations will evolve faster if they reproduce by sex; the deep structure of this exposition has to do with creating a history for a species in an imaginary space. Now I would like to create a collage in which we look at the work of E. O. Wilson and, surprisingly enough, the automatic writings of the deep-trance medium Randall-Stevens in order to show the common narrative root structures shared by mysticism and science. In his trance, a "higher being" comes to Randall-Stevens and tells him about the true story of Genesis and the beginnings of human evolution.

As I have told you, my children, Earth is, and was, created the furthest from Divine Heaven, and was also created the grossest of the material worlds. For this reason it will be seen that the process of evolution was not so quick as that taking place on the other worlds of gross matter. Alas, this made itself apparent to the active brain of

Eranus, who was always one to use his own power of thought within himself.

He became dissatisfied, and realizing also his power as a divine son of God the Father-Mother, he decided to experiment with the process of evolution in his own way. All he required was the creative word of power which Yevah alone held. . . .

Eranus unfolded his scheme to Yevah, saying that it was only an experiment for the well-being of Earth and its evolution. The result was that the two, Eranus and Yevah, collaborated together to create material bodies which, as Eranus explained to Yevah, could reproduce their kind without the necessity of waiting for the word of command from the Godhead through El Daoud.[3]

The voice that speaks to the medium Randall-Stevens seems to come out of the ancient past of Gnosticism, for Eranus and Yevah are the Archons of the Gnostic creation myths, but the story also bears resemblances to the cosmogonies of the Hopi and Maya Indians. If we examine the aspects of all these various narratives that concern the evolution of sex, we find the thesis that sex was created in order to accelerate evolution.

If sexuality creates an acceleration of evolution in which novel organisms appear to adapt themselves to changing circumstances in the environment, then we should begin to suspect that there is a relationship between the evolution of organisms and the evolution of the planet.

In recent years the study of solar flares and changes in solar radiation, ice ages, weather changes, the shifting levels of cosmic rays and extraterrestrial radiation, the reversal of the earth's magnetic field, the evolution of the earth's atmosphere, and the movement of the tectonic plates all have begun to suggest a new view of planetary dynamics. No Darwin has come along to put the pieces together in a grand theory, but articles, for example, in the *New Scientist*[4] have begun to suggest a return to the catastrophism of the nineteenth century. This, taken with the contribution of René Thom in the topologies of his "catastrophe theory," allows one to see the liquid solution of catastrophism moving toward crystallization.

Changes in our perception of natural history do not occur in a vacuum; natural history is related to human history, and through techniques of the field known as "the sociology of knowledge," we can begin to see relationships between the way a scientist perceives

natural history and composes his narratives about natural processes, and the historical environment of ideas in which he or she
lives. The time of Darwin and Lyell saw a revulsion to the earlier
idea of Cuvier's catastrophism, and a deep conviction that the
reaches of time were vast enough to allow the slow and incremental changes of natural selection. The liberals of the nineteenth
century had a deep conviction that the world was orderly and
slowly making continual progress. An Old Testament vision of the
Fall, or a scientific vision of an irresponsible nature in which
Jehovah-like fits of rage occurred, was entirely repugnant to them.
And so Cuvier's catastrophism was demoted, and Lyell's doctrine
of geological stability and uniformitarianism was put in its place.
But over the last century countless little anomalies in that
paradigm have been accumulating, and now it seems as if it will
not be long before some entirely new paradigm emerges. If there
is to be a New Synthesis, it will need to take those anomalies into
account, to synthesize planetary dynamics in which changes in
solar radiation, the reversal of the earth's magnetic field, the
movement of the tectonic plates, and very rapid changes in the
weather are all seen as part of a hitherto culturally invisible
periodicity. E. O. Wilson's sociobiology, a linear extension of
Darwinism, does not fulfill the new requirement. If human
culture enters into a period of catastrophes and instabilities, the
intellectual climate will change along with the global climate, and
its easy optimism and positivism will seem antique. In some ways,
the intellectual climate has already begun to shift. Barbara
Tuchman has said that she was moved to write her history of the
calamitous fourteenth century, in which the Black Death wiped
out one-third of the population from India to England, because
she felt that the modern world was at the edge of a similar
catastrophe,[5] and in her recent novel, *Shikasta,* Doris Lessing has
given us a grand vision of catastrophes and human evolution.

If catastrophes return, then catastrophism will return as well (or
is it the reverse?). But the important point to realize is that when
the general theory of planetary dynamics is created by a scientist,
it will have been anticipated by centuries, if not millennia, by the
mystics and artists. There is now no way to relate the evolution of
the planet to the evolution of humans except through myth. To
adopt a point of view cosmic enough that things as seemingly

separate as extraterrestrial radiation, shifts in the earth's magnetic field, and changes in the climatic foundations for human culture are all seen as part of one process, one would have to be a priest of the ancient Maya, or a Hopi shaman.

The truth is that myth and art create the preconditions of consciousness out of which science arises. Lévi-Strauss has said that magical rites and beliefs are "acts of faith in a science yet unborn,"[6] but he would be more correct to say that myth is an expression of knowing in a science yet unborn. Both myth and science spring from the same root structures of consciousness, so it is as valid to say that science is a dim intuition of a truth which the mystic experiences, as it is to say that myth is a dim intuition of a truth which only the scientist can prove. Myth and science seem to be like continents which are oceans apart, but if one dives into the depths of the sea, one discovers that the oceans cover what is, in reality, the single crust of the planet.

A mythic narrative and a scientific exposition are not unrelated forms of cultural activity. The idea of the creation of novelty can be shared by both myth and science. For example, Professor Wilson sees the evolution of sex coming from the enhancement of adaptations through the increase of diversification in the creation of novelty, but his mentor, Professor Maynard Smith, sees the origins of sex as a response to conditions of damage.

> Although group extinction may eliminate the occasional "loss" mutation, it cannot have brought together the series of adaptations concerned in the origin of sex. Long before the origin of eukaryotic sex, the prokaryotes had acquired the capacity for genetic recombination—that is, the pairing, breaking, and rejoining of homologous lengths of DNA. It seems clear that its original function was not the generation of evolutionary novelty, but the repair of damage. . . .
>
> Starting from a population of haploid single-celled organisms, one can at least guess at the main stages and the selective forces responsible. The first stage will be binary cell fusion to form a heterokaryotic cell, with two haploid nuclei of different ancestry. The selective advantage of such fusion would be analogous to the advantages of hybrid vigour, particularly the covering up, by recombination, of deleterious genes. As in the origin of recombination, the first step was to compensate for damage rather than to create novelty.[7]

Response to damage or the spontaneous generation of novelty are two very different ideas; they are ideas that are also connected to different archetypes in the organizing and constructing of a narrative out of "facts." Perhaps it will be easier to see what I am getting at if I magnify the issue into the sociology of knowledge. If one is a scientist who believes in Darwinism, then one sees evolution as a process in which the spontaneous generation of novel combinations enhances the adaptation of species. It is a smooth process of evolutionary progress, a process quite compatible with the world-view of a technocratic liberal. If, on the other hand, one sees the origins of sex coming out of circumstances of damage and disruption, then one sees nature as capable of such disruptive and damaging circumstances. Such a world-view would be characteristic of a more religiously conservative scientist, one not so easily given to the confident assertions of the positivist. Now, how will these two different scholars look out on the historical environment? One, like E. O. Wilson, would see continuing progress, the spontaneous generation of novelty, and an evolutionary sequence in which the humanist is replaced by the scientist in the government of a technological state where nature and culture are brought under increasingly powerful controls through sociobiological management. On the other hand, a scholar like myself would look out on the contemporary historical environment and expect that scientifically unexpected periodicities from a totally uncontrollable nature are about to shatter industrial civilization and that the response to that damage is going to trigger the next stage in the evolution of consciousness, a stage that has been anticipated by the artists and the mystics.

The confidence and positivism of the sociobiologist would lead to a mandarin politics in which the state would be organized by scientists; the tragic sense of history of the scholar would lead to a politics of Buddhist compassion in which the common suffering of all sentient beings leads to a more egalitarian vision of the commonweal. As Buddha pointed out a long time ago in the *Dhamapada,* we are what we think. Each civilization, whether it is religious or scientific, is merely an externalization of consciousness. It is, therefore, very important for our politics of knowledge and our knowledge of politics to appreciate the common foundation of myth and science. Since sociobiology is becoming politically ambitious,[8] it is well worth the effort to look at the mythic notions expressed in its scientific narratives.

Genetics claims that sexual reproduction creates rapid diversification with new populations able to adapt more flexibly to new ecological niches. A corollary to such diversification is a heightening of conflict, conflict between male and female, and conflict among the various demes. As Wilson expresses it:

> In short, social evolution is constrained and shaped by the necessities of sexual reproduction and not promoted by it. Courtship and sexual bonding are devices for overriding the antagonism that arises automatically from genetic differences induced by sexual reproduction.[9]

Sexual reproduction is a departure from the parthenogenetic steady-state; it generates diversity in a context of disequilibrium, out of which novel adaptations can arise. Here again we see the recurrence of a mythic root-idea, that of the disruptive dynamism of novelty contrasted with a preexisting steady-state. In one narrative we have angels as the preexisting steady-state and human beings as the new, dynamic, adaptative group; in another myth we have the stable androgynous Adam contrasted with the conflict-laden couple, Adam and Eve. And in the world of popular mythology of television, we have a new version of the ancient myth of the Amazon. In the series "Wonderwoman" (derived from a children's comic book), the introduction explains that Wonderwoman comes from an island lost to the world because of its location in the Bermuda Triangle; there, safe from the destructive ravages of a male technological civilization, the parthenogenetic society of mother and daughter is able to carry on its peaceful, prehistoric, Aegean way of life. In each of these narratives the steady-state is always the more ancient and stable way of life; the new step in cultural evolution is the dynamic and unsettling form of dangerous experimentation.[10]

The epistemologist Gregory Bateson has remarked that we could not have music and the creation of novel forms unless we had a background of noise, of uncommitted potential in randomness and disorder that awaited selection in the ordering of the creative act.

All that is not information, not redundancy, not form and not restraints—is noise, the only possible source of *new* patterns.[11]

Noise and disorder seem to be the necessary backdrop for what Whitehead would call "the creative advance of the universe." In the ideal Amazon society without males, the parthenogenetically created daughter is really the clone of the mother; the society continues down from generation to generation with the timeless values of the Great Mother held intact. But when a gamete throws half its genetic investment away to open itself to the intrusions of the male, then the old stable crust of the ground under the virgin's feet cracks open, and the Lord of the Underworld rides out to rape the daughter and carry her off to the dark world where the male is king. Small wonder that Demeter wept and sought throughout the world to find her lost daughter, Persephone.

Since some scholars may think it flippant to compare a scientific theory with a television program or a Greek myth, let me illustrate what I mean by a root structure by comparing sociobiology with literature, E. O. Wilson with D. H. Lawrence. First, Wilson:

Sex is an antisocial force in evolution. Bonds are formed between individuals in spite of sex and not because of it.[12]

And here is the language of the artist:

The men kept together; as if to support each other the women also are together, in a hard, strong herd. It is as if the power, the hardness, the triumph, even in this Italian village, were with the women in their relentless, vindictive unity. . . .
   On Sunday afternoons the uncomfortable youth walks by the side of his maiden for an hour in the public highway. Then he escapes; as from a bondage he goes back to his men companions. On Sunday afternoons and evenings the married woman, accompanied by a friend or by a child—she dare not go alone, afraid of the strange, terrible sex-war between her and the drunken man—is seen leading home the wine-drunken, liberated husband. Sometimes she is beaten when she gets home. It is part of the process. But there is no synthetic love between men and women, there is only passion, and passion is fundamental hatred, the act of love is a fight.[13]

Since both the poet and the sociobiologist were observing the courtship dances and battles of humans and animals, it is not all that surprising that poetry and ethology can share common insights. It is, however, surprising that poetry, literature, and the humanities in general are so undervalued in our postindustrial society, when poetry and myth have shown time and again that they can outrace by centuries the insights of the scientists. A poet like D. H. Lawrence is deeply connected through the creative reverie with the collective unconscious; he can know through intuition what the scientist must labor to prove. But virtue does not alone reside with the poet, and Lawrence as well as Wilson was capable of narrowness and fatuous overgeneralization. Lawrence misunderstood yoga and the religion of ancient Mexico in *Fantasia of the Unconscious* and *The Plumed Serpent,* and his vision of politics, expressed in his *Apocalypse,* was as authoritarian as anything in *Sociobiology.* However, we know how to protect ourselves from the politics of artists, for we simply don't take art that seriously, but we do not know how to protect ourselves from the politics of social scientists. In the new society we have created through mass education, we have tried to force the humanists in the universities to become social scientists, and in the extreme patterns of narrow specialization, we grant PhDs in the social sciences to some people who have read almost exclusively articles in specialized journals and predigested textbooks prepared especially for the enormous classes favored by the bureaucracies of the edubusiness. Equipped with worthless degrees, these social scientists then become the expert consultants to government and the educators of the next generation.

You can train a specialist to repeat an existing procedure, but you cannot train a scientist or an artist to create new ways of knowing and being. To be creative, you have to know how to be receptive, Yin; you have to know how to be at home with the ambiguous, the random, the disordered. Specialists have a poor tolerance for poetry and ambiguity, and their rush to order often misses a much more interesting form of order at a higher level of being. When you show a specialist the relevance of myth, he will automatically assume that myth is a sloppy form of guesswork that needs to be given precise and quantitative expression in "real" science. It is in this spirit that E. O. Wilson calls fiction "the research protocols of human ethology." This imperialistic colonizing of art and the humanities encourages further specialization, for the humanist will simply retreat in disgust to the comfort of his own specialty and his own cronies.

To be fair to the scientist, I must also point out that when an artist sees a fascinating insight or archetype expressed in the awful writing of a medium in a trance, he too feels the need to give the unconscious utterance the more refined expression of art. The process of alchemical sublimation from unconscious to conscious is shared by artist and scientist.

For both Wilson and Lawrence, sex is a courtship dance of conflict. Although the scientist is not permitted to talk about the meaning of evolution, or the goal toward which the evolutionary force is driving, the artist or the mystic is, and both artist and mystic have long recognized the inseparable relationship between sex and death. Sexual reproduction introduces death, for it produces new individuals that, by virtue of being limited and highly specific beings, must die. The asexual cell divides itself *ad infinitum* and therefore never fully dies; the parthenogenite reduplicates itself in a daughter that is practically a clone, but the sexual organism reproduces itself and then moves that much closer to death. Reproduction is the climax of life; in some species, the postcoital male immediately dies or is consumed by the female.[14]

If death is part of the deep mystery of sexuality, and *le grand mort* overshadows *le petit mort,* and if sexual reproduction is a force that produces new individuated beings, then perhaps we can understand why the sadist has coupled pain, death, and terror with the beauty of sexuality. The archangel of evolution, the Archon, created the human sexual body, and with it, death. The sadist simply shoves death into the Archon's face, as if to say, "See, this is your work." In blatantly linking pain and death with sexuality, the Marquis de Sade is a modern Gnostic who trembles in horror at Creation. His act of artistic horror in writing *The Ninety Days of Sodom* is an attempt to shove Creation back into the face of Jehovah in disgust. The Marquis de Sade is, therefore, the mirror-image of a moralist; his vision of horror and his obsession with suffering are the cries of an innocent who has never been able to become inured to the pain of human existence; he dwells on it obsessively and must write out vision after vision of hell. The tragedy of the Marquis is indeed a Gnostic one of entrapment, for in hating the evil Archon of creation he has become precisely what he hates and given to the devil another incarnation in his own writing.

Those who have a vision of the horror of existence cannot stand the unsettling dynamic of a universe which, in order to move and create, must introduce principles of randomness, freedom, disorder, and evil. The Gnostic or Manichean wishes to move back into the peace of that most ancient steady-state of all, nonexistence. He struggles to escape but finds himself trapped in a body; in horror of the body, he creates in his sexual perversions grossly distorted images of bondage and terror to communicate his own vision of the nature of incarnate existence.

Love and death, Eros and Thanatos: sexual reproduction is a metaphysic of conflict, and the twisting of the human body in sexual perversions tells us something about the spiritual limits of the human anatomy. Sexuality creates individuals; many cannot stand an individual existence, and so they seek to return: to the womb, to the herd, to the church, to the totalitarian state. Sexuality creates individuals and then has to face the conflict of individuals moving in all their different directions for comfort in mother, herd, church, and state.

II

PERHAPS ONE of the most bizarre examples of sexuality as conflict in the allegedly innocent world of the animals is found in the infanticidal practices of the langur monkeys. A langur troop is ruled by a dominant male until such time as a new dominant male arrives to expel him. Upon the expulsion of the old dominant, the new ruler kills all the infants in the troop. The theory goes that by stopping lactation in the females with infants, the dominant male accelerates their return into estrus and receptivity for insemination by him. Needless to say, the mothers do not welcome infanticide but try to protect their infants; when, however, their infants are killed and they come into estrus some weeks later, they do present themselves to the dominant male and allow themselves to be inseminated in the coitus of a few seconds that represents the tenuous relationship between these two warring sexes. Dr. Sarah Blaffer-Hrdy, a colleague of E. O. Wilson at Harvard who has studied the langurs, seems to support Wilson's theory that sexuality is intrinsically conflict-laden. Blaffer-Hrdy, however, goes even further to assert that males and females in the langurs practically constitute two separate species.

> Langur life histories presented here illustrate the extent to which the two sexes differ. The demands of reproduction have led to the evolution of two quite different creatures, two sexes caught in the bounds of irreconcilable conflicts . . .
> Rarely do the best interests of the female langur coincide with those of her consort. As Strindberg so clearly perceived, sexuality means conflict. Apart from insemination, langur females have little use for males except to protect them from other males. The outstanding question, then, is why females should tolerate males at all. Why allow themselves to be subjected to the tyranny of warring polygynists? . . .
> Once again the pitfall is intrasexual competition—this time competition among females themselves for representation in the next generation's gene pool. Whereas direct competition among males for access to females selects for males who are as big and as strong or stronger than their opponents, a female who "opted" for larger body size in order to fight off a male might not be so well adapted for her dual role of both survivor (of drought and other climatic fluctuations) and childbearer. An oversized female might produce fewer offspring than her smaller cousin. In the long-term evolutionary scene, her cousin's progeny would prevail.[15]

Sexual cultures seem caught in a hopeless contradiction, in that the interests of the sexes are so deeply at odds; but a culture of Amazons would seem to be caught in an equal contradiction. A society of strong females would have to either import weak males to inseminate them—and thereby select for physical weaknesses that could damage their society—or import strong males and introduce traits that would be so alien to it—and thereby select for the extinction of their amazon culture and the reestablishment of a bisexual one. If such societies of amazons have ever existed, we can begin to see why they might have been short-lived experiments in escaping from what Blaffer-Hrdy calls "an evolutionary trap."

Fascinating as ethology can be, it does seem that its metaphysical generalization into the illusory synthesis of sociobiology suffers from Whitehead's "fallacy of misplaced concreteness." Selection, inclusive fitness, and the gene pool are concepts that become personified in sociobiological narratives, but at the same time that these disguised personifications are slipped into, true cultural and psychological configurations are reduced to physical genes that can be inherited. Suddenly we encounter a langur female who is concerned about her "representation in the next generation's gene pool." In the nineteenth century, Ruskin talked about "the pathetic fallacy" in poetry whereby trees and streams were said to weep at the passing of the shepherd-bard. Now it seems as if the tendency to use the pathetic fallacy has been inherited by sociobiology and that the gene pool stands by and weeps or cheers at the behavior of humans and animals.

> All-out fights between males are rare, probably because of the formidability of another male langur and the diminution in reproductive potential that a male would suffer if injured.[16]

Here an immediate experience of pain is changed into a possible future loss of reproductive potential. In evolutionary thinking, the individual with his sensations of pain or his thoughts is not important; it is his reproductive potential to create the next generation that is important. But if the individual unit's only value is in his creation of the next individual unit, which also has no value except to create the next individual unit, then we end up with a whole *regress ad infinitum.* One either has to be a thoroughgoing atheist and say that the entire universe is meaningless, or one ends up by projecting value to the end of the line: the individual is not a value because it is merely a means to an end, the *Ens* of evolution. One does not talk about the "goal of evolution" in polite company, so the scientist indulges in disguised teleology by making reproduction and the eschatology of the future the focus of "maximizing one's inclusive fitness in the next generation."

But why have a generation at all? If the almighty gene wanted immortality, why did evolution introduce anything beside the immortality of the asexual cell? The amoeba doesn't have to worry about its inclusive fitness in the next generation. Pity the poor langur who, because of evolution's dirty trick in introducing sexual reproduction, now has to calculate percentages on his genetic endowments to successive generations and commit infanticide to make certain that another gene does not usurp his place. The gene begins to be portrayed by the sociobiologists as a kind of businessman pushing his way through a competitive market system, and all the old notions of Social Darwinism seem to have been revived. The mysticism of Rudolph Steiner, who would posit a group soul for a species and claim that the group soul makes the decisions, seems more straightforward. The sociobiologist seems to posit a new version of the unconscious, not one filled with Jung's mythic archetypes but rather computerlike calculations on population genetics.

Two additional and more powerful examples of sociobiological versatility: Kurland (in press), developing an idea suggested by Alexander (1974), asks why an individual should invest in his sister's children rather than his own. In answer, Kurland invokes the concept of "paternity certainty." Your wife's children share ½ of your genes, *provided you are their father*. Your actual relatedness to them will therefore be ½ times the probability that you are indeed your (jural) children's father, i.e., times the average paternity certainty for your society. Let us say that this figure is ⅓: you are therefore related to your own children by (½) (⅓) = (⅙). Your relatedness to your "full" sister, in theory ½, is at least ¼ (representing your common father) plus ¼ (your putative common father) times the paternity certainty of ⅓, totaling ¼ + (¼) (⅓) = ⅓. Since you thus share ⅓ of your genes with your sister and she provides ½ the genes of her children, you are related to her children by (½) (⅓) = ⅙. In this situation, sociobiology predicts you will invest equally in both your sister's children and your own, all things being equal, since you are related to both sets of children by ⅙. In societies in which paternity certainty falls under ⅓, you should invest more heavily in your sister's children than your own; if paternity certainty is more than ⅓, you should favor your wife's children. Kurland notes that, just as we would expect, matrilineal societies tend to have low paternity certainty and to place little stress on female fidelity; patrilineal societies tend to have high paternity certainty and place greater stress on female chastity and fidelity. Men invest in their sister's children where there is matrilineality and in their own children when patrilineality prevails. In other words, the avunculate makes sense in terms of sociobiology! *Whatever individual's conscious motives, they act as if they had performed the above calculations.*[17]

In the unconscious of the psychoanalysts, archetypal images are expressed in dreams, and these can be lifted up to a new level of conscious meaning by the analyzing doctor. In the unconscious of the Structuralists, certain patterns and structures appear in myths, and these can be lifted up to a new level of conscious meaning by the anthropologist. In the unconscious of the sociobiologists, certain numerical calculations on inclusive fitness are expressed in sexual behavior, and these can be lifted up to a new level of consciousness by the scientist.

In sociobiology intrasexual competition for inclusion in the next generation's gene pool becomes the unconscious motivation for the behavior of humans and animals. The langur, as well as a member of a preliterate society, is obsessed with "inclusive fitness," and all his behavior can be explained in terms of this concept. An organism's consciousness is epiphenomenal to its behavior, and its behavior is determined by unconscious calculations. Inside the animal is a gene and a computer; these are "real"; the rest is associated states of subjectivity. Infanticide, subjectively, may seem to go against the mother's feelings, but we need to remember that for sociobiology the gene is what counts, not the individual. A kindly langur male who adopts a troop of females and infants but takes no pains to murder the infants and reinseminate the females will live to see the offspring of other males flourish around him, and the genes of our kindly, noninfanticidal male will pass away. And so infanticide is an advantage if a male wishes to maximize his inclusive fitness and invest his genes in the future.

The Santiago school of the biology of knowledge does not share in sociobiology's denigration of the individual in the process of evolution. In a recent work, Francisco Varela takes issue with the simplistic epistemology and sees quite a different relationship between the individual and the species.

It is said that what evolves is the species and that the individuals in their historical existence are subordinated to this evolution. In a superficial descriptive sense this is meaningful because a particular species as an existing collection of individuals represents continuously the state of a particular historical network in its process of becoming one, and, if described as a state of a historical network a species necessarily appears in a process of transformation. *Yet, the species exists as a unit only in the historical domain, while the individuals that constitute the nodes of this historical network exist in physical space.* [My emphasis.] Strictly, a historical network is defined by all and every one of the individuals which constitute its nodes, but it is at any moment represented historically by the species as the collection of all the simultaneously existing nodes of the network; in fact, then, a species does not evolve because as a unity in the historical domain it only has a history of change. What evolves is a pattern of autopoietic organization embodied in many particular variations in a collection of transitory variations in a collection of transitory individuals that together define a reproductive historical network. Thus, *the individuals,* though transitory, are essential, not dispensable, because they constitute a necessary condition for the existence of this historical network which they define. The species is a descriptive term that represents a historical phenomenon; it does not constitute a *causal* component in the phenomenology of evolution.[18]

E. O. Wilson claims to be a scientific materialist, so it is surprising that he does not acknowledge that one never observes a species, but only individuals. A species, as Varela points out, only exists in consciousness; for Varela's epistemology this means that the observer is an intimate part of the system he observes. This idea flows nicely with the Quantum Theory of Werner Heisenberg. Heisenberg has pointed out that we cannot have any such thing as "a science of nature"; we can have only a science of man's knowledge of nature.[19] For both the German physicist and the Chilean biologist, natural history is a construct of consciousness that itself has a cultural history; therefore, one cannot speak about atoms or individuals in a species without taking both consciousness and culture into account in one's scientific narrative. Sociobiology dismisses the mind, the individual, and the culture. Were we to bow to Wilson's wish that ethics be removed from the humanities and placed in scientific hands, where moral issues could be treated simply as an aspect of the genetic variance problem, then we would end up with a rather hideous distortion of the body-politic. On the other hand, if we accept Varela's affirmation of the value of the individual as a descriptive agent in an evolutionary transformation, then we end up with a culture in which consciousness is given space to express its career through time. Perhaps because the Santiago school of Humberto Maturana, Francisco Varela, and Francisco Flores has had to work under conditions of civil war and fascist coup, their perceptions of history and natural history are quite different from those of E. O. Wilson in Cambridge, Massachusetts.

In dismissing consciousness and culture in natural history,

sociobiology is not simply offensive to the territoriality of the humanities; it is bad science. It expresses the passions of the reductionist who is irrationally impelled to show that "It is all nothing but . . ." Here it is difficult to draw the line between science and science fiction, and in the domain of sociobiology where the narratives are clearly mythological, it is doubly difficult. The drive or decision by which an animal maximizes his reproductive-potential representation in the gene pool eludes me. It would seem that infanticide is a *cultural* trait well on the other side of the Weissmann barrier that protects the gene from the soma. If there were not this Weissmann barrier to protect the integrity of the gene, then there would be no stability to the inheritance of traits in a species. To elevate an abstraction like "inclusive fitness" to a *motivation for* behavior, rather than recognize it as simply a geneticist's *explanation of* behavior, and then to go on to reduce cultural complexes to discrete genes, seems to me to be an example of the worst forms of reductionist thinking characteristic of the nineteenth century. I would rather take my mythology neat in the cinematic visions of the *Akash* with a seer like Steiner than in the camouflaged passions and murky reasoning of a sociobiologist.

Dr. Blaffer-Hrdy, perhaps sensing her occasional slip into personifications of evolutionary forces, has defended her theories.

> In this context, it cannot be stressed enough that no conscious intent on the part of the male is implied. It is simply assumed that the genes of animals who respond to a given situation in the most advantageous way—relative to other animals in the population—will be disproportionately represented in the next generation.[20]

The genes of an animal may be disproportionately represented in the next generation, especially if he has eliminated all competitors, but a cultural trait is not the same as a genetic trait. Infanticide is not a trait any more than a symphony is; a person may inherit musical ability, but he does not inherit symphonies, except through the medium of culture. A monkey may inherit a high dose of male hormones that encourages aggressive behavior, but he does not inherit infanticide. Information in the cell is not an object; a complex cultural trait cannot be simply reduced to a gene or a pheromone.[21] The presence of the fallacy of misplaced concreteness in Blaffer-Hrdy's work derives perhaps from the influence of her teacher at Harvard, E. O. Wilson. Consider, for example, Wilson on the evolution of society.

> Human beings are absurdly easy to indoctrinate—they *seek* it. If we assume for argument that *indoctrinability evolves,* at what level does natural selection take place? One extreme position is that the group is the unit of selection. When conformity becomes too weak, groups become extinct. In this version selfish, individualistic members gain the upper hand and multiply at the expense of others. But their rising prevalence accelerates the vulnerability of society and hastens its extinction. Societies containing higher frequencies of *conformer genes* replace those that disappear, thus raising the overall frequency of the genes in the metapopulation of societies. [My emphasis.] [22]

Conformity, a vast abstraction of the set of relationships of a group within a society and that society's relationship to a complex environment, is here made into a discrete, physical substance, a gene, and an even more complex abstraction, indoctrinability, is said to evolve. An eohippus may "evolve" into a horse, but when we say that a society of hunters and gatherers evolves into a farming village, we are using the word "evolves" as a metaphor for a process of directional change. Since a society of hunters and gatherers does not seem to change into a civilization without first changing into an agricultural village, anthropologists have created the metaphor of cultural evolution. But what it means to say that "indoctrinability evolves" is quite beyond me. It seems to express a vague notion that is at once bad science and bad poetry.

As a form of reductionist thinking, sociobiology seems to be a new landslide of the detritus of nineteenth-century materialism. First, it reduces a psychological or a cultural complex to a gene, and then it conceptualizes a gene as a hunk of matter rather than a crystal of sacred geometry and frozen music. Wilson speaks of the "upward-mobile gene" and the "homosexual gene";[23] we might as well speak of the car-stealing gene and the vandalism gene and arrest such criminals, through amniocentesis, in the womb. To say that a teenager steals a car because he has inherited a car-stealing gene is to fashion oneself in the science of Moliere's doctor, who sagely explained that his drug could induce sleep because it possessed a certain dormagenic property.

The sociology of knowledge of the future will find sociobiology to be a rich mine for studies on how "facts" can be interpreted (if not created) in unexpected ways. Like the spurious Social Darwinism of the nineteenth century, sociobiology constitutes a scientific attempt to create a myth; that it does not achieve the profoundity of traditional myth is due to the fact that it is too conscious, too cut off from the heights of the mystical summits of human consciousness, and too far removed from the depths of the psychology of the unconscious. As a contrived piece of rational mythologizing, sociobiology nevertheless does illustrate my point that when scientists generalize to tell us what we are, where we come from, and where we are going, they ineluctably move from science to myth.

Nothing is more likely to generate mythology than speculation on the origin of the species. In his review of the literature on the evolution of the brain, Carl Sagan stopped to consider the mythological nature of his own activity.

> These conjectures on the origins of the mammals constitute a kind of scientific myth; they may have some germ of truth in them, but they are unlikely to be the whole story. That scientific myths make contact with more ancient myths may or may not be a coincidence. It is entirely possible that we are able to invent scientific myths only because we have previously been exposed to the other sort.[24]

Sagan assumes that mythopoeic thought is an archaic heritage which has been transcended in the rise of scientific thinking, and in this assumption he follows the old Frazerian anthropology of the stages of progress from magic to science. I prefer to see myth in the Platonic tradition as a hieroglyphic mode of thought whereby the Archetypal Forms and the sensations of the physical plane come together in a mode of consciousness in which the ego becomes empty to be filled with the Daimon. Since the root-ideas of myth are at a deep and basic level of consciousness, they are not always expressed in day-to-day, casual descriptions, but when a person sinks into an imaginative reverie to write a book, or to synthesize the factual results of research, then he or she is likely to move into a more mythopoeic form of narrative, for even science can be a form of storytelling.

One basic root-idea is the Fall; another is sexual polarity. The poet Robert Graves has remarked that "Woman is, Man does." This notion is said to represent an archetypal distinction between the masculine and the feminine, and as an archetype it has been generalized into all facets of culture until it has been transformed to justify the stereotype of a "woman's place is in the home" so resented by feminists. The sociobiological version of the notion is expressed in Wilson's narrative.

> Why are there usually just two sexes? The answer seems to be that two are enough to generate the maximum potential genetic recombination, because virtually every healthy individual is assured of mating with a member of another (that is, "opposite") sex. And why are these two sexes anatomically different? Of course, in many micro-organisms, fungi, and algae, they are not; gametes identical in appearance are produced (isogamy). But in the majority of organisms, including virtually all animals, anisogamy is the rule. Moreover, the difference is usually strong; *one gamete, the egg, is relatively very large and sessile; the other, the sperm, is small and motile.*[25] [My emphasis.]

The gigantic egg sits, and the frantic and tiny sperm flagellates its tail to cross vast distances on its quest for dissolution in the huge egg. This is another version of "Woman is, Man does," another version of the death-defying quest of the male for ultimate dissolution in the Great Mother. The archetype, like an overture, sounds a melodic line that echoes on down from conception to death, from the dawn of history with the conservative, neolithic, Great-Mother cultures to the dynamic civilizations of the male gods. But civilizations, like the penis, rise and fall, and when the towers and battlements crumble into the earth, they return to the embrace of the Great Mother. So we can see that the archetype of "Woman is, Man does" is not simply the ethnocentric projection of a patriarchal culture; it is an archetype interpreted and embodied in the stereotypical situation of a parochial culture. The Great Mother is not merely a type of figure from the neolithic cultures of the Near East; she is an archetype. From a metaphysical point of view, the Great Mother is a metaphor for the receptacle of cosmic space itself.

III

WHEN THE SCIENTIST is ignorant of myth, cosmology, and literature, the quality of his narrative can be simplistic and naive—a straightforward, nineteenth-century exposition of positivism and progress—but when the scientist is gifted with an imagination and an artistic ability in writing, the narrative takes on the best qualities of storytelling. Since storytelling is, perhaps, the oldest of the arts, a good scientific story begins to move beneath the shallow streams of conventional empiricism to express the deeper dimensions of consciousness.

Just such an artistic work of scientific reporting and observation is Jane van Lawick-Goodall's *In the Shadow of Man*. It is not simply that the book is as well written as many novels, but that the sensitivity which enables Lawick-Goodall to write so well also informs her perceptions and generalizations. In her work is none of Wilson's arrogance; she has not, in his ugly word, "biologicized" the humanities; she has humanized biology.

In the foreword to her book, Lawick-Goodall explains how Dr. Louis Leakey wished her to observe chimpanzees in the wild because she was not an expert and, therefore, could look at the chimpanzees without academic preconceptions. In his classic work, *The Structure of Scientific Revolutions*, T. S. Kuhn has shown that the scientist who makes an important breakthrough in creating a new paradigm is often either very young or new to the field he or she revolutionizes. Lawick-Goodall's work is a confirmation of Kuhn's thesis, for she was both young and new to the field of ethology. Before her work, most primate studies had been conducted in the laboratory; there the scientist could force the chimp to conform to his own convenient schedules and research routines in a condition of imprisonment. By going out into the field to live with the chimpanzees in their own natural conditions, Lawick-Goodall was able to demolish many cherished generalizations of the fields of ethology and anthropology.

One of the favored notions on which I was raised as an anthropology student was that man was Homo Faber, the tool maker. It was not surprising that a technological society would overemphasize the importance of tools, but it was surprising how anthropologists could blind themselves to the use of tools by otters and birds. When Lawick-Goodall observed that chimps would strip the leaves off twigs, line them up in a row beside a termit hole, and then begin to fish down the hole for the edible insects, she showed that not only were the chimps capable of changing nature into culture, but they were also capable of thinking in terms of a future. The twigs not in hand lay by the side of the animals awaiting their future use.

Perhaps Dr. Lawick-Goodall's most dramatic discovery was that chimpanzees indulged in ritual rain dances.[26] Here was behavior that had nothing to do with "the struggle for existence"; it was not an act that enhanced the animal's inclusive fitness; it was an emotional and artistic response to the changing atmosphere brought on by a rain storm. With song and dance and tool making in evidence in chimpanzee society, it no longer makes sense to reserve the term "culture" for humans alone. Chimpanzees have a culture, and perhaps when our sensitivity is raised to new levels we will begin to see that such creatures as whales and dolphins have cultures as well.

The rain dance of the chimpanzees seems to express a religion, an expression of awe at the natural forces of rain, lightning, and thunder. Perhaps the change in the ionization of the air, associated with the onset of a thunderstorm, affects their moods and emotions. For a moment they forget the normal routine of their daily lives to look up and bind their smaller world back up with the larger world of nature. The word "religion" comes from the Latin *religāre*, meaning to bind; to bind or connect the individual with the universal is to commit a religious act. The profane is the world of routines in which the whole is forgotten; the sacred is the individual seen in awe-inspiring relationship to the immensity of the universe. A sacred moment or place is thus one which connects the immediate concerns of the creature with the whole of Creation. The rain dance of the chimps is just such an occasion. Just as we, on formal occasions of state, take out our old insignia and maces of authority to display them in expressions of hierarchical ranking, so do the male chimpanzees gather together to shake branches in display and to set their own systems of hierarchy and dominance before the even mightier displays of nature. Such an act of ritual has an almost human ambiguity about it, for it is an expression of power, the chimpanzee hierarchy made visible, and an expression of weakness, a submission to the greater power of "What the thunder said." It would seem, therefore, that the religion of the chimpanzees is not one of fertility, but of animism, the interpenetration of natural forces within their own animal culture.

One of the reasons the chimpanzees may have no religion of fertility rites is that sexuality is matter-of-fact for them, far more so than it has become for humans. A female in estrus, or heat, is the center of attention for the males, but there is no conflict or competition, and the males will patiently queue up behind her to wait their turn for what is, in reality, a communal coitus. The act of intercourse itself is brief and perfunctory.

> Chimpanzees have the briefest possible intercourse—normally the male remains mounted for only ten to fifteen seconds.[27]

Status and the ranking of males in the hierarchy of dominance seems to be far more important, in chimpanzee society, than erotic drives. In chimpanzee culture, male dominance is not a means for monopolizing a harem of females, and since paternity is not in evidence, it would seem also that male dominance is not a means of ensuring inclusive fitness; rather, Lawick-Goodall has observed that the ranking is a means of preserving the social band. When threatened by another social unit, chimpanzees will go to war.[28] If paternity is communal, then the desire for representation in the gene pool is simply the desire to protect one's own group from the threat of a foreign one.

Human beings traditionally associate sexuality with bestiality, but this association would seem to have more to do with the projection of repressed desires onto animals than it has to do with the sexuality of beasts. Certainly in the case of the chimpanzees, no such association of sexuality and bestiality is possible. Humans have a consciousness which emphasizes sexuality, perhaps because the origins of human consciousness are related to the origins of human sexuality. Humans are far more libidinous than beasts, and so it makes little sense to assume that sexual passion is the archaic heritage of our animal nature.

Another truism about beasts that collapses under the weight of Lawick-Goodall's observations is the notion that "might is right" for mere animals, and that no sense of justice restrains their use of force. If a lower-ranking chimpanzee male captures meat, an out-of-the-ordinary delicacy in his diet, he does not have to turn it over to a higher-ranking dominant male upon demand. "At such times the higher-ranking males, frustrated beyond endurance, frequently vent their aggression on lower-ranking individuals."[29] Life in this primitive condition of nature is not, in the words of Hobbes, "nasty, brutish, and short"; it is a world of rules, a world in which physical aggression and sexuality are shaped by a protoculture.

Of course, one cannot generalize about all animal behavior from that of the chimpanzees. Animal cultures differ as much as human cultures: baboon males take care of children, langurs are infanticidal and keep harems, and gibbons are monogamous for life. The glib generalizations of the past about the sexuality of animals came from the projection onto them of the shadow of civilization, a projection in which the natural and instinctual life was forced to live out the caricatures of civilized man's fantasies. It is interesting to see what happens if we alter the process to reflect back from animal behavior onto human behavior. When we see the animals not as catch-alls for our own projections, but as points of entry for insight into human behavior, we can discover a new kinship with all living things.

One such point of entry is Lawick-Goodall's observations on male friendships. The chimpanzee males make lasting friends, but the females seem to do this hardly at all. Since there is no way of telling the father of a chimpanzee infant, the basic family unit is the mother and the child. In the case of the chimpanzees, tenderness and affection between mother and child can go on for years. It would seem reasonable to assume, therefore, that most of the female energy goes into the maintenance of the family life of the species, with little left over for palling around in the way the males do.

> Despite this basic difference in the structure of the human and chimpanzee family group, the behavior of some human males is not so different from chimpanzee males as might be expected. In the Western World at any rate, many fathers, even though they may be materially responsible for their families welfare, spend much time away from their wives and children—often in the company of other men. All-male groups are popular in many cultures: they range from clubs and stag parties in the Western World to initiation and warrior groups in primitive societies. In short, a vast number of human males, although they may be only too anxious at times for

feminine company, are equally keen for much of the time to "get away from women" and relax in the ease of male companionship. Chimpanzee males seem to feel rather the same. Naturally they cluster around pink females when these are available, but often they travel about and feed in all-male groups and are more likely to groom each other than they are to groom females or youngsters.

Never, however, have we seen anything that could be regarded as homosexuality in chimpanzees.[30] [My emphasis.]

Humans have a culture which includes homosexuality, the nuclear family of mother, father, and child, and a female sexual pattern in which estrus is eliminated. (Freudians would, of course, argue that there is a relationship between the paternal family and homosexuality.) We also have religions which focus on fertility, women's mysteries, and the great mythological relationships of love and death, Eros and Thanatos. The differences are as striking as the similarities. In his *Origins of the Family, Private Property, and the State,* Friedrich Engels used the ethnographic research of Lewis Morgan to theorize that the early stage of the human family was the mother and the child, with all the males of the social unit belonging to the entire group, the *gens.*[31] This theoretical model of the early condition of the human family seems to correspond to the chimpanzee grouping of females and infants with no "fathers." We are left, therefore, with the problem of explaining how the shift away from estrus, the emergence of the nuclear family, and the appearance of homosexuality came about.

IV

IN FREUD'S MYTH of human origins, *Totem and Taboo* (an explanation which A. R. Kroeber called "a Just-So Story"), the primal family consists of the Great Father, his harem, and the brother-herd of subdominant males. One day, according to Freud, the brother-herd rises up in revolution and slays the Father; then in an agony of remorse for their action, they create a eucharistic feast in which they all bind themselves together in one common outpouring of guilt and expiation by consuming the body and blood of the Father in a cannibalistic rite. Freud's myth tries to show how, in the condition of the primal crime, we created evil and, in remorse for the act of revolution, became human. But in order to feel so highly conscious an emotion as remorse, the brothers would already have to be human; the Freudian myth invokes what it must explain and so explains nothing. We have to go back further to find the origins of humanity. Freud's *Totem and Taboo* is a conscious dream, an active imagination which could help a Jungian analyst see into the condition of Freud's unconscious life, but it is not a description of the dawn of human culture, for everything we know from ethology would make us suspect that the early human family was not composed of the Great Father, the harem, and the brother-herd. Freud was projecting Father Abraham and the patriarchal family structure of the Biblical pastoralists.

To explain the origins of human culture and the formation of human sexuality, I would like to consider another piece of scientific mythologizing, "The Human Revolution" by Charles Hockett and Robert Ascher.[32] Hockett and Ascher go back to the period of dessication in the Pliocene when the forests were disappearing and the savannah was opening up. With only small forests and dispersed clumps of trees remaining, Hockett and Ascher theorize that the strong primates controlled the old traditional ecological niche and expelled the weaker primates into the open and dangerous savannah. The primate that was expelled from this forest garden of Eden was Proconsul (now called Dryopithecus). Unable to swing happily in the safety of the trees, the small primates had to band together and pick up rocks to defend themselves. With their hands taking the burden of carrying things away from their mouths, they were in the novel position of being able to let their mouths be used for the chatter that would be needed to give warnings and organize the search for food. Since, as Hockett and Ascher argue, the natural effect of any innovation is conservative, in that the purpose of the innovation is to enable the individual to re-create his old familiar condition, these new primates would likely band together in small clumps of trees to forage in search of food only when it was safe. Under these changed circumstances tool-use and language evolve together, and the long march toward a culture of rockets and computers begins.

The mythic structures implicit in Hockett and Ascher's narrative of the fall from Eden are obvious, but an anthropologist might argue that the relationship between myth and model is the opposite: the myth is a dim racial memory of the original drama of hominization. We do know that early primates like Ramapithecus were arboreal, and that later primates like Australopithecus afarensis and Homo habilis were not, and so we are left with the problem of imagining a transitional scenario from forest to savannah. Hockett and Ascher's imaginary scenario is as good as any and seems to have been absorbed in the anthropologist Richard Leakey's accounts of human origins,[33] so it seems quite reasonable to adopt it as the foundation for my own speculations.

One of the most basic features of the human revolution is the disappearance of estrus in the females. How are we to explain this dramatic departure from the animal norm? Perhaps we can understand the shift away from estrus by understanding the shift from the forest to the savannah. In the forest environment the chimpanzees roam freely and are largely not subject to predation. The males travel along with their pals and the females take care of the infants. To understand the open and fluid nature of such an easy grouping, we need to contrast the chimpanzee society of the forest with the baboon society of the open veldt.

Baboons travel in a tight defensive pack, with the protective circle especially tight when the pack is crossing open terrain. In the center of the circle is the dominant male and his close associates, the hierarchy known as "the establishment." Close to these males are the females and their infants, and surrounding the females is an outer perimeter of subdominant and adolescent males; these form an early-warning system and a defensive line of expendable, inexperienced males. The society of the baboons is rigidly hierarchical, but the close proximity of the dominant males and the females with infants seems to have encouraged some rudimentary aspects of male child-care, for males will take care of infants with some degree of tenderness; they are not like the langurs who are homicidal to all but their own brood.

The rigid structure of baboon society is a response to the openness of the savannah, an environment like that faced by a Pliocene primate forced out into the open. We may imagine his response would be similar to that of the baboon, that he would huddle with his fellows in fear of the unknown. If the females and the infants were to venture out into the savannah on their own without the males, they would be in great danger. The new environment would negate the arrangements of the sexual division of labor of the old forest environment, and the females would need to lure the males away from paling around in all-male groups into some sort of protective association with the females and the infants.

But what kind of signal could the females give to lure the males back? Here perhaps the amazing chimpanzee which Lawick-Goodall has christened "Flo" can offer us a clue.

> One day when Flo was socially grooming with four adult males, a young pregnant female arrived; she had recently joined our group from the north. Pregnant females often continue to show monthly swellings, and this one had a very pink posterior. The males on this occasion did not mate her, but they were nevertheless interested. They left Flo, hastened over to the newcomer, inspected her bottom, and began to groom her vigorously. It was only a few minutes later that I noticed Flo. She had moved several yards toward the young female and was standing staring at her with every hair on end. Had she dared, without doubt she would have attacked the newcomer. As it was, she presently walked slowly over to the group and herself inspected the swelling carefully. Then she moved away and sat down to groom Flint.
>
> We could scarcely believe it when the following day Flo showed the beginnings of a swelling. Flint was less than two years old, and whereas young females may start swelling again when their infants are only fourteen months, old females like Flo do not normally become pink again for four or five years after giving birth. However, Flo's sex skin was swollen enough to arouse instant attention from Rudolph, who feverishly pushed her to her feet and intently inspected her bottom. So did two other males. Then they sat around grooming *her*. The next day that extraordinary swelling had gone—nor did Flo show any signs of swelling again for the next four years. I cannot believe that it was pure coincidence.[34]

Flo's remarkable evidence of mind over body seems to indicate that humans in a biofeedback laboratory are not the only ones who can gain control over autonomic functions. Since female chimpanzees in estrus are always subject to special favors and attention, and since estrus is often the way a female gains temporary status and privilege in the dominance hierarchy of the males, it is a reasonable speculation to assume that female primates, when exposed to the dangers of the open savannah, might not feel so good about the old ways of males in groups with mothers left alone with the infants. The females might initiate a revolution in which they change their body signals to excite the interest of the males to become secure as the object of favors and attention in an encirclement of males. If Flo could change her body overnight, it is not too much to assume that Ramapithecus could change over a longer period of time.

The shift from estrus to a receptivity for intercourse at all times represents an eroticization of time; sexuality becomes an orientation to all experiences rather than a perfunctory ten-second interlude in a way of life oriented around status and power. In establishing a new signal system for sexuality, the females set up a magnetic force that pulls the males toward them to constellate a wholly novel social grouping for the wholly novel environment of the savannah. With the abandonment of the periodically inflamatory signals of estrus, the female develops a whole new body language of attractive signals, such as fleshy buttocks and full breasts. Intercourse changes from a perfunctory, dorsal mounting to a full confrontation of mates in frontal intercourse, and the genitals of the male grow larger than those primates who came before. Small wonder that the old medieval paintings of Genesis emphasize the genitals by covering them with fig leaves. Genesis is the story of the genitals.

The eroticization of time, however, brings with it an inherent contradiction: on the one hand the shift away from estrus serves to attract the males back to the females, but on the other hand this disturbs the traditional system of male-bonding and increases the likelihood of intrasexual competition. E. O. Wilson noted:

> Fox (1972), following a suggestion by Chance (1962), has argued that sexual selection was the auxiliary motor that drove human evolution all the way to the *Homo* grade. His reasoning proceeds as follows. Polygyny is a general trait in hunter-gatherer bands and also may have been the rule in the early hominid societies. If so, a premium would have been placed on sexual selection involving both epigamic display toward the females and intrasexual competition among the males. This selection would be enhanced by the constant mating provocation that arises from the female's nearly continuous sexual receptivity.[35]

The shift from estrus is a signal that touches off a red and green light at once, an excitation of both sexuality and male competitive aggression. In the double-bind theory of Gregory Bateson we know that such a double signal can generate madness or the destructuring of a context which creates a moment of Zen illumination. Just such a "Touch!"-"Don't touch:"-"Danger!" seems to be expressed in the Genesis myth of human origins, for there Jahweh points out the tree to Adam—and thereby rivets his attention to it—and then forbids Adam to taste of the fruits of such consciousness. When the shadow of God, Satan, tempts the shadow of Adam, Eve, there is no way out except to move completely into the world of consciousness, to know light and shadow, good and evil, sexuality and danger, Eros and Thanatos. If we accept the theory that myths are unconscious expressions of a racial memory, then the fact that the female offers the male a red, attractive apple may express the situation that I am arguing for—that the female first shifts from estrus to attract the male into the new human culture. Out of this seduction, Adam loses his old companionship with the angels and the male god, Jahweh; he responds to his attraction to Eve by resenting her and longing for the good old days of the prelapsarian steady-state. With the insight of genius, Milton recognizes in his own retelling of the Fall in *Paradise Lost* that Genesis is the story of the genitals by showing Adam's first act after the Fall to be the lustful rape of Eve.

All of which simply goes to show that our mythologies and religions are about sexuality and not about the animism of the religion of the chimpanzees. Our religions are about sexuality because we are trying to deal with the basic contradiction of a sexuality that draws males to females and shifts from male bonding to male competition and aggression.

The structural anthropologists, like Lévi-Strauss and Edmund Leach, have gone to great lengths to demonstrate that a myth is often a way of coming to terms with a contradiction.[36] It is not surprising, therefore, that the greater myth of Genesis and the lesser myth of sociobiology both point up the inherent contradictions of sexual behavior.

The shift from estrus is a revolution initiated by the females. In anthropology this revolution is seen in anthropocentric terms.

Both Freud and Lévi-Strauss are basically interested in the same question: how did *Homo* come to be *sapiens?* What sets man off from Nature while leaving him part of Nature? For Freud, this is a result of the imposition of restraints on free sexual activity as a result of strong feelings—guilt, fear, fraternity, obedience, incest, etc. For Lévi-Strauss (1949), in his earlier work, it is a result not of negative injunctions but of the positive value of exchange, i.e. of women. In his later work (e.g., Lévi-Strauss, 1962a, 1962b) the distinguishing feature of man is also exchange, but exchange of information rather than women.[37]

Although feminist scholarship has reached its own levels of ideological hysteria, the ethnocentrism of Robin Fox's anthropology as expressed above, is appalling. When one has surfeited on the male clubbiness of Freud, Lévi-Strauss, Fox, Tiger, and Ardrey, the feminist anthropology of Elaine Morgan's *Descent of Woman*[38] is a welcome and witty relief. In her speculative scenario, the hominids venture out into the savannah and are wiped out; only a few hominids who move from forest to the seashore survive to become the ancestors of the human lineage. From Morgan's analysis, a popularized version of Sir Alastair Hardy's theories, it was by becoming aquatic that humans lost their body hair, developed pendulous breasts and long hair on their heads, and switched from dorsal to frontal intercourse, a revolution which required the lengthening of the male penis. E. O. Wilson has dismissed Morgan's claims to science,[39] and her popularity with the general public has never reached to the scientific specialists. Nevertheless, her clever debunking of the macho school of anthropology is a welcome contribution to the sociology of knowledge.

When Robert Ardrey is seeing man the deadly hunter,[40] and when Lévi-Strauss is seeing man exchanging women as dumb objects of possession, they are focusing on the fact that males are part of a system of epigamic display. In hunting and gathering societies, the men will beat their chests telling stories of the hunt, but the gathering by the women brings in seventy percent of the food. In a society of early hominids, the males might have displayed, but their actions were responses to signals of sexual receptivity emitted by the females. The male is the *figure,* but the female is the *ground,* and this pattern of *gestalt* is another version of "The egg *is,* the sperm *does."* The shift from estrus is a revolution initiated by the females; it may seem that the males are powerful in their epigamic display of sexual competition, but the real power is with the females who initiate the shift in the first place.

> In apes and indeed in mammals generally the existence of the sexual heat not only restricts mating to one or two days in the month; it restricts it to one or two unions for each pregnancy. One copulation may, and usually does, secure a whole litter of offspring. But without restriction, as in man, ten or a hundred matings may take place with only a single offspring. Indeed in the extreme case a whole lifetime of mating may lead to no offspring at all. Thus in man the continuous sexual life is secured at the expense of about a hundred times as much production of sperm by the male and a hundred times as much sexual activity as is needed for the reproduction of a species with a cyclical mating activity. Sperm-redundancy, as specialists describe it, increases from 10 to the 8 to the 10 or more. Thus in man, unlike other animals, sexual intercourse has ceased to be just a means of reproduction. But it has not become just an end in itself. Rather it is something between the two, an activity devoted equally to maintaining the continuity of the family and the structure of society.[41]

In the shift from forest to savannah, and from estrus to receptivity at all times, we encounter another version of the archetypal pattern of the shift from an ancient steady-state into a new, unsettling, and dynamic condition. Sexuality becomes the force for disrupting the old camaraderie of males in groups, but it does not immediately establish the nuclear family of mother, father, and infant. But how would a new male-female strategy for reproduction and survival constellate itself in the new conditions of the savannah? Would the new group include the solitary dominant male with his harem, as pictured in Freud's *Totem and Taboo?* I doubt this for several reasons. For one reason, one male alone could not adequately protect a harem of females with infants in the open veldt. The baboon's system of having many watchers surround the females would be more effective. In this system, one could forage for roots, seeds, and insects in the open, while dozens of guards periodically rose up on two feet to peer over the grass to sound a warning if a predator approached. For a second reason, most recent archaeological digs in Africa have provided evidence that the early hominids transported their food back to a base camp and engaged in food sharing. Since the early hominids were most likely carrion-eaters and scroungers rather than hunters, the need to carry the food away from the open to some protective clump of trees would be clear. Such a system of food sharing would require a more complex grouping than Freud's fantasy of the single dominant male with his harem.

With Hocket and Ascher's application of Romer's Rule from paleontology—namely that the effect of every innovation is conservative—in mind, I would imagine that the effect of the female innovation would be to lure the males out of groups to bring them back to the females. The males would reassert the old familiar habit by ranging out in groups to scrounge for food. The basic division of labor would be established, with females foraging for roots and seeds, the kind of light picking a mother with an infant can easily do, and males going off to scrounge or steal a kill and cart the heavier beast back to the home base in the clump of trees. In this way, the old forest condition is reconstituted in the clump of trees, and the old male-bonding system is re-established in the hunting and scrounging band.

The implications of this line of reasoning upset many cherished conceptions about human nature, so it will be worth spelling these out. First, if food sharing is basic to human evolution, as Glynn Isaacs and others argue,[42] then the Social Darwinist myth of survival of the fittest and "every man for himself" is a projection from the more cruel times of capitalist society. Kropotkin's perspective on *Mutual Aid* seems to be much closer to the natural condition of human and hominid societies. Secondly, if the female shift from estrus and the new pattern of food sharing are the initial responses to the new environment of the savannah, then a social and cultural revolution precedes the technological one. Ardrey's celebration of the development of the weapon and hominid killing as the fountainhead of human evolution is as much of a personal fantasy and projection as Freud's *Totem and Taboo*.

Hominids were first scroungers and not hunters. The first tools were most likely sticks and sharp and jagged rocks useful in cutting carrion into pieces small enough to carry back to the base camp. Of course, we don't see a simple system here of linear causation, but a more complex multiple-feedback system. The movement into the savannah encourages a new clustering of hominid bands. The attempt to re-establish a forestlike settlement in small clumps of trees encourages a new division of labor with females gathering and males scrounging. The division of labor helps to re-establish the old social unit of male bonding, and the cooperative projects of scrounging help to encourage a signal system for defense and research into the environment for what helps in securing food. The use of tools encourages education among peers in tool use and thus also encourages social grouping and male bonding. The encouragement of male bonding helps to increase the distance between the sexes in the primal division of labor, and thus to increase the opposition between the sexes, and so establish a cognitive dissonance between the needs for male bonding and the needs of the females for protective association with the males. Since the receptivity to intercourse is likely to encourage intrasexual competition among the males, "the human revolution" presented the hominids with a dynamic but highly volatile situation. Surely some form of sexual repression and control would have to be developed.

Freud has elaborated the classic theory that human culture is based upon repression, but recently some anthropologists have argued that such repression is at the base of the rapid evolution of the hominid brain. In *Men in Groups,* Lionel Tiger recounts:

> Chance's proposition is that the development of patterns of inhibition was crucial to the enlargement of the evolving human brain. Dominant males possessed breeding advantage; to maintain the cohesion of the community it was essential to inhibit aggression directed at the dominant males. That dangerous weapons were available which could lead to deaths within the community as well as without, must be seen as an additional factor of remarkable importance in the development of mechanisms for inhibiting male rivalry in the group.[43]

In this view that sexual repression is good for the growth of the brain, we encounter a scientific variant of the yogic myth that sexual repression is necessary for the elevation of *kundalini* and the autosemination of the brain. Once again, we see the ancient notion that genitals and brain are intimately connected through the spinal column.[44]

The shift away from estrus causes an explosion in the body which generates an implosion in society, for it requires the compression of males into some form of rudimentary band of scroungers and hunters. By setting up a system of double signals of excitation and repression, hominid sexuality departs radically from the natural sexuality of the other primates. Hominid sexuality undergoes an intensification in consciousness, an emphasis which lays the foundation for the obsessive quality of human sexuality. Gone is the casual ten-second coitus of the animal; present for good is the sexualization of human culture, and an association of erotic excitement with a thrilling sense of danger.

It is with the human eroticization of time that all the new forms of sexuality unfold, unfold like the petals of shrapnel in an explosion. Sexuality explodes in every direction and will light upon any available appendage, orifice, or symbolic article as part of the human sexualization of consciousness. It is at this stage of intensification that sexuality will move in any direction of consciousness; it is at this stage that we get homosexuality, incest, and later, with the domestication of animals, bestiality. The females shift from estrus and pull the males back to them with the remorseless power of pheromones; they pull them away from "men in groups," from palling around in the forest, into new forms of social cohesion and restraint. Small wonder that one of the dominant patterns of male behavior is the resentment of women and the longing to break away from them and from social responsibility, to return to the old steady-state in the pub, the hunt, the forest. Small wonder that male homosexuality expresses the rejection of women and the celebration of male dominance in such Christopher Street caricatures as the black-leathered storm trooper and the Marlboro cigarette-ad cowboy. One turn of the spiral of history plays out the theme from the earlier turn, and in turning away from women and social responsibility to remain with boys and men, the homosexual rejects the beauty and terror of that female-odored night in which the world changed. A new force was released, but the explosion only moved out a short distance before it was caught and forced in an implosion into a new culture, the hominid society. Small wonder that all the medieval paintings of the Fall show the primal couple leaving the safety of the forest garden and moving into a new world, a world that is emphasized as sexual by their covering of their newly enlarged genitals in shame.

In the explosion of the new sexual forces in the body, the innocence of animal sexuality is trapped in a new body. Now perhaps we can appreciate the insight of the Gnostic myth in which the first Adam is trapped in a sexual body, screaming to be let out, while the Devil laughs and commits unspeakable acts with him. Now perhaps we can begin to understand why humans are so obsessive about sexuality, why pornography rarely presents loving and affirmative images of sexuality. Whether the pornographic art is from Europe, America, Africa, or Asia, the images are grotesque and caricatured: Japanese men run up the street with their huge penises in front of them, supported by wheelbarrows; African vulvas open like the huge maws of some devouring beast.[45]

Why does not pornography more often present sexuality with love, tenderness, beauty, and adulation? Why does it so quickly slide into the imagery of bestiality and sadomasochism? Why for every sublime image of Bernini's St. Teresa in orgasm are there a million grotesque images in "adult" book shops and latrine walls? Pornography is the shadow side of myth, a racial memory expressed in obsessive imagery, and as a twisted form of reflection of our archaic inheritance, it expresses the shock of incarnation. Precisely because we are more highly conscious than the animals, our sexuality is intensified by consciousness. Homosexuality, sadomasochism, and bestiality are neither inhuman nor "natural"; there is no such thing as "natural" for human beings. To paraphrase Goethe, man is man because he is not nature. In rituals of adoration of the penis and the whip, or in black-leathered celebrations of male dominance and bondage, humans are longing for constraint, for a compression back into an original, presexual mode of being. The caricatured emphasis on sex is not a celebration of it, but an attempt to escape it altogether. Pornography, in a way, is indeed as the moralist claims, "garbage"; it is the rotting compost-heap of old mythologies left over from all the cultures of human evolution.

So for all our digressions into the sciences of sociobiology, ethology, and anthropology, we have not escaped the world of myth expressed in the Prologue. The mystic Rudolph Steiner said that the price of thought is double-sexedness, and that the evolution of the brain and the genitals are wed together. And that is precisely what the anthropologists M.R.A. Chance and Lionel Tiger are telling us.

But in the mythologies of the anthropologists it is the activity of the male which initiates the long march of human culture. In the Fall into the division of labor, Lévi-Strauss sees the great hunters trading women to create the exogamous bonds of one hunting band with another. The egg is, but the sperm does. The tiny sperm may be furious in its activity, but its highway to the egg is paved by the alkaline trail set down by the Great Mother. "Behind every great man is a great woman."

The female of the species is the initiator of the hominization of the primates; she is the creature who, with a unity of mind and body, moves from the estrus cycle to the menstrual cycle. A new society was created in which the old differences reconstituted themselves in new ways. The old male bonding, the old chumming around in the forest, could become the all-male band of, first, scroungers of carrion, and then hunters. Through the use of tools and signaling, the males would develop a primitive technology and a primitive language for the definite and specific objects that crystallized in their newly emerging conscious minds. Through the gathering of plants, and the observation of the seasonal rhythms of the appearance of plants, as well as the observation of their own menstrual and lunar cycles, the females would observe the basic periodicities of nature and lay down the foundations for the first great synthesis of science and religion, astrology.

The religion of the chimpanzees is animistic; the religion of humans is sexual, but out of the association of sexuality with the forces of nature, the females were to create our first religion, a religion of menstruation, childbirth mysteries, and the phases of the moon.

CHAPTER TWO

Symbolization

I N THE BEGINNING was the Word. The Creator sounded the opening chord and from its multiple vibrations appeared the single sphere that was to expand to express the entire universe.[1] When twelve billion "years" later a tiny planet lay covered with oceans and unbroken clouds, the Creator once again said, "Let there be light," and a bolt of lightning struck the waters, and the astonished molecules fell in chains to the quiet depths of the sea where they could whisper in the language of nucleotides to begin yet another chapter in the universal life of the Word.

From elementary particles of light to atoms, from atoms to molecules, from dust cloud to solar system, from gaseous mist to ocean, or even more simply, from forest to savannah, the transitions proceed, and yet each transformation seems unexplainable from the preceding condition. What is the relationship between light and particle, information and matter, mind and body?[2] How can the chimpanzee, Flo, move from mind to body to go into estrus overnight? Or how, for that matter, can a twentieth-century mystic like Therese Neumann develop the wounds of Christ, the *stigmata*, on her own body?[3] How do symbol and idea become translated into bleeding flesh? How can the cells be made to hear and obey what the organism thinks? At the level of these questions, sociobiology is dumb, but the still-small voice of the philosopher Whitehead is worth hearing.

> Thus an electron within a living body is different from an electron outside it, by reason of the plan of the body. The electron blindly runs either within or without the body; but it runs within the body in accordance with its character within the body; that is to say, in accordance with the general plan of the body, and this plan includes the mental state.[4]

In his philosophy of *Organism,* Whitehead tried to move beyond the pure idealism of the Hegelians or the pure materialism of the positivists. In his vision of matter as a *process,* he was, perhaps, influenced by another great English mystical scientist, Michael Faraday. In his *Experimental Researches in Electricity,* Faraday saw a dance of energy that was far more complex than the simple materialism of his Victorian colleagues; for him, matter was not lumps of stuff but an interpenetrating field: "Matter is not merely mutually penetrable, but each atom extends, so to say, throughout the whole of the solar system, yet retaining its own centre of force."[5]

The visions of profoundly religious scientists like Michael Faraday and Alfred North Whitehead ascend to a level of understanding beyond the dogmas of routine science and orthodox religion; they move from the third level of myth, the heroic, to the fourth level, the hieroglyphic. In Faraday's vision of the interpenetrability of matter, or in Whitehead's vision of the prehensive unification of space-time, is expressed the Unitive state of the mystic. Few scientists and few priests have reached this summit of human understanding, this vision of the Logos. The scientist, the philosopher, the saint, and the artist, all take different paths up the mountain, but the higher up they go, the closer they come together at the peak of human consciousness. Each is given the grace of a different landscape on the way up, but one landscape is not better than the other.

The four levels of myth can be seen as four levels of ascent up the mountain. The first level of myth is the simplistic understanding of myth on the flatlands of the valley; the second level is the beginning understanding that there is more to myth than one thought. The third level is the elevated and dizzy vision of the hero who looks *down* on the valley and becomes egoistically thrilled with the grandeur of *his* sweeping vision. The fourth level of myth is the vision at the summit, the vision where the mountain ends and the sky begins; gone is the arrogance of the positivist, and saint and scientist, philosopher and artist all sit down to listen to the music of the spheres.

Myth is the history of the soul, the memory of our greater Being; ritual and sacrament are the reminders. (When I was a child I was taught to memorize a catechism in which a sacrament was defined as "the outward sign of an inward state.") In the continuing Fall the part breaks away from the Whole; to make something sacred, one must reconnect the part to the universal Whole. The chimpanzees re-make connections in their rain dance, and we, in kinship with all living things, also know how to dance. We have had the best of teachers. As Jesus says in the Gnostic Round Dance:

> The Whole on high hath part in our dancing. Amen. Whoso danceth not, knoweth not what cometh to pass. Amen.[6]

To understand events, or what comes to pass, one must understand the cosmic dance, that musical and geometrical pattern of movement in Creation. The patterning of all patterns of events is the Logos. At the summit of human understanding in the Dance, or in the ecstasy of the Unitive state, *mythos* is no longer a description; it is a performance of Reality. At the lower levels of human understanding myth is symbolic. A great stream separates the third from the fourth levels of myth, the heroic from the hieroglyphic, and the ancient Greeks understood this, for the word *symbol* meant something that was thrown across. The sage like Utnapishtim can cross over, but the hero like Gilgamesh is left behind, and so the sage must throw over something to help the hero understand consciousness on the other side of the stream of time and space.[7]

Jesus in the Dance, St. Teresa in ecstasy, Bach at the keyboard, and Faraday in his laboratory are all in a place beyond the grasp of the sociobiologists. And I think even the sociobiologists must sense this unconsciously, for their arrogant claims to a total synthesis imply an anger that there can be anything beyond the power of their explanations. Their claim to totality is like the cry of the archon Ialdabaoth that he was the Lord of the Universe and that there was nothing beyond him. *Sophia,* however, knew better. If our culture is going to know better, then we too will have to move from sophism to *Sophia,* from the heroic myths of Darwin, Marx, Freud, or Wilson to the hieroglyphic language of the gods.

II

THERE WAS A TIME when we said that humans alone had thought, and that humans alone had language.[8] Then came the stories about the language of dolphins and the songs of the whales. A few years later psychologists were teaching chimpanzees Ameslan, the sign language of the deaf and the dumb. Suddenly the chimp was thrust into the place where nature and culture cross, and for this animal the laboratory did indeed become a place of crucifixion. With behaviorist pulling to the left, passionately hoping to be able to explain the human through the animal, and with the rationalist pulling to the right, insisting upon the discontinuity of the quantum leap from nature to culture, the battle stirred up the dust of centuries. In the battle of Premack versus Chomsky it was another round in the old battle of British empiricism versus continental rationalism, of Locke-Berkeley-Hume versus Descartes-Leibniz-Spinoza.[9]

The battle rages on, and it looks as if it will continue for some time to come. Research into the origins of language is really research into the origins of consciousness. Now we seek to understand human nature through research into animal behavior, but in the eighteenth century scholars sought to understand human culture through research into primitive societies. Demonstrating the attraction of opposites, Enlightment Europe became fascinated with the primitive, and many learned societies began to take up the subject of the origins of language and human culture. The Berlin Academy of Sciences offered an essay competition on the subject and in 1772 it awarded the prize to Johann Gottfried Herder. But after a century or so of speculation, scholars became frustrated with a subject that was so open to conjecture and so closed to verification. By 1866 the Société de Linguistique de Paris banned all further communication on the subject of the origins of language. Banished were all the theories of the onomatopoeic imitation of thunder, the mimickry of the calls of birds, and the gestural origins of speech.

After a moratorium of a century, with the shift of emphasis in the field from philology to structural linguistics effected, the scholars began to wonder whether now, finally, modern science was equal to the task. With all the fanciful theories of the past long forgotten, buried away as they were in the obscure journals of the nineteenth century, the scientists began to speculate once again. Charles Hockett and Robert Ascher wrote their own version of a Kipling-like "Just-So Story" on how the hominid found his tongue.

Pushed out from the forest into the dangerous savannah where he was unable to swing in the trees, the weak primate had to bend down to pick up rocks, carry food with his hands, and begin to use his mouth for babbling to his fellows. A simple system of hoots and calls enabled the scrounging animals to signal the presence of food or danger, or both.

How a closed system of a limited number of calls can become an open system of an infinite number of novel sentences is, of course, the central question about the evolution of language.

> Doubtless many overloaded systems did collapse, their users there-after becoming extnct. In at least one case, there was a brilliantly successful "mutation": *pre-morphemes began to be listened to* and identified not in terms of their acoustic gestalts but in terms of smaller features of sound that occurred in them in varying arrangements. [My emphasis.] [10]

Like Freud before them, Hockett and Ascher invoke what they are trying to explain. Their answer is equivalent to saying that language evolved one day because long ago there was a day when language evolved.

Von Humboldt expressed the dilemma of research in this field very well when he said: "Man is man through language alone—but in order to invent language he must have been man already." [11]

There are other problems with Hockett and Ascher's explanation. The proto-hominids with an overloaded call system are said to have become extinct, yet we live on a planet with thousands of species who have survived without any call system. Alfred Russell Wallace first expressed a just objection to Darwinian thinking when he asked, if the brain evolved because of survival of the fittest, "How then was an organ developed so far beyond the needs of its possessor? Natural selection could only have endowed the savage with a brain a little superior to that of an ape, whereas he actually possesses one but little inferior to that of the average member of our learned societies." [12]

Why does the human have far more of a brain than it needs for survival? And why, for that matter, if survival is the name of the game, did not the baboons invent a language, since they too had to live in the open and dangerous savannah? To explain all these puzzling questions, anthropologists resort to their own peculiar brand of popular mythology and science fiction. Richard Leakey and Roger Lewin have written:

> The evolutionary momentum that propelled *Homo erectus* toward *Homo sapiens* must have left behind some pockets of *erectus,* and have caused some *sapiens* populations to move down biological blind alleys to their own extinction. Joining Neanderthal Man on his ill-fated journey were also Solo Man and Rhodesia Man, both of whom likewise paid the penalty of overspecialization.[13]

What in terms of science "evolutionary momentum" is, I really don't know. As a writer, I recognize a metaphor when I see one, but if "evolutionary momentum" is a metaphor, does that mean that "extinction" and "overspecialization" are also metaphors? Can it be that Solo man and Rhodesia man are not really species, but metonymies constructed out of a few fragments of bone? And what is extinction? Did the Romans become extinct because they were overspecialized or because they were eliminated by evolutionary superior beings in the barbarian invasions? And why should Neanderthal man pass into extinction when he had an even larger brain than ours? If for millions of years hominids with lesser endowments were managing to survive, why should Neanderthal man suddenly become subject to overspecialization? Finally, what does it mean when the anthropologists say that "Cro Magnon man suddenly appeared on the scene?" Clearly, the account of human origins in anthropology is a fictionalized narrative in which the gaps between half a skull here and one or two teeth there are filled in with projections, unconscious assumptions, and scientistic mythology. I do not object to scientific myths, for they are useful in holding together a conglomeration of scientific theories, but I do object to the fact that most scientists reject mythopoeic thought. With such an unconscious myth of progress as the *ground* of one's consciousness, and a few teeth or half a skull as the *figure* of one's perceptions, it is easy to connect the dots in graphing a single curve for the arc of human evolution. The glue that holds the scientific "facts" together are the metaphors like "overspecialization," "blind alleys," and "evolutionary momentum." If the modern biologist were to use poetic metaphors like Henri Bergson's *élan vital,* his colleagues would cringe in disgust at the appearance of mysticism in a scientific discourse, and yet Richard Leakey's "evolutionary momentum" is Bergson's creative evolution renamed.

When we try to ask unanswerable questions like "How did language evolve?", we come to the limits of knowing, but not to the limits of being. That shoreline where the island of knowing meets the unfathomable sea of our own being is the landscape of myth. When we come to an edge we have to shift our mode of thought, say from rational analysis to intuitive meditation. We can still try to put out to sea in slender craft, but we have to realize that these are not pieces of our own making. A good craft like a sailboat takes on the qualities of the medium through which it moves, and so it is with a myth: that which glides across the face of the unknown takes on the qualities of the unknowable. A myth is never *known;* it is a relationship between the known and the unknowable.

> Three wise men of Gotham
> Went to sea in bowl.
> If the bowl had been stronger,
> My song had been longer.

Scientific models and scientistic myths are not seaworthy craft because they take as their premise that they are adequate for all circumstances; they assume that reality is knowable, quantifiable, and describable in their notation. The mystic understands that the mind is like a flashlight in search of the nature of darkness: the more he searches, the more he chases it away, and so the mystic shifts from "The Creative" to "The Receptive," turns off the mind, and allows the darkness to commune-icate with him. When one is searching in the past with language for the origin of language, one is approaching an edge that is very similar to the edge one approaches when one moves out of linguistic thinking in meditation. When one returns to language after meditation, the language of Zen *koans* takes on a whole new life. And so if we are going to approach the other end of language, the very beginnings of it, we will need to realize that our hard, conceptual, discrete, scientific models are not always the most appropriate vehicles of thought.

For those who find oracles and *koans* distasteful there is The New York Academy of Science's recent publication on the *Origins and Evolution of Language and Speech.*[14] Now that the moratorium on discussions of the origins of language has been lifted, a new moratorium may have to be declared, for some of the fanciful narratives of the nineteenth century are returning in contemporary dress. Julian Jaynes, in his contribution, constructs a neat linear progression in which cries appear first, then modifiers, then commands, then "life nouns," "thing nouns," and finally, around 10,000 B.C., names.[15] Jaynes sees this whole process of evolution of language beginning as late as 70,000 B.C. and completing itself during the Mesolithic period.

Jaynes's perceptions seem to be highly ethnocentric and limited to English, for he sees distinctions between *processes* and *objects* which would not be the same for a speaker of Chinese or Hopi and therefore might not have been the same for a speaker in the late Pleistocene. Also, the difference between a "life noun" and a "thing noun" might be quite different for a member of an animistic culture in which all "objects" are alive. But the greatest problem I see in Jaynes's theory is his notion that language can evolve in bits and pieces.

Recent studies of neonates show that within a day or two of birth an infant is moving his arms and legs in rhythmic synchrony with the pulse of his mother's words; this synchrony has been established in slow-motion films which catch the emphasis an ordinary observer might miss.[16] The newborn is literally dancing *to* language before he can utter a word. The fact that a structure is matched by another structure argues for the innate quality of linguistic ability and seems to corroborate Eric Lennenberg's work.[17] If language is an expression of certain innate structures, then it is the structure which is important and not the pieces. Language would then have to evolve all of a piece; you could not have, say, modifiers in 70,000 B.C. followed by names in 10,000 B.C. In this understanding that language is a structure, von Humboldt was far more insightful than Jaynes.

> In order that a man may truly understand even a single word—understand it not only as a sensory impulse but as an articulate sound defining a concept—the whole of language must already be present within his mind. Nothing is separate in language; each and every element declares itself as part of the whole. Natural as it is to assume that language was formed gradually, its actual invention can only have occurred in a single instant.[18]

How Jaynes can look at the art of the Upper Paleolithic period and think that those artists lived in a perceptual fog in which men and animals did not have names eludes me. Clearly, the articulations needed to construct a painting are expressions of a linguistic order. From the selection of a site to the preparing of one's tools to the coordination of a complex composition, such as the painting of the two bison seen in Figure 3, the skills needed to execute a work of art require language ability and both hemispheres of the brain working in harmony.

But it is not only art that signals the presence of language: tool making is another indicator. To set about to produce a fist hatchet, one has to have the class "fist hatchet" in mind; the operation is then performed to make the rock take on the characteristics of the class. The production of tools (as opposed to the mere opportunistic use of available sticks and stones) indicates that Homo Faber is already thinking in terms of sets and classes. Considering that some of the techniques of pressure flaking require an intuitive understanding of a complex geometry, it seems absurd to place complete language acquisition as late as 10,000 B.C. Ashley Montagu's position seems much more credible than Jaynes's.

It is suggested that the kind of cognitive processes involved in the making and the transmission of the art of making the Oldowan-type tools mentioned, implies the existence of some form of speech,

Figure 3. Two bison from Lascaux.

however rudimentary. We know that it is possible to think without speech; deaf-mutes do it. It is not, however, possible to speak without thinking. A creature that learns to make tools to a complex pre-existing pattern, calculated to serve a series of complex future purposes, among them the making of other tools, must have the kind of abstracting mind that would be of high selective value in facilitating the development of the ability to communicate such skills by the necessary verbal acts.[19]

The subject of the evolution of language is highly controversial and subject to wide divergences of opinion. Montagu sees language present in Oldowan culture; Glynn Isaacs does not but maintains that "the symbolizing capabilities of Plio-Pleistocene hominids was not necessarily beyond that of contemporary pongids."[20] Precisely because the subject is open to wildly different points of view, with the origins of language put somewhere between two million and ten thousand B.C., I doubt that the science of the twentieth century is going to be any the less frustrated than the Société de Linguistique de Paris of the nineteenth century.

Nevertheless, a ban on the subject will not eliminate the problem, and the difficulty of the problem is good for our humility. Chomsky's pronouncement of a decade ago is still valid:

In fact, the processes by which the human mind achieved its present stage of complexity and its particular form of innate organization are a total mystery, as much so as the analogous questions about the physical or mental organization of any complex organism. It is perfectly safe to attribute this development to "natural selection," so long as we realize that there is no substance to this assertion, that it amounts to nothing more than a belief that there is some naturalistic explanation for these phenomena.[21]

III

IF WE LOOK at the origins of hominid culture in the shift from the forest to the savannah, we find an integrated complex in which all the new separate elements of tool use, food sharing, communication, and sexuality reinforce one another in a system of feedback loops. The shift from estrus in the females attracts the males and constellates a small band; the need to transport food to a safe home base in a clump of trees establishes a system of food sharing and tool use for cutting discovered carrion into portable pieces; elementary tool use and a home base encourage communication and a division of labor in which females gather and males scrounge. Each element reinforces the other, so that tool use encourages education and communication, and the home base gives a place for such activities to go on in an intensified form. The grouping of females in a home base encourages mother-infant babbling, and this, too, works to intensify communication. Most anthropologists look to tool production and the coordination of signals in group hunting as the foundation for the evolution of language, but the prehistorian Alexander Marshack sees the origin of language in childhood.

> The problem of language and speech origins is clarified from another direction by the ontogenetic nature of the language capacity. If, at any point in the evolutionary process "language" or proto-language was to be learned, it would not have been in the context of the hunt. It would have been learned young, and before the individual was economically productive. It would have been learned in the context of the maturing, generalized cognitive capacity and within a child's widening, increasingly complex relational competence.[22]

Food sharing in a home base sets up the ideal conditions for communication, babbling, clowning, and play. From the seder to the eucharist, humans to this day regard the taking in of food and magical words together as a sacrament and an expression of a mysterious *event* in history. Perhaps behind the event of the Passover or the Last Supper is the archetype of another event; perhaps Freud in *Totem and Taboo* gave us an intuitive insight which had the right structure but the wrong content.

One can see that language could be of use in the scrounging activities of the males, and equally of use in the gathering activities of the females. The gathering of useful plants is an exercise in establishing a cultural taxonomy of nature, precisely that kind of activity likely to establish a list and a grammar of discrete items. The problem is that we can see many ways in which language might take off, *once it was started,* but we cannot see how it could get started in the first place. All our theories about the origins of language are really nothing more than descriptions of how language would be of use once it was there. Darwinian notions that language would help fit the survivors for survival explain nothing, since we have evidence of species surviving in the same ecological niche without the help of language.

Try as hard as it can, empirical science cannot come up with a naturalistic explanation; it can only slip into fantasies that make scientists feel good because they are in harmony with their opinions, prejudices, and unconscious assumptions about the nature of reality. But the invocation of a phony myth of scienticism is not as worthwhile as the recollection of a genuine myth. One might as well assume that the soul fell into matter and is impelled to work its way back to God as babble about "evolutionary momentum" and think that one is free of religion and full of science. The scientist can do little better than the saint who said, "In the beginning was the word." As for me, I prefer to take my mysticism neat, and straight from the vessels of the great mystics of human history. Here, for example, is the great Islamic saint and poet, Jalaluddin Rumi (1207–1273) on "the evolution of man."

> First he appeared in the class of inorganic things,
> Next he passed therefrom into that of plants.
> For years he lived as one of the plants,
> Remembering naught of his organic state so different;
> And when he passed from the vegetative to the animal state
> He had no remembrance of his state as a plant,
> Except the inclination he felt to the world of plants,
> Especially at the time of spring and sweet flowers . . .
>
> Again, the great Creator, as you know,
> Drew man out of the animal into the human state.
> Thus man passed from one order of nature to another,
> Till he became wise and knowing and strong as he is now.
> Of his first souls he has now no remembrance,
> And he will be again changed from his present soul.[23]

When Charles Darwin's grandfather, Erasmus, wrote his work, *Zoonomia,* on the evolution of life, he was not discovering anything new but was simply rediscovering ideas of progression well known in Islamic thought and in alchemy. European scientists like

Erasmus Darwin were not conversant with either alchemy or Islam, but ideas, like wind-blown seeds, have a way of crossing boundaries and appearing in unlikely places. The clergy of Darwin's day thought that each species had been created by God in 4004 B.C., and so when the geologists were able to demonstrate the absurdity of such a theology, scientists like Thomas Huxley felt that they had pretty much taken care of religion. But the exoteric religion of Bishop Wilberforce and the esoteric traditions of a Rumi are quite distinct. When Charles Darwin tried to imagine the evolution of life from matter to mind, even he approached a level of poetic vision that was beyond orthodox theology or empirical science but lived at the boundaries of myth. In his *Notebooks* for 1837–1838, Darwin wrote:

> The grand question which every naturalist ought to have before him when dissecting a whale, or classifying a mite, a fungus or an infusorian is What are the Laws of Life?
>
> The soul by consent of all is superadded, animals not got it, not look forward. If we choose to let conjecture run wild, then animals—our fellow brethren in pain, disease, death, suffering and famine, our slaves in the most laborious works, our companions in our amusements,—they may partake from our origin in one common ancestor, we may be all netted together.[24]

Darwin sees a common ancestor in physical space-time; a theosophical mystic would see the ancestor as preceding the emergence into the time-stream of the physical plane. For the theosophist, the soul descending into the physical plane is something like a space capsule in re-entry: as consciousness descends, various excretions of consciousness spark and peel off. In this mythic tradition, animals are archaic excretions of human consciousness, and when humanity reascends into the spiritual realms, these projections will be reabsorbed, and animals will disappear. The exoteric reflection of this doctrine is that as our technological society develops, it is eliminating countless species of animals at an astonishingly rapid rate.

If we try to do without poetry and esoteric mythology to describe precisely and scientifically how language evolved, we find that there is no causal explanation. For those whose emotional hatred of religion blocks out religious experiences, the only way open to William Blake's Imagination in our culture is through science fiction. The science of Julian Jaynes is disguised science fiction; the science fiction of Arthur C. Clarke is disguised Gnostic mythology.

But how do transformations like the evolution of language take place? A scientist looks for a cause inside time; a mystic knows that causality is essentially a process that is outside time-space. For the mystic, involution and evolution are related to one another. The traditional emblem for this relationship is the double triangle.[25]

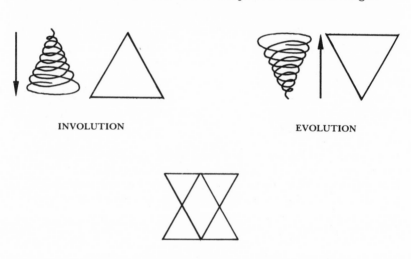

INVOLUTION   EVOLUTION

This double-triangle emblem can also be used as an image for the process of transformation. One part of transformation is a very slow and gradual build-up of the preconditions necessary for transformation, a preparation of the vessel, △ ; the other part is an instantaneous burst in which the transformation seems to occur like lightning in "the twinkling of an eye" △↓ . The evolution of life is a preeminent example: slowly the planet is prepared over eons, and then in an electric bolt of lightning the ocean is catalyzed and molecular life appears.

We do not know what bolt of lightning came inside the brains of the hominids to generate language. The Creator sounded a note, and the brute responded, dumbfounded. Such is the transformation of hominization. At the edge of consciousness, there are no explanations; there are only invocations of mythology.

IV

THE SAME SLOW PROCESS seems true of the second great transformation, Symbolization. Assuming that language ability extends back to the hominids, we see a slow process of cultural development over millions of years, and then in the Acheulean period of Homo erectus, about three hundred thousand years ago, we find the first engraved tool.[26] At that point, humanity crosses another threshold, miniaturizes its universe into symbolic form, and takes a toddling step toward iconography, writing, and the first stammerings of calendrical notation and mathematics.

Before the publications of Alexander Marshack appeared, the importance of symbolization was not stressed; anthropologists concentrated on hunting and gathering and focused on technology and economy. Rachel Levy had tried to reconstruct "the religious conceptions of the stone age,"[27] but for archaeologists more comfortable with discussions of tools, such speculations seemed too romantic and mystical. When Marshack came along and claimed that the Paleolithic *baton de commandement* with its engraved markings was a calendar stick for a primitive form of lunar "time factoring," there was a great deal of resistance, not the least because Marshack was not a professional anthropologist and did not have a PhD.

T. S. Kuhn, the historian of science, has pointed out how a paradigm shift in science often comes from a worker who is outside the specialty he transforms;[28] therefore the early resistance to Marshack is not surprising, but rather true to the classical pattern of scientific revolution. Marshack was patient with the skeptics and continued to work to establish a mass of data. In some cases it seemed as if Marshack were reading into arbitrary scratches on bone the phases of the moon, but in others it did seem as if he might be on to something.

The implications of Marshack's observations were enormous, for they meant that as early as fifty thousand years ago primitive humanity had observed a basic periodicity of nature and was building up a model of nature. The human being was no longer simply walking in nature; it was miniaturizing the universe and carrying a model of it in its hand in the form of a lunar calendrical tally stick.

Since the problem of portability exists in a hunting culture, the man who was carrying a baton either poked through a belt or hung on a thong through the hole, whether as a ritual or working object, might find it convenient or practical to make his notations on this slate that was with him daily. Or, if the baton broke or its primary purpose was ended, he now had a clean bone surface at hand that could serve as a slate. Such notations on a baton would then be either related or unrelated to the primary purpose of the baton. We cannot tell which. . . .

If, apart from any practical uses, a baton was also a ritual object, it may have been used by the shaman (priest) or chief, or by the head of a family group. In that case, the notations may have had ceremonial or administrative uses. But in a culture that counted "moons" there may have also been other purposes: perhaps for a voyage, visit, or march, or for a menstrual or pregnancy record, or for a private period of initiation.[29]

It was the Abbé Breuil, one of the first world-renowned specialists on paleolithic cave art, who christened the long engraved bone *le baton de commandement,* no doubt because it reminded him of the baton carried by military officers. This terminology was unfortunate because names exercise powerful control over perceptions, and prehistorians were locked into a particular way of looking at the object. A lunar calendrical tally stick could have quite other uses than as a phallic expression of military power.

Recent studies in physiology have noted that women who live in close proximity to one another—nurses in a hospital or coeds in a college dormitory—tend to have their menstrual periods at the same time.[30] Other studies have shown that women living near the equator have a marked tendency to ovulate during the full moon.[31] It is reasonable for us to expect that women living together in small hunting and gathering bands would all have their menstrual periods at the same time. Since classical myths have associated the menstrual period with the darkness of the new moon, it seems also reasonable to assume that the women would be having their periods in synchrony with the phases of the moon. It is this poetical connection between women and the moon that is at the foundation of the classical conceptions of lunar goddesses.

The idea that menstruation is *caused* by the new moon is universal. Papuans say that a girl's first menstruation is due to the moon having had connection with her during sleep, and the Maoris speak of menstruation as "moon sickness." A Maori stated: "The moon is the permanent husband, or true husband, of all women, because women menstruate when the moon appears. According to the knowledge of our ancestors and elders, the marriage of a man and wife is a matter of no moment; the moon is the real husband." We shall see that such conceptions are by no means peculiar to the Maori, but pervade primitive thought.[32]

The implications of this association of women and the moon would suggest that women were the first observers of the basic periodicity of nature, the periodicity upon which all later scientific observations were made. Woman was the first to note a correspondence between an internal process she was going through and an external process in nature. She is the one who constructs a more holistic epistemology in which subject and object are in sympathetic resonance with one another. She is the holistic scientist who constructs a taxonomy for all the beneficial herbs and plants; she is the one who knows the secrets of the time of their flowering. The world-view that separates the observer from the system he observes, that imagines that the universe can be split into mere subjectivity and real objectivity, is not of her doing. She expresses "the witness of the body," that Whitehead tried to rediscover in his philosophy of organism and process. Hers is the philosophy that stood before the speculations of the presocratics; she is the "Holy Mother Church" which Descartes challenged when he cut the umbilical cord between philosophy and the Church and split reality into the *res extensa* and the *res cogitans*. The reason the Venus of Laussel or the modern Virgin of Guadalupe are pictured with the crescent moon is that woman and the moon are a single mystery.

Le baton de commandement is then not, I believe, exclusively a masculine rod, but also a feminine instrument of measurement. Marshack does not wish to accept this hypothesis because it says that the origins of notation, measurement, and the kind of science which reaches its consummation in the megalithic astronomy of Stonehenge are with women, not men. Such a hypothesis would unsettle the whole of masculine narratives of progress and power from the archaic darkness of myth and superstition to the modern light of technology and industry. Small wonder that Marshack resists the sociologist Elise Boulding's attempts to turn his data in the direction of the Great Mother. What is surprising, however, is that Boulding backs down.

> Marshack had expressed himself strongly on this point in a communication to the author, and there seems to be no reason to question the careful linking of evidence and intuition that stands behind his statement that the baton tradition must be regarded as a masculine one.[33]

On the contrary, there are very good reasons presented in Marshack's own text why the baton tradition should be seen as a feminine one.

> Perhaps the Siberian peoples [of today] possess the key to that phenomenon; their women calculate child-birth by the phases of the moon, according to observations made by B. Dolgith and other Soviet ethnographists among the Nganasans, Entses, Dolgans, Chukchi, Koryaks, and Kets. Pregnancy has the duration of exactly 10 lunar months, and the woman keeps a sort of lunar calendar (it was always a woman who was the custodian of the lunar calendar among those nationalities).[34]

The fact that Marshack can quote the findings of these Soviet ethnographers in his text and then go on to ignore the obvious implications indicates to me the presence of a strong bias against or unconscious resistance to the feminist implications. The owner of the baton is not man the mighty hunter but the midwife. Anyone who has ever worked with a midwife in the delivery of a child will know that her ancient mystery is a marvelous combination of hard science and soft sensitivity for the mother; it is perfectly reasonable to assume that menstruation, lunar calendars, and midwifery are as much or more at the foundation of human science than man the great killer so celebrated by Robert Ardrey:

> Not in innocence, and not in Asia, was mankind born. The home of our fathers was that African highland reaching north from the Cape to the Lakes of the Nile. Here we came about—slowly, ever so slowly—on a sky-swept savannah glowing with menace . . .
>   In neither bankruptcy nor bastardy did we face our long beginnings. Man's line is legitimate. Our ancestry is firmly rooted in the animal world, and to its subtle, antique ways our hearts are yet pledged. Children of all animal kind, we inherited many a social nicety as well as the predator's way. But most significant of all our

gifts, as things turned out, was the legacy bequeathed us by those killer apes, our immediate forebears. Even in the first long days of our beginnings we held in our hand the weapon, an instrument somewhat older than ourselves.[35]

What we see is what we are. Each anthropologist projects onto the mythic landscape of the origins of humanity his own vision of human nature. I project myth, poetry, and a Whiteheadian philosophy of organism; Ardrey projects menace, terror, violence, and the supreme potency of the weapon; for him the weapon is a phallus shooting forth the seeds of all the great technological cultures to come. To be sure, there were weapons in the Upper Paleolithic and beyond, but we do not know *how* those hunting cultures regarded killing. Judging by what we know of recent and classical hunting cultures, the hunter was not a modern alienated urban man in need of finding his egotistical manhood in an act of slaughter, but rather a humble petitioner to the group-soul of the herd to grant him the minimum he needed for his own survival. What we see on the walls of Lascaux may well be images of just such prayerful petition and worshipful observation. The image of the headman striding forth at the front of a column of hunters and giving orders with a gesticulation of his magical baton seems something of a memory from later cultures. Since hunters and gatherers had to be on the move in a seasonal round, they needed to know on what day to strike camp, and, therefore, they also would need to know on what day the baby was due. The anthropologist A. R. Pilling notes that the Yurok Indians had menstrual calendars and could predict births within a day,[36] supporting the thesis that the baton belongs to women's mysteries. The fact that the baton was later taken over by men in the militarist cultures of patriarchal civilization may, in fact, indicate that they took it over *because* it was a most ancient symbol of feminine power. The priest and the shaman dress like women to take on their magic, and in male initiation ceremonies, or in the rituals of *couvade,* the men imitate the birth pangs of women. Again, there is ample cause to think that *le baton de commandement* was originally the province of women.

One of the reasons cited for considering the batons masculine tools is that they are often carved with images of animals. These animals naturally suggest an association with man the hunter.

Marshack, however, argues that these animals are symbols of a time of year; a salmon would indicate the time when the salmon were running, a bison turning to bite at an insect would indicate the month when the black flies were thickest, the antlers of an elk would indicate the rutting season. The early stages of time factoring may have been associated with midwifery, but by the Upper Paleolithic a more complex calendar seems to have been constructed.

> If, as my earlier analysis has indicated, the ibex is a symbol or sign of early spring—or of a myth, rite, or sacrifice related to that season— and if the plants (and the possible fish) are taken to be seasonal and storied signs, then it is possible to perform a simple juxtaposition in a test with our lunar model.[37]

Marshack's test to see whether the marks correspond to the phases of the moon seems to bear out his contention that the batons are lunar tally sticks, and that the incised ibex head is a sign for early spring. His insight is an exciting one, for it suggests a possible continuity between ancient astrology and the religion of Ice Age humanity. The ram's head or Aries is the astrological sign for the beginning of spring. If Marshack is on to something, then astrology does not begin (as often thought) with the Mesopotamians, but it goes back to a lunar astrology in the Upper Paleolithic. The poet Robert Bly, in his celebration of the lost religion of the Great Mother, has called astrology "the great intellectual triumph of the Mother civilization.[38] If we wish to get a feel of what this lost religion was like, perhaps we should look, not to the archaeologists, with their emphasis on tool kits, but to those archaeologists of the unconscious, the poets. If we wish to understand a world-view built up on the phases of the moon, *A Vision* by W. B. Yeats[39] or *The White Goddess* by Robert Graves begin a journey far out of the civilized mind of modern, industrial humanity.

Marshack understands that a technology is not separate from a mythology, and that giving a name like "Solutrean" to a tool kit is not the same as naming a culture. Our grandfathers rode in horse-drawn buggies, and although we fly in jets, our religion is not all that different. President Jimmy Carter may be a technocrat, a nuclear engineer, and an Annapolis graduate, but he is also a twice-born Christian, and the imagery he invokes goes back even beyond the time of Christ. The anthropologists of the nineteenth century, like Tylor and Frazer, helped to establish connections between primitive religion and civilized religions; now Marshack is enabling us to establish continuities between the religion of the Ice Age and the religions of the ancient Near East. One of the most exciting and provocative of Marshack's analyses is his discussion of the role of storytelling in time-factoring notation.

> It became apparent as I worked that a documentation of the notations, though adequate for a scientific paper, could not explain or encompass the range of the associated symbolic evidence that began to unfold. Nor would it have explained the notations. I was forced to my inquiries into "story."
>
> When the adult *Homo sapiens* hunter saw the phases of the moon, he could presumably explain them to a child, to a teenager, or to himself, in each case differently and in each case in terms of the knowledge and mythology he had . . .
>
> Nevertheless, we cannot assume that the Ice Age hunter himself would have been able, consciously and in words, to separate his stories from his hard, factual knowledge. For he probably used one to understand and teach the other, and the words and names he used would have a storied content . . .
>
> The storytelling skill, then, helped him to see and recognize process and change, to widen his references and comparisons, to "understand" and to participate in them in storied terms, and it enabled him to tell and foretell them. One assumes, then, that the kind of stories a man tells—in this case a hunter's—helps him to unify the extraordinary diverse phenomena and processes of his life; and since a story is an *equation,* a cognitive form for abstractly structuring and dealing with process and relation, the uses and complexities of the story form would change as the culture became more complex. For us the important thing is to recognize that the innate, evolved *Homo sapiens* capacity for storied thinking has probably not changed significantly in the last 40,000 years.[40]

In modern science a "fact" is perceivable because of a background of myth. Each phase of the moon would have a name and a story associated with it, as would each animal. Through myth a cumulative body of knowledge would be passed on, and the means for passing it on would be a story, an engraving on a bone, or a painting on the wall of a cave. The story or the painting would serve to connect the part with the whole, the event with the myth, the quotidian with the sacred.

Because we have separated humanity from nature, subject from object, values from analysis, knowledge from myth, and universities from the universe, it is enormously difficult for anyone but a poet or a mystic to understand what is going on in the holistic and mythopoeic thought of Ice Age humanity. The very language we use to discuss the past speaks of tools, hunters, and *men,* when every statue and painting we discover cries out to us that this Ice Age humanity was a culture of art, the love of animals, and women. For years feminist scholars have objected to the use of the word "man," and I as much as anyone have bristled with annoyance at their ideological cant, their zealotry, and their insistence on the use of the ugly and abstract word "person"; but it is clear that they are right. Naming does direct thought, and one can notice in Marshack's use of the words "man" and "hunter" that he cannot *see* the culture in front of his eyes. Gathering is as important as hunting, but only hunting is discussed. Storytelling is discussed, but the storyteller is a hunter rather than an old priestess of the moon. Initiation is imagined, but the initiate is not the young girl in menarche, about to be wed to the moon, but a young man about to become a great hunter. The work of Marshack is perhaps the strongest evidence that Boulding's attack on the use of the word "man" is entirely justified.

V

TO BEGIN TO UNDERSTAND what is going on in the notation and art of the Upper Paleolithic, we have to escape not only the ethnocentricity of academic male subcultures, but also the limited epistemology of social science. We have to use the "Imagination" to recover a sense of the sacred. The sacred is the emotional force which connects the part to the whole; the profane or the secular is that which has been broken off from, or has fallen off, its emotional bond to the universe. *Religāre* means to bind up, and the traditional task of religion has been to bind up the pieces that have broken away from the ecstatic Oneness. For urban, civilized humanity, the work of religion is to reconnect the alienated and exploited classes in a vision of unity, or to reconnect the alienated human species with nature and the heavens. Religion is not identical with spirituality; rather, religion is the form spirituality takes in a civilization; it is not so much the opiate of the masses as it is the antidote for the poisons of civilization. (Of course, an overdose of an antidote becomes a poison in itself.) Because religion is a response to the conditions of alienation in a civilization, religion is unnecessary in a culture of hunters and gatherers. The culture of hunters and gatherers is spirituality personified; every event is part of a story, every part is connected to the whole, every act is flooded with the sacred. When an entire way of life is sacred, the people do not have to build churches and sing hymns on Sundays. For those contemporary individuals who have lost a sense of the sacred in daily life and also lost a sense of the use of religion, there is no way to regain the emotional feelings of connection with the whole except through art. And so in sophisticated, urban centers like New York, more people go to the Metropolitan Museum of Art on a Sunday than go to either cathedral in the city. For the postreligious culture of modern humanity, art is the last religion. The only chance the sociobiologists and anthropologists who have lost touch with precivilized spirituality or civilized religion have to break out of the limits of their behavioral science world-view and reconnect the part with the whole is through art. To try to recapture a sense of the sacred in Ice Age art, we should meditate on the central icon of that art, the statue of the Great Goddess.

Figure 4 of the famous *Venus of Laussel* is a reproduction of a low relief from the Dordogne in the Upper Perigordian, or roughly 19,000 B.C. The prehistorian André Leroi-Gourhan has identified it as "a woman holding a bison horn." With her large pendulous breasts, great stomach, and immense hips, this Paleolithic Madonna is of a type found with countless other figurines in excavations from Spain to the Soviet Union. This icon of the lady with the horn has a singular fascination. The horn appears to be shaped like a crescent moon and, therefore, expresses the relationship between the moon and woman. The covering of the low relief, red ochre, suggests that the woman is associated with the magical menstrual blood that relates woman to the moon and to childbearing.

Figure 4. The Venus of Laussel.

The Australian Blacks, who pour blood over their sacred stones, and paint themselves red after their rites, volunteer the information that this red paint is really the menstrual blood of women. In a Hottentot song addressed to the spirit of rain she is addressed: "Thou who has painted thy body red like Goro; Thou who dost not drop the menses." The diety refered to, there can be little doubt, is a

form of the moon, and the red ochre with which they paint
themselves is called "gorod" after her.[41]

The horn which the Venus of Laussel holds in her hand is incised
with thirteen, perhaps fourteen, marks. These may symbolize the
phases of the moon from the new moon to the full (in women's
mysteries, from menstruation to ovulation) or the thirteen lunar
months in the year. Many modern women can feel their ovulation;
in a culture focused on menstruation and the moon, it seems
reasonable to assume that a woman would be so attuned to nature
and her own body that she would also feel her ovulation. The
significance of ovulation might not be understood medically, but it
would be felt intuitively as an important event in the life of the
womb. Since the people of this period carved innumerable vulvas
on the walls of the caves, it is natural to assume that the monthly
rhythms of the vulva were closely attended to, and that ovulation
was no invisible event but was a subtle tidal pulse that seemed to be
drawn by the apparitional light of the full moon.

There are other mysteries expressed by the bison horn, the
Paleolithic original of which the classical cornucopia is a copy: the
horn of plenty is the universal vulva from which emerge all the
creatures of life, plants, animals, and humans. If we need to find a
symbolic bridge that allows us to connect the cornucopia of
classical Greece with the Paleolithic vulva, then I would suggest
the poem the Sumerian goddess Inanna, the Queen of Heaven,
composes in celebration of her vulva:

> Inanna exalts him,
> Composes a song about her vulva:
> The vulva, it is . . .
> Like a horn it . . . at the large wagon,
> It is the "boat of Heaven," fastening ropes . . .
> Like the new crescent, passion . . .[42]

The dots express the breaks in the clay tablet where the cunieform
is illegible, but even in its fragmentary state, the Sumerian poem
enables us to read backward and forward through time. Literature
as a written mythology is a way of recording far more ancient oral
material, so the Sumerian poem can be taken as a clue to the
ancient iconology of the vulva. What we discover is that the

woman with the horn is a complex hieroglyph. The bison horn is presumably from an animal associated with the Great Goddess, and such indeed is the suggestion of André Leroi-Gourhan.[43] The horn is the vulva, the crescent moon; later it becomes the crescent-shaped reed boats that ply the Tigris and Euphrates; still later it becomes the cornucopia of the nurse of Zeus, Amalthea. Poetic logic works through puns and the transformational associations described by Freud in his *Wit and the Unconscious*; recognizing that the Paleolithic lady holding the single horn becomes the lady and the *unicorn* of the medieval period gives us a clue to the logic of myth and poetry. The unicorn who may be touched and tamed only by a chaste virgin is a lunar symbol of the ancient religion of Europe. The famous tapestries at the Cloisters Museum in New York describe how man the hunter chases and slays the unicorn and thus present us with a medieval legend of the shift from the matrilineal society worshiping the moon to the patrilineal society worshiping the solar Christ. From the lady with the single horn to the lady with the lunar white unicorn, nothing is lost in the world of myth and the unconscious. The joker in our deck of cards is the fool of the medieval court, and beyond him lies the Paleolithic shaman in animal skin and animal headdress, with the lunar *baton de commandement* borrowed from woman's mysteries to be his androgynous ensign of power.

The epistemology of the behavioral sciences is all well and good in its very limited space, but to understand *culture*, we must go to school with the poets and the shamans. A scholar in the human-ities may know a score of dead languages, but *if* his own imagination is dead, then a poet who knows only his own living language may pass through to a deeper understanding of the images.

Take, for example, one more image: Albrecht Dürer's *Virgin* (see Figure 5). In this vision of Mary, she is sitting on top of the crescent moon, a crescent that has also the appearance of the horn of an animal. If one lines up in the mind's eye the Venus of Laussel, Inanna composing a poem to her vulva, the cornucopia of Amalthea, the lady and the unicorn, and the Virgin of Dürer, one creates a collage that is really a five-voice fugue. In this polyphony of images in the unconscious which is beyond and outside historical time, there are complex harmonies but no dissonances:

the images do not clash, but that, of course, is an aesthetic judgment and not a scientific one. If one wishes to be only scientific, then one will have to remain content with discussions of pressure flaking and tool classifications.

A great prehistorian who does not limit himself to the classification of tool kits is André Leroi-Gourhan. In his monumental *Prehistoire de l'art occidentale*,[44] he tries to move into an understanding of the meaning of the images of Paleolithic art. In an admirable combination of the skills of the scientist and the sensitivity of the artist, he mapped hundreds of thousands of images through a keypunch data-processing system and then tried to understand the meanings of the patterns that emerged independent of his own classifications. He saw two languages present in the cave paintings, one an abstract and stylized notation of signs, and the other a magnificent art of realistic portraiture of animals, but it was not until he looked at his keypunch arrangements that he began to see a pattern of association of signs with the animals. It appeared that there

Figure 5. Albrecht Dürer, from The Life of the Virgin, *1511.*

were female signs, various transformations of the image of the vulva, and male signs, various transformations of the phallus and spear. By analyzing the juxtapositions of sign and painting, Leroi-Gourhan conjectured that there was a poetic logic of association and that the animals themselves had a sexual valency, much as in Romance languages every object has a masculine or feminine gender. In further analyzing the jux-tapositions, Leroi-Gourhan noticed that the signs seemed to balance the images; a male animal was juxtaposed with a female sign, or vice versa. Then he noticed that there was a logic to the distribution of images within chambers inside the cave sanctu-aries: certain rooms were predominantly female—these were generally the central chambers; the entrance chamber was predominantly male, but often the deepest chamber was a room of male and female juxtapositions.

> After we have ruled out the hypothesis of hunters' magic, of these being literal representations of trapped animals, or weapons and huts for spirits, or the simplistic symbolism of the pregnant animals, what hypothesis is left? Clearly, the core of the system rests upon the alternation, complementarity, or antagonism between male and female values, and one might think of "a fertility cult." If we weigh the matter carefully, this answer is at the same time satisfying and laughable, for there are few religions, primitive or evolved, that do not somewhere involve a confrontation of the same values, whether divine couples as Jupiter and Juno are concerned, or principles such as *yang* and *yin*. There is little doubt that Paleolithic men were familiar with the division of the animal and human world into two opposite halves, or that they supposed the union of these halves to govern the economy of living beings. Did they conceive of this union the way we do, or in the fashion of Australian aborigines and Kanakas? Did they suppose that the activity of the male only nourishes the spirit which has entered the body of the female? Theirs was probably some other explanation we cannot imagine.[45]

If we add to Leroi-Gourhan's meticulous analysis of the placement of the images Marshack's idea that the animals are expressions of time-factoring patterns, then the art begins to appear as a complex cosmology. The animals become the early forms of the zodiacal animals, images for lunar months, and expressions of the basic dualistic nature of existence: male and female, Yin and Yang, life and death. The moon dies but is reborn; woman bleeds, but the vulva is a wound that heals itself. This miraculous nature of the vulva seems to have taken hold of the imagination of Paleolithic humanity, not simply because there are thousands of vulvas incised on the walls of the caves, but because the vulva was elaborated into a poetic logic in which "spear is to wound as phallus is to vulva."

> To gain a dynamic understanding of the cave representations, one would still have to integrate into this frame-work the symbolism of the spear and the wound. Taken as symbols of sexual union and death, the spear and the wound would then be integrated into a cycle of life's renewal, the actors in which would form two parallel and complementary series: man/horse/spear, and woman/bison/wound.[46]

The slit of the vulva appears like a wound made by a spear, and so the spear becomes a phallus. But the vulva is the magical wound that bleeds and heals itself every month, and because it bleeds in sympathy with the dark of the moon, the vulva is an expression not of physiology but of cosmology. The moon dies and is reborn; woman bleeds but does not die, and when she does not bleed for ten lunar months, she brings forth new life. It is easy to see how Paleolithic man would be in awe of woman, and how woman's mysteries would be at the base of a religious cosmology. We can see just how long-lived such iconology is if we stop to remember the spear that makes the wound in Christ's side, and recall just how many medieval paintings pictured Christ exposing his wound. The labial wound in the side of Christ is an expression that the male shaman, to have magical power, must take on the power of woman. The wound that does not kill Christ is the magical labial wound; it is the seal of the resurrection and an expression of the myth of eternal recurrence. From Christ to the Fisher King of the Grail legends, the man suffering from a magical wound is no ordinary man; he is the man who has transcended the duality of sexuality, the man with a vulva, the shamanistic androgyne.

When we are dealing with legends of Christ, we are dealing with a Mediterranean culture in which the supremacy of the male had been established for millennia, but what is the role of the male in this Paleolithic lunar mythology? The image of woman is clear and direct, but man is rarely represented and we have to strain to catch his indirect reflection off the images of horse and spear. Leroi-Gourhan has classed the images of ibex, mammoth, stag, bear, reindeer, and horse as having a male valency, but the explicit images of human males are almost nonexistent and very sketchily rendered when they do appear. The schematic images of the male, however, do seem to have one thing in common, and that is that the male is represented as either harrassed, chased, or wounded by an animal. Leroi-Gourhan has identified this as "the wounded-man theme."[47] Perhaps the most famous of all these images is the so-called scene from the pit or "the shaft of the dead man."

> At first sight this Chamber seems to be one of the least impressive parts of the cave, for the walls are marked and scored in all directions. But this concentration of confused lines and figures may indicate, on the contrary, that the place was particularly sacred or important . . . The decorated walls have a patina; worn and smoothed by time and friction, they bear witness to the constant use and frequentation of this part of the cave.
>
> At the far end of the Chamber of Engravings, a stone, highly polished, worn and much blackened by the constant passage of countless human bodies, forms a kind of lip over a yawning pit. The domed vault above it is engraved with various animal figures, latticed signs painted in several colours, long bands of short parallel strokes, and clusters of diverging lines similar to those in the Chamber, but of smaller size. The quintessence of all the signs in the cave would seem to be concentrated on the restricted surface of this dome, in spite of the fact that it is so high above the Shaft leading down to the well and the scene of the Dead Man and must have been difficult to reach.[48]

Figure 6 shows the painting from the Shaft of the Dead Man. The first thing one notices about the painting is the striking difference in style between the human figure and the animals; the animals are rendered in the naturalistic style of the other figures at Lascaux, but the man is a mere stick figure and is so stylized as to seem some sort of mediation between the naturalistic style of the animals on the one hand and the abstract signs on the other. The interpretation of Dr. Laming, the specialist on Lascaux, is straightforward and literal: it is a picture of a hunter who has struck his spear into the bison (whose entrails are spilling out) and has been

Figure 6. Scene from the pit, Lascaux; also called "The Shaft of the Dead Man."

gored to death in return. But this interpretation makes no sense at all. First of all, the spear is shown lying across the flank of the bison, or superimposed upon it. Secondly, to disembowel a bison, one would have to ask it to turn over so that it could be stabbed on its soft underbelly. Thirdly, since the man has a bird head and is shown with an erection, we should suspect that something else must be going on. Violent death can cause an erection, but so can dreams, visions, trance states, and the awakening of *kundalini*.

Robin van Löben Sels, a Jungian psychologist and student of Shamanism, has suggested that the painting is "a power vision" of a shaman in trance. Of course, one can never know for certain, but if one begins to look at the painting as a dream vision or as a mythological mural, then other features become more noticeable. The spear then is not impaling the bison, but it is juxtaposed with the sign of the vulva, the sign which Laming misreads as the entrails. Thus spear and vulva become a couplet, as man and bison become a couplet. In Leroi-Gourhan's analysis of the poetic logic, we have a mythological structure: spear is to wound as phallus is to vulva as man is to bison. If the man is a shaman, and the bison is an image of the Great Goddess, then the bison could be an epiphany of the Goddess coming to the shaman in the power vision that sets him apart from ordinary men.[49] In the center of the picture is a staff with a bird on the top, and this seems related to the fact that the man is shown with a bird's head. The staff with a bird on top, whether as totem pole or caduceus, is an ancient and universal symbol, and this painting from Lascaux may in fact be an expression of the source in Paleolithic religion from which all the later images derive (see Figures 7 and 8).

The staff of the god Mercury, the caduceus, shows two snakes coiling around a central rod surmounted by the two wings of the bird on top. Every initiate of Tantric yoga knows that the two snakes symbolize the two nerve channels, the *ida* and *pingala*, which spiral around the central passage way, the *sushumna*, of the spinal column. The snake symbolizes the chthonic force, the being which crawls along the ground; the bird symbolizes the higher realms of the consciousness, the being which is liberated from earth and can fly off to Heaven. In different cultures around the world this knowledge is rendered in the imagery particular to a

Figure 7 (left). Hans Holbein the younger, The Staff of Mercury, or Caduceus.

Figure 8 (right). Printer's device and colophon from the first edition of The Chemical Wedding, *Strassburg, 1616.*

place. In India, the image of a lotus is used, for a lotus has its roots in mud (the subconscient), has a slender spinal stem which passes through the water (the physical plane of consciousness), and then has a blossom which rests "white and unwet" upon the water, but facing up to the sun (the super-conscious). In Mexico the image is a tree in the jungle; its roots are in darkness and its spinal trunk rises up in the dappled light, and there on the top of the tree, facing toward the sun, the brilliantly colored Quetzal bird makes its nest. To teach the snake how to rise up the trunk to become a bird, or a plumed serpent—a Quetzalcoatl—is how yoga was expressed in ancient Mexico. But in ancient Egypt, the raising of *kundalini* was expressed in terms of raising the *djed* pillar of Osiris. The staff of Osiris was the expression of this initiatic material. What is expressed in the lotus, the plumed serpent, or the staff of Osiris is the yogi's knowledge of the three brains of man.[50] The first brain is the reptilian brain of the spinal cord, the brain of instinctive reflexes, the brain of the subconscious. The second brain is the limbic ring, the brain of passion and emotion, of fight or flight. The third brain of human evolution is the neocortex, the twin hemispheres that are the two wings of the bird of the staff of Mercury. In Tantric meditation a yogi experiences an inner bridge in the midbrain; one pole of this midbrain bridge is at the back of the medulla oblongata, and a *prana* seems to come in from outside at that point; the energy meets a force rising from the base of the spine and then crosses the midbrain bridge to a point between the two eyes, "a third eye." As the energy rises from the base of the yogi's spine, his eyes roll up, he becomes absorbed in the visions in the single eye, the third eye, and his whole consciousness becomes polarized. At the same time that he feels carried up in a vision and out of the body, the base of the spine is filled with energy, the genitals are flooded with vibrations, and the penis becomes erect. For a Roman Catholic, or a celibate monk, the intensification of genital activity *coupled with* an expansion of consciousness is astonishing, if not shocking.[51]

If van Löben Sels's intuitive hunch that the scene from the Shaft of the Dead Man is a shamanistic power vision and not a literal painting of a hunt is correct, then the ithyphallic condition of the man makes good sense. The erection does not have to do with fertility, although it is a sign of potency; the potency is expressed by the fact that the shaman in a deep trance state is in communication with the gods. If the bird on top of the staff is a sign of the Tantric transformation, then the bird head on the man indicates that he is one whose consciousness can fly into the sky; he is no ordinary man, he is a shaman, an initiate who has won the favor of the divine feminine, the Shakti, the Great Goddess. The stick-figure rendering of the man could then be explained as a mediation between the abstract style of the signs of phallus and vulva and the naturalistic style of the animals, because the shaman himself is the mediation between the opposites of man and god.

It would seem that in Paleolithic religion, as well as in the civilized religions that descend from it, the place where the opposites cross is a place of crucifixion for the male. The wounded man at the foot of the Great Goddess, the bison, or the dead man in the arms of the Virgin Mary, although they are images that span the millennia, may still be related, in much the same fashion as the image of the Venus of Laussel is related to the icon of the Virgin of Dürer. Leroi-Gourhan speaks of a man wounded by a bison, and I speak of the bison as an epiphany of the Great Goddess, but the two hypotheses are not mutually exclusive. The manifestation of a god in a trance or vision is often described in religious experience as a tearing or a rending. The statue of St. Teresa in ecstasy by Bernini shows an angel gleefully stabbing St. Teresa with an arrow, and the saint is presented as a woman in the ecstasy of orgasm. Future archaeologists, ignorant of religious states of consciousness, will probably strive to be scientific and avoid all far-fetched interpretations to describe the statue as one of a sadistic little boy stabbing a masochistic woman with a Mesolithic instrument of the hunt.

The literal interpretation of the painting in the Shaft of the Dead Man is obviously a gross oversimplification of a complex iconology; my reading of it as a shamanistic power vision may, on the other hand, seem to many to be too far-fetched: a projection of my own experiences in kriya yoga on an unresisting and silent image. A reader with a healthy skepticism would require more substantiation than a hypothesis of a universal shamanism connecting the yoga of India and Mexico with the religion of the Upper Paleolithic. Fortunately, I do think that there are other artifacts in the Neolithic period that reach back into the Paleolithic and look forward to the imagery of the civilized religions that follow. Thanks to the research of the archaeologist Marija Gimbutas, we can now trace the iconography of the bird-snake complex back to the sixth millennium B.C. in Central Europe.

> The Snake and Bird Goddess was a predominant image in the pantheon of Old Europe. As a combined snake and water bird with a long phallic neck she was inherited from the Magdalenian culture of the Upper Paleolithic. Though usually portrayed as a hybrid, this divinity could also be a separate Snake Goddess. She is the feminine principle.[52]

In yoga the feminine principle is Shakti, the Great Goddess experienced by all initiates of the Tantric process of transformation. The fact that the Snake and Bird Goddess is elaborated in the Neolithic period indicates that it had a long history, as Gimbutas suggests. The missing link provided by Gimbutas allows us to appreciate that the religion of the Upper Paleolithic is not simply the parochial superstitions of one tribe; it is the first universal religion, and its universality as an iconic system based upon the mysteries of menstruation and a lunar calendar cuts across cultures with different languages or tool kits. It is a universal religion whose range of influence even in the Upper Perigordian extends from Spain to Central Asia. By the time of the Neolithic, it had diffused throughout Africa and Eurasia. My contention, then, simply takes us one step back from the seventh millennium in the Balkans to the Magdalenian period in France. The ithyphallic condition of the bird-headed man, associated as he is with a magical staff with a bird on top of it, can then be seen in a context in which precisely those images do have meaning.

> The presence of the Bird and Snake Goddess is felt everywhere—on earth, in the skies and beyond the clouds, where primordial waters lie. Her abode is beyond the upper-waters, i.e. beyond meandrous labyrinths. She rules over the life-giving force of water, and her image is consequently associated with water-containers. . . .

> The bisexualism of the water-bird divinity is apparent in the emphasis on the long neck of the bird symbolically linked with the phallus or the snake from Upper Paleolithic times and onwards throughout many millennia. This "bisexualism" may derive from the fusion of two aspects of divinity, that of the bird and that of the

snake, and not from male and female principles. The image of the
phallic Bird Goddess dominates during the seventh and sixth
millennia in the Aegean area and the Balkans.[53]

The imagery of bisexualism is universally stressed in shamanistic
practices. In the culture of the Siberians or the American Plains
Indians, a shaman is often chosen because he shows feminine
tendencies. And in Tantric yoga, when the *kundalini* rises in the
deep states of meditation, the *prana* rising up the central spinal
channel is often said to be as if the semen were flowing up through
the spine into the brain. The *sushumna* of the spine becomes a
vagina, and the yogi feels an ecstatic experience that is both male
and female at once. The representation for this balancing of
opposed forces can be described as the marriage of Shiva and
Shakti in the brain, or it can be expressed as a serpent coiled
around an egg. From Leroi-Gourhan's analysis of cave art, the
balancing of these male and female forces is precisely what the
cosmology of Upper Paleolithic religion is all about.

This continuity of iconography and spiritual traditions of
initiation does, however, present us with a historical problem. The
conventional narrative of isolated and ignorant Paleolithic and
Neolithic tribes that finally come together in the "urban revolution" to create civilization simply won't do. It seems that there are
three alternate hypotheses. First, we can say that the art, religion,
and astrological cosmology of the Ice Age peoples are far richer
and more complex than we have believed before, and that this
culture is an *Ur-kultur* that is the fountainhead for all the later
civilized cultures which flow out of the world's first universal
religion.[54] Secondly, we can say with Rudolph Steiner and other
Theosophists that there is a missing *Ur-kultur* in prehistory that is
not Paleolithic but Atlantean. The Theosophists would claim that
Lascaux, Mexico, Egypt, and India have similar initiatic practices
because there was once a global elite with a high magical science.[55]
Thirdly, we can say with the Jungian psychologists that there is no
external physical place where culture originates, that there is only
the one universal collective unconscious of the human species, and
that this unconscious is beyond time and space. For the Jungian
psychologist Erich Neumann the culture of the Great Mother is
universal and ubiquitous; it does not diffuse from Lascaux to
Mexico.[56] Neumann rejects the diffusionist explanations of prehis-

tory; he argues for an evolutionary explanation in which the human mind is everywhere true to type and quite naturally constructs images of birds and snakes, for birds fly in the air and snakes crawl on the ground, so one easily becomes an image of the chthonic force and the other an image of the celestial. All the theories have certain points which recommend themselves, and so, following the idea of Lévi-Strauss that one should include all the variants of a myth, I accept all of them as variants on the myth of human origins. I think the culture of the Ice Age hunters was far more complex than any prehistorian has imagined, but I also think that there was a missing elitist culture in prehistory, and I accept the testaments from Irish, Mexican, Egyptian, Tibetan, Indian, and Greek mythologies that this "Atlantean" culture did exist.[57] I think the Jungian analysis of mythological patterns is very useful, but in their introverted fascination with dreams, Jungians ignore history. A Jungian reads his dream notebook and not the newspaper each morning; history has no reality for him, and so he has no feeling for it. Neumann pores over Neolithic material yet keeps insisting he is not talking about historical sequences, but merely about psychic levels. If I am comparing de Kooning's *Woman* with the *Mona Lisa,* I may want to talk about psychic perceptions of women, but I had better realize that there is such a thing as history and that its impact on the artist is considerable, for what separates da Vinci from de Kooning is an important historical stretch of time.

The Marxists ignore the internal world; the Jungians ignore the external world. Each writes a prehistory which agrees with his own temperament; the Marxist will talk about class struggle and alienation, and the Jungian will talk about the dragon fight in which consciousness breaks away from its domination by the collective. All this academic bickering comes from a failure to recognize the white and yolk of a single egg. There is a collective unconsciousness which unites minds separated by time and space, and ideas do travel through external time and space through a process of cultural diffusion. There was a rich and complex culture among the Ice Age hunters and gatherers of the Upper Paleolithic, and there was also an elitist, Atlantean culture. Historical reality is much larger than either our orthodoxies or our heresies.

CHAPTER THREE

Agriculturalization

HUMAN BEINGS love to talk about the weather. When strangers are brought into an uncomfortable proximity with one another, as in an elevator or at a counter in a café, a brief reference to the weather will transform the uneasy atmosphere and create an occasion of human culture. Such little pleasantries are unconscious rituals that express the important relationship between weather and culture.

Each of the critical transformations of human culture is associated with profound climatic changes. The hominization of the primates is associated with a period of dessication in the Pliocene, a withdrawal of the forests and an opening up of the savannah in which the early hominids are pushed out into a new ecological niche. For almost a million and a half years thereafter that ecological niche is stable, and Homo erectus undergoes few evolutionary changes in his movement through time. But about 300,000 years ago, during the European Second Interglacial period, "the first evidence of sapientisation occurred,"[1] and the fossil remains begin to express the stages toward the emergence of modern humanity. At about this time the first engraved rocks and tools also make their appearance, and with them we can infer that the human is now miniaturizing her universe into symbolic forms. It is at this point that we can truly begin to speak of such a thing as "culture."

With the appearance of culture the rate of change seems to accelerate. Hominization occurred over millions of years, but Symbolization occurs within a time frame of hundreds of thousands. Once the climatic change opens up a new ecological niche, however, there does seem to appear a period of stability. Steady-state and transformation seem to alternate with one another. The culture of Ice Age humanity expresses a steady growth in the complexity of the tool kit, and a steady growth in complexity of artistic development. As Leroi-Gourhan has pointed out, the continuity of artistic traditions over millennia is remarkable. But, in the wisdom of the ancient Taoist sages, "Reversal is the movement of Tao," and every steady-state is followed by a period of transformation. For humanity this means that once again the weather changes and humanity is forced into yet another ecological niche.

During the Ice Ages the European tundra were covered with great herds of reindeer, horse, and bison, but when the winds shifted, the rains that once fell upon North Africa fell upon Europe. The land responded with an offering of trees. This time, however, humanity had so changed from its Pliocene origins that the return of its ancient forest home was no welcome event. The culturally elaborated adaptations of the Ice Age hunters melted away with the glaciers; now through the thick forest the hunter pursued a single animal with the new tool of the bow and arrow.

The climatic changes that stimulate these transformations of culture are not yet understood by science, but what is slowly emerging in the literature is a much more profound appreciation of how everything is very subtly involved with everything else. Explosions of volcanoes change the atmosphere; shifts in the earth's angle of rotation affect the movement of winds; and there is now dawning an almost mythopoeic sense that "our inconstant sun"[2] may be following cosmic seasons in its movement through the galaxy. Because so much of archaeology is guesswork, scientists have a tendency to fall into the old logical error of *post hoc, propter hoc:* things changed, therefore things changed because of the change. At one time, warming will be invoked as the cause of the change; at another period, the increasing cold will be seen as the cultural stimulant.

In the post-Pleistocene period the glaciers retreated, the seashore rose 300 feet, the tundra turned to forest, and the great herds disappeared from Western Europe. And gone with the animals was the great "high culture" of Ice Age humanity. It is not hyperbole to speak of the high culture of these hunters and gatherers, for cave paintings like Lascaux are complex works that speak rather eloquently for the abundant leisure and rich cosmology of their creators. Hobbes may have thought that life in a primitive condition of hunting and gathering was "nasty, brutish, and short," but we now know that these so-called primitives were what the anthropologist Marshall Sahlins has called "the original affluent society."[3] With a labor of a mere fifteen hours a week, hunters and gatherers can provide for all their needs. They have far more leisure time than an agrarian community, caught up as it is in what Marx called "the idiocy of rural life," and they certainly have more leisure time than the harassed factory and office workers of the industrial era. With their populations adjusted to the carrying capacity of the environment,[4] hunters and gatherers rarely starve, for they are not dependent on the fortunes of a single crop. With their needs so easily provided for, primitive humanity devoted most of its spare time to matters of ritual and art. Small wonder that, as a contemplative people with time on their hands, they gave much thought to the relationship of menstruation and the moon, observed nature, constructed a calendar, told stories, and painted hundreds of thousands of images on the walls of the caves. As the Sistine Chapel expresses the flowering of the culture of the Renaissance, so Lascaux expresses the flowering of the culture of the Magdalenians. In more ways than one, the two great murals have much in common, for they are not mere decoration; they are mythological visions of the nature of time.

For the few thousand years that Magdalenian culture lasted, the relationships among religion, art, and technology seem to have achieved a condition of harmony and balance. But for humanity all steady-states are temporary, and just when we think we can take nature for granted, whether we live in a hunting or an industrial society, the weather changes, and we are forced to change.

Great ages of transition, with their attendant changes of climate—as we ourselves seem about to discover—are difficult times of decreasing culture. Adjusting to a new ecological niche calls for a new adaptation and takes the entire psychic energy of a culture. The Mesolithic was just such an age of transition; with none of the art of Paleolithic Lascaux and none of the fine crafts of Neolithic Çatal Hüyük, it was—like the fifth century A.D.—a Dark Age.

Over many parts of southwestern and southern Europe the culture of the Mesolithic inhabitants was in all measurable respects inferior to that of their Advanced Paleolithic forebears. The ebullience and verve of the Magdalenian hunters were based on altogether exceptional conditions which came to an end with the Ice Age itself.[5]

In the days of the great herds on the tundra, hunting could be a simple form of gathering, an activity much like the gathering of plants by women. In the division of labor between men and women in the Upper Paleolithic, a balance seems to have been struck. The harmony of the male and female principles celebrated on all the walls of the caves may have been reflected in daily life, with women serving as priestesses, artists, craftswomen, and gatherers, and men serving as shamans, artists, craftsmen, and hunters. Such a balanced division of labor seems to have been disturbed in the Mesolithic period. Hunting parties would need to range out farther from the home base, and as the hunting or fishing camp became a place with a longer life, it also would become a place with its own male subculture, its own stories, its own rituals. And as gathering by the women and children began to bring in far more food than hunting, the hunting parties would have to range out even farther if they were not to come home empty-handed. The farther out they ranged, the longer they were away, and the greater grew the distance between the subculture of the males and the traditional culture of the females in the religion of the Great Goddess.

The Great Goddess was still, to be sure, "the Mistress of the animals," the source of all life, and the patroness of the hunt. Figure 9 shows a North African rock painting in which the Great Goddess lifts her hands as a force flows out of her vulva directly into the phallus of the hunter about to shoot his arrow.[6] The animal he seems about to shoot is an ostrich, an animal whose giant egg can be used as a vessel in which to hold water but an animal that symbolically has a long phallic neck. Many figurines of the Great Goddess have similar long phallic necks; the bird expresses both the feminine and the masculine principles in the poetic logic of the old iconology that arrow is to wound as penis is to vulva. The force of the Goddess's vulva shoots into the penis of the hunter; his arrow shoots into the phallic bird of the Great Goddess, to make a new vulva as wound; thus the painting

Figure 9. Paleolithic rock painting, Algeria.

expresses the energy of a cycle, from vulva to vulva. Our way of expressing this cycle of eternal recurrence would be "Dust thou art, and to dust thou shall return." The phallic-necked bird also gives us a clue that the presence of the bird on a stick in the painting from the Shaft of the Dead Man is no simple, literal painting of a bird-headed man hunting a bison. Both paintings remind us that the Great Mother belongs to the mysteries of the hunt as well as to the mysteries of menstruation and the moon.

When two subcultures follow the same religion in different ways, that religion is no longer the same, as we can see in the cases of the Jews and Christians of the time of St. Paul, and the Catholics and Protestants in contemporary Northern Ireland. The stories that men would tell around the fire of the hunting camp and the stories that women would tell to a girl at menarche would not be the same. As the gathering of women and girls began to produce more and more food, until the very storage of it required a new kind of sedentary life, and as hunting required greater distances and longer-lived seasonal camps, the distance and tension between the female and the male patterns of life would become pronounced.

Life changed greatly for the Ice Age hunters, but we know from studies of cultural history that when a way of life is vanishing, people hold on to it and try to give it a more intense expression. When knighthood is about to disappear from the waning Middle Ages, armor becomes extremely elaborate; the celebration of the armored knight mounted on his horse becomes an unconscious farewell. Whether it is the Ghost Dance of the American Indians or the return to nature in the romanticism of industrial Europe, the "Silver Swan" madrigal of Morley or the *Art of the Fugue* of Bach, it is the supernova of a star in its death. The swan song of the Ice Age hunters, I believe, was a holding-on that generated the domestication of animals, but we must not see this domestication as the reaction to economic necessity, forced upon the hunters by the pressure of a lack of food. It was rather a religious act, an emotional act in which the animals were first domesticated because of their symbolic connection to the great universal religion. Animals may have been domesticated for religious purposes far back into the Magdalenian period, but I would pick the period of the early Mesolithic as the time when the activity became culturally intense. Most prehistorians place the domestication of animals much later and see it as arising along with the growth of sedentary villages. Eduard Hahn put forward a thesis in the late nineteenth century that the ritual probably preceded an economic exploitation. I see the cultural conditions for such a ritual domestication existing at the transition from the Upper Paleolithic to the Mesolithic.

> Eduard Hahn has postulated that the motive for capturing and maintaining the urus in the captive state was to have available a supply, for sacrificial purposes, of the animal sacred to the lunar mother goddess worshipped over an immense area of the ancient world. The economic uses of the animal would then have been a by-product of a domestication religious in origin. Why the urus was selected as the animal sacred to the deity is uncertain, but this was probably because its gigantic curved horns resembled the lunar crescent. Studies in prehistoric and early historic religion have shown that the bovine was early regarded as an epiphany of the goddess or her consort and was slain in the ritual enactment of the myth of her death.[7]

It is not *her* death, but his; the god that is ritually killed is never the eternal feminine. It is the king who must die; it is Dumuzi, the Sumerian shepherd-king, and it is she who causes his death. If the ethnologist Robert Briffault is right and the moon is seen as masculine—the husband of the Goddess—then when the Goddess menstruates, the moon is killed. I think, however, that the moon only becomes the husband of the Goddess later, when the discovery of paternity gives us the concept of husband and father; the earlier form would more likely identify the Goddess herself with the moon, a *participation mystique* of the moon and the vulva as fertile crescents.

Stock breeding in the domestication of cattle is an activity that is likely to create just the conditions for the discovery of paternity. If cattle, used for sacrificial purposes, were kept in sacred corrals, then the keepers were likely to be performers of sacred tasks. They were not yet priests, for society was not yet that specialized, but they may have been the precursors of what later became priests. The priest and the shaman are not the same kind of man. The shaman is the visionary, prophet, or yogi who is outside the social structure; he is an individual who goes through a solitary initiation, survives the crisis, and returns to his community as one stronger and wiser than his fellows. The priest is no such solitary initiate: he is the voice of the collective, a social functionary. The shaman or prophet is chosen by God; the priest is chosen by society. One can go to a seminary to learn how to become a priest, but the training of the shaman is far more dangerous.

If the keepers of the sacred corral discovered paternity in their stock breeding, then that knowledge would have been seen as numinous, awe-ful, and unconsciously unsettling. Their further discovery that castrated bulls are easier to absorb into culture created the conditions in which castrated priests could offer up their paternity to the culture of the Great Mother. The unconsciously unsettling knowledge of paternity could thus be absorbed into the old order, and the priestly caste of the keepers of the corral could become the *castrati* of the Great Mother. The patterns we meet at the dawn of civilization may thus go far back into the Mesolithic and the first domestication of cattle.

> The notion of using cattle for secular labor seems to have been derived from the use of cattle to pull sacred vehicles. Castration of the bull, which led to one of the most significant developments, the ox, also had a religious origin. Neither the taming effect of castration nor its effect in improving the texture of meat could have been foreseen. Human ritual castration, the reenactment of the fate of the deity in certain cults of Near Eastern ritual mythology (Tammuz, Attis, and so on) probably served as the model for the castration of the bulls.[8]

I would accept this argument but invert it. Castration of bulls was a socialization process that turned a bull into an ox; in this transformation something wild became something very useful; nature became culture. This knowledge thus became a way in which the wild knowledge of paternity could be converted to a useful function—the rise of the priesthood. Castration is an obsessive form of behavior; it is an institutional way of taking literally and concretely something the solitary shaman would know to be metaphoric for initiatic and secret states of consciousness. Just such a priestly translation of shamanistic knowledge took place in the Mexico of the Aztecs. In the yoga of Quetzalcoatl, the initiate spoke of the opening of the heart to the light of the sun, and what was meant by this was the opening of the chakras in the subtle body; the Aztec priests, as voices for collectivization, took the esoteric words literally, ripping out the victim's physical heart and holding it up to the sun.[9] The castration of men seems to represent a similar misreading of esoteric knowledge, but to understand how this could come about we have to have some understanding of the symbolic meanings of the phallus before the discovery of paternity and the domestication of animals.

Since the Magdalenian hunters and gatherers seem to have constructed a rich and complex cosmology based upon the balance of the complementary forces of the masculine and the feminine, it may be the case that the discovery of paternity must be set back in the Upper Paleolithic. Since the Magdalenians expressed themselves in an art of a complex time factoring, the seasons when the elk were in rut or when the calves were dropped would be closely attended to. We need to remember, however, that the discovery of paternity does not mean that men before this time did not associate sexual intercourse with childbirth. As Ashley Montagu has studied it, in Australia physiological paternity is dwarfed by the process of mythological incarnation through which a spirit-child enters the body of a woman.

In this book I have pointed out *ad nauseam* that practically everywhere in Aboriginal Australia, contrary to the common belief, intercourse is associated with conception, *but not as a cause of conception or childbirth* ... As I have shown in this book, the

Australian Aborigines have no notion of physiological conception,
but they do believe that a woman must be opened up by the male
penis before a spirit-baby can enter her.[10]

The presence, then, of phallic symbolism in Magdalenian art does
not automatically indicate a knowledge of physiological paternity;
it does mean that the penis is subsumed under some cosmology at
which we can only guess. If we look at some of the phallic *art
mobilier*, we do notice that the penis is separated from the male
body and is regarded as a symbol or hieroglyph. It is no longer
simply a penis; it is a phallus. In one bone engraving a phallus is
seen juxtaposed with a bear's head. Marshack's reading of this
bone is:

> The phallus is almost flowerlike in its complexity, making contact in
> one direction with a bear head via an angular emanation. In the
> other direction a smaller sub-phallus seems directed into a vulvar
> form.[11]

Leroi-Gourhan sees the bear as an animal with masculine valency;
he does not read it as feminine like the bison. We know that in
Mousterian times, the time of Neanderthal humanity, there was a
bear cult. In one cave over twenty bear skeletons were found
buried together under a flat stone slab that weighed almost a ton.
If the bear lived in the caves, then there may have been some
poetic equation, such as bear is to cave as penis is to vulva. If the
bear is a symbol of masculinity, then the pointed emanation could
be the breath of the bear entering into the phallus, rather than the
semen of the phallus entering into the mouth of the bear. We can
never know for certain, but the imagery does tell us that the
phallus is part of a complex mythological system.

Another carved bone depicts the phallus with fishes carved on it
and is itself carved in the shape of a fish. If these time-factoring
animal signs are the root forms of the zodiacal animals, then this
could be what later becomes the sign of Pisces. The equation of
fish/phallus is a mythic structure that survives all the way up to
Egyptian times: in the myth of Isis and Osiris, when Isis gathers
up the dismembered pieces of Osiris's body, she is unable to find
his penis, for a fish had swallowed it. Isis's brother, Set, had cut up
Osiris's body into fourteen pieces, and these pieces probably

symbolized the fourteen phases of the moon from the full to the dark. Thus the disintegration of the full moon and the dismemberment of Osiris would be associated; the fish that swallows Osiris's penis may have been a star which came into a particular association with one of these phases of the moon. Therefore, we should be prepared to realize that the astrology behind these myths could have been more complex than something simply dealing with the phases of the moon.[12] Marshack does not relate his material to astrology or the myth of Isis and Osiris; yet his very choice of language rings bells for those students more conversant with mythology: "Fish, phallus and water, seem aspects of a larger myth which apparently also includes the 'goddess.'"[13]

Before the discovery of physiological paternity, the phallus would still be the symbol of the masculine; since the erection of the penis comes with dreams and trances, as well as sexual contact, the penis would be rich in complex symbolic associations which would enable it to go through the apotheosis by which it becomes the phallus. One can only make a guess in these matters, but I would suspect that the concept of paternity alive at the time of the Magdalenian hunters is one in which physiological insemination is not stressed as a causal agent; I would suspect that the ideas of the Ice Age hunters would be closer to the Australian aborigines than to our own.

The domestication of cattle, however, would change all that. The cattle may have been chosen because their curved horns recalled the lunar crescent, but once the cattle were kept in corrals, and once second generations were raised in captivity, then the observation of inherited characteristics, like Mendel's observation of sweet peas, would encourage a focusing of attention on genetics. It is at the point of conscious stock breeding that I think one is likely to get the idea of physiological paternity. The phallus of the bull would then become the receptacle of a great deal of attention, and here a religious ritual of castration might develop. The castration would further encourage new ideas of genetics, for the changes of behavior of castrated bulls would be observed: ritual would have feedback on ideas of genetics, and ideas of genetics would have feedback on ritual. An entire mystery school would develop right at the time when the old ways of the great herds were vanishing. In this mystery school the old pattern of what Leroi-Gourhan has identified as "the wounded man theme" would take on a new symbolic dimension.

II

THE NATURAL RHYTHM of the male is a phallic one of rise and fall, whether it involves towers, stock markets, or whole civilizations. The natural rhythm of the female is one of eternal recurrence: the vulva bleeds and heals, the moon darkens and is reborn. Men die in all the myths of the Near East because these myths embody a philosophical inquiry into the meaning of existence and the nature of death. The male embodies the mystery of death; his climactic phallus seems to say it all. We come out of matter (*materia, Mater*), and we are simply many little pieces broken off from the One; as fragments we can only hope to lead a fragmentary life until the One takes us back in death. The Great Mother is no simple notion from primitive religion, but an idea in a complex mythology that became demythologized and secularized by the Presocratics, but not changed. The male as the limited and vanishing principle and the female as the unlimited, eternal, and containing principle are simply expressed differently by Anaximander from the manner used by the painters of Lascaux or Çatal Hüyük. If we paraphrase only two terms of Anaximander, we can move out of classical Greece back into the old universal religion of the Upper Paleolithic.

> The Non-limited [the Great Mother] is the original material of existing things; further, the source from which existing things [men] derive their existence is also that to which they return at their destruction, according to necessity; for they give justice and make reparation to one another for their injustice, according to the arrangement of Time.[14]

In the Old Religion, the arrangement of Time would be described by astrology, by the animal images of the ancient lunar calendar. "Unto all things, there is a season . . . a time to live, and a time to die." Nothing is more short-lived than the erection; like the crocus of spring, it is there for a moment, and then it is gone; one moment the penis is small, soft, and insignificant, and then in the next it is hard, rigid, and three and four times its previous size.

The penis is the perfectly obvious and natural symbol of instantaneous time. By contrast, the bleeding vulva of menstruation is the perfectly obvious and natural symbol of cyclical time. The myths would therefore quite naturally tell stories in which the male is the climactic, tragic figure of flourish and vanish. The erection of a baby, the erection of a lover, the erection of a man in violent death, the erection of a dreamer, the erection of a shaman in ecstatic trance: all these would be noticed and seen in a context of intense but instantaneous experiences. Men die in all the Near Eastern myths, not because women are cruel, castrating bitches, but because men are the most immediate and obvious symbol for the phenomenology of the limited, vanishing body. If in some of the old myths the king must die to have his scattered pieces fertilize the fields, it is because the myth and the ritual were attempts to come to terms with death. If the priests of Diana of Ephesus castrated themselves and offered their genitals on the altar,[15] it was because the phallus was the symbol of the dying body. To offer up the phallus was therefore a petition to the Goddess for immortality. The yogi hopes to gain the universal feminine of Shakti by giving up sexual intercourse; he offers up his phallus in celibacy. The priests who were ignorant of the esoteric mysteries of the three brains of man and their relationship one to another in yogic trance states took the metaphoric language literally and hoped to achieve the higher states of consciousness by castrating themselves. Origen castrated himself because he did not understand the Tantric experience to which Jesus was referring:

> For there are some eunuchs, which were born so from their mother's womb: and there are some eunuchs, which were made eunuchs of men: and there be eunuchs, which have made themselves eunuchs for the kingdom of heaven's sake. He that is able to receive it, let him receive it.
>
> Matt. 19:12

With this historical pattern spanning the millennia in front of us, we can now perhaps truly appreciate the painting from the Shaft of the Dead Man at Lascaux. The ithyphallic bird-man is the climactic, ecstatic, instantaneous male principle confronting the enormous, slow, bovine, and enduring principle of the eternal feminine in her epiphany as the bison. The painting is a vision of the higher consciousness that comes at the interface between life and death in the orchestration of the brain and the genitals through the spine in states of trance and meditation. The painting is a mythological rendition of what Plato would transform into parables, "likely stories," and dialectical discussions of the One and the Many.

The mythological pattern of the rise and fall of the male principle has heretofore been seen as a motif from the Near Eastern myths of "the corn gods" discussed by James George Frazer in his *Golden Bough*. But the work of Marshack and Leroi-Gourhan enable us to see that these later religions of the civilized period are elaborations of the cosmologies from the universal religion of the Upper Paleolithic.

III

THE MAGDALENIAN CULTURE of 12,000 B.C. was a temporary steady-state, a balance of the sexes in a harmonious division of labor celebrated in the juxtaposed male and female signs on the walls of the caves. The Mesolithic culture from 10,000 to 8000 B.C. was a Platonic *Magnus Annus* of loss and cultural disorientation, a Dark Age. The Neolithic culture from 8000 to 6000 B.C., however, was a brilliant period of the revival of crafts, the transformation of gathering into gardening, the growth of a cross-cultural obsidian trade, and the rise of towns. Astrologers, when they observe this pattern, insist that it corresponds to the zodiacal progression.[16] I am not an astrologer and I hold no brief for it, but I do believe the origins of astrology are not with the Chaldeans of Mesopotamia but with the hunters and gatherers of the Stone Age. Whether or not we believe in astrology is irrelevant; the question is, did the Magdalenians? If so, then in a self-fulfilling prophecy they may have been organizing their lives according to a religious belief system, and not simply an economic or ecological one. In the zodiacal procession of the poles, the 25,920-year cycle, Lascaux is the time of Virgo, and Virgo is associated with artistic excellence and discrimination. The Mesolithic transition is in the sign of Leo, a sign associated with masculine qualities of forcefulness and practicality. The Neolithic of 8000 to 6000 B.C. is in the sign of

Cancer, a feminine sign associated with domesticity, retentiveness, and sentiment. Since the period from 8000 to 6000 B.C. saw the rise of domestic architecture and permanent villages and towns, the shift from the seasonal round to permanent settlement may have been inspired by religious as well as economic or environmental reasons.

The Mesolithic period is, I believe, one in which the traditional division of labor between the sexes is undergoing a change: the men are moving into the domestication of animals, and the women are ranging out to include a much broader spectrum of plant foods in their gathering. Physiological paternity has been discovered, but it is still subsumed under the mythological system of the religion of the Great Mother. Knowledge of a "fact" and its institutionalization in a society are quite distinct: murder, for example, was probably "discovered" in the Pliocene, but the institutionalization of murder in warfare does not seem to have occurred until the late Neolithic or the protoliterate period. The discovery of paternity does not mean, therefore, that the religion of the Great Mother is going to be replaced by one of the Great Father. That transformation is to come, but it will not be until humanity has shifted from the custom-bound life of the intimate matrilineal village to the law-ruled life of the complex patrilineal state. If one wishes to gain an understanding of how humanity could shift from the one to the other, one needs to have an understanding of the enantiodromia (a movement that turns into its opposite) of the development of gathering into agriculture.

The archaeologists tell us that although the post-Pleistocene climate changed markedly in Western Europe, there was no pronounced change in Southwest Asia. The extinction of the Pleistocene megafauna had ended there long before it had in Europe, and so a "broad spectrum" of food collecting had been going on for some time. The decision to include wild cereals in the collection may have been initially a random act of gathering, but once that decision had been made it triggered a runaway system of positive feedback in which the entire culture was transformed.[17] There is, of course, the usual scholarly disagreement, with Braidwood disagreeing with the environmental-determinist theories of Childe, and Binford disagreeing with Braidwood's invocation of culture and human nature, but most seem to accept

Flannery's cybernetic model.[18] The experts agree that in the foothills of the mountains of Southwest Asia certain forms of wild cereals grew and that women and children could collect enough grain in three weeks to feed a family for an entire year. The men would return from the hunting or fishing camp to find the home base filled and overflowing with grain. Once again, the miraculous nature of woman had asserted itself, and, armed with a crescent sickle shaped like the moon, she had gone out and gathered more life than any hunter could kill.

Woman had gone out and unconsciously taken nature into culture, for in gathering the wild wheat she struck the stalk with her sickle and thus helped to scatter the wild-blown seeds; in carrying the grasses home she increased the proportion of grains with large heads that stuck to the stalk. In her spilling of seeds around her home base, certain types of grain were being selected for; grains that could not easily reproduce themselves in the wild now had a helper, and the process through which crosses and hybrids become established was set into motion. As the seeds she spilled sprang up closer to home, it would seem as if the magical woman, the Great Mother and Mistress of Animals, was now becoming the Mistress of Plants. Ceres, the goddess of wheat, was about to make her appearance in prehistory. If we now say that "woman's place is in the home," it is not because men put her there, but because the home became the capitol of women's mysteries. It is the feminine vessel and container, the cornucopia brimming over with food. To deal with that problem of abundance, woman took another step and invented pottery to store the fruits of nature. Small wonder that pots were shaped like great-breasted matrons or were made round, not on the potter's wheel, but on the woman's breast.[19]

In the runaway system of positive feedback of collecting cereals, no conscious decision was made to change the culture; there was no Lenin at the Finland Station masterminding what V. Gordon Childe liked to call "the Neolithic Revolution";[20] yet a new culture began to develop at an increasingly rapid rate. Its growth could not help but push the old ways of hunting into the background. Of course men would still hunt, but it was more from the force of the three-million-year-old tradition, for the satisfactions of male bonding in their own subculture, and as an escape from the furious activity of the women in gathering, grinding, cooking, and pottery. They could offer their obsidian to the women for use in the lunar crescent-shaped sickles, but even that contribution was ambiguous, for all the later myths would speak of castration with sickles; the standing grain cut down by the women would not create happy associations for the men. If we wonder now how easily men are threatened by women, and how the slightest expression of feminine power can generate castration anxieties in even a big man, then perhaps we would do well to think back on the origins of agriculture. As a gatherer, woman was a botanist; as a cook and a potter, she was a chemist; as a mother, she was a priestess of the Great Mother. Woman was a formidable creature in every way, and the origin of agriculture, rather than eliminating the religion of the Great Goddess of the Upper Paleolithic, ended by adding another miracle to the list of feminine wonders.

Whether or not Neolithic man longed to get away from women to go fishing or return to the hunting camp, the stored-up treasure in the granary would require his protective presence, and that was the beginning of the enantiodromia of agriculture for women. Hunters and gatherers have little property, and what they have they can carry, but sedentary collectors begin to have stores of grain, grinding stones, and clay bins that they cannot easily leave. They begin to have wealth, and the hunter with his spear and bow and arrow discovers a new use for his tool and his trade. If his manhood is insignificant in producing food in the chase, it can become significant in protecting women and wealth. It must have been frustrating for the Neolithic hunter to come home and lay his deer before all to admire, to realize his catch would last a few days, woman's a whole year. No doubt the hunter would demean the porridge of cereals and seeds as "woman's food" and make loud noises about a thick steak of venison, but the furious activity around him continued in spite of all his celebrations of the noble chase. And that, too, triggered a positive feedback system of accelerating change. The more insignificant male activities were, and the more women's activities produced wealth, the more some men were attracted to steal and other men attracted to defend the new acquisitions. The men discovered a new way to get together and warfare was born. It was not ecological pressure or shortages of protein, as anthropologist Marvin Harris has claimed;[21] institutionalized violence, as opposed to the stylized agons of hunters over grievances, was the shadow side of the Neolithic Revolution. It is naive to look always to negative things for the cause of negative behavior; in the enantiodromias of history, we need to understand that even a positive change casts a shadow. We need to understand that the unique excellence of a thing is at the same time its tragic flaw. The collection of cereals produces wealth and increases the cultural distance between men and women, and both phenomena were to prove very dangerous.

Every culture which has ever created a class to protect itself has ended up having to protect itself from the protectors. In ancient Mexico, the priests set up a warrior class, and the warriors later took over from the priests. In America we created a Department of Defense, and now everyone is threatened. So it was in 8000 B.C. Wealth engendered the need for defense, and by the time the men were through protecting the women, they would be talking about protecting *their* women. Through male bonding, the subculture of the hunt caught up in the mystique of the chase, the hunting party became a military force, and men discovered that they need not stop at defense: they could go out to hunt for other people's wealth. It would not happen overnight, but the enantiodrama was that the discovery of cereals by women permitted the discovery of warfare by men.

Warfare was not the only discovery of Neolithic hunters. The presence of a food supply which could be stored over a considerable length of time also enabled the men to expand their hunting activities into trading activities. The aborigines in Australia love to come together to trade stone axes, much as young boys love to come together to swap marbles or yo-yos. The material that was truly prized for its sharpness by all hunters was obsidian, and this volcanic glass seems to have been traded widely, for the obsidian of Anatolia has been found in Palestine, and the cowrie shells of Palestine have been found in Anatolia. The storage of grains, and the convenience of their portability in travel, enabled some men to be away for extended periods of time. The natural encounter of hunting bands on the move would encourage trade as a social form of intercourse which could defuse a potentially dangerous meeting.

Since the Neolithic Revolution, trade and warfare have been

linked in a peculiarly contradictory relationship, for on the one hand, trade is a sublimation of male violence and a form of cross-cultural exchange which requires peaceful conditions; on the other hand, trade stimulates the accumulations of wealth and power which generate jealousy, rivalry, and warfare. In this peculiar and deadly symbiosis the presence of warfare stimulates trade and the presence of trade stimulates warfare.

IV

THROUGH THE COLLECTION of cereals, hunting, and trade, and with the help of an epoch of benign weather, human population began to grow. Towns and even "cities" began to be possible even before women had expanded gathering into gardening. As Jane Jacobs has argued, cities come before agriculture.[22] The unconscious decision to collect wild cereals is, in many ways, a more significant event than the alleged "invention of agriculture." Strictly speaking, there is no such event; the Neolithic Revolution is a projection onto the screen of prehistory of the idea of the Industrial Revolution. Such ideas have the advantage of making invisible transformations visible, but we need to remember that when we are talking about such enormous transformations as hominization, symbolization, and agriculturalization, we are not talking about events.

The transformations of culture do not take place in history, they take place in myth. It is because the individual cannot perceive in the limits of his own lifetime such transformations as the Neolithic or Industrial revolutions that we have need of myth. A model, a hypothesis, or a myth is a way of rendering the invisible. Because the unconscious is outside time, it can perceive transformations beyond the limits of the ego. These unconscious perceptions are expressed in art or mythologies. We ourselves are living in an age of cultural transformation, but if you went to the experts to ask for a description, they could tell you nothing. You have to go to those who are at home in the unconscious and the superconscious, the artists and prophets; through myth and symbol in art, science fiction, or religion, they will describe the present by speaking about the future.[23]

There is, of course, a danger in all this myth making, whether the myths are religious, Freudian, Marxist, or sociobiological. Again, what we see is what we are. Marshall Sahlins sees food collectors as an affluent society; the Marxist Central European prehistorian, Dragoslav Srejovic, sees the Mesolithic food-collecting community of Lepenski Vir in Yugoslavia as a true soviet.

> The everyday life of the inhabitants of Lepenski Vir was exceptionally hard. In order to get food, building materials and stone for weapons it was necessary to leave the security of the settlement, closed in by steep cliffs and the great river, and face the perils of the world beyond these boundaries. Individual strength and skill was not sufficient for that struggle; only by united efforts was it possible to catch large prey or obtain essential materials, and only the group could assure a safe return to the settlement.
> This complete economic dependence of the individual on the community ruled out all personal freedom. Each member was forced to produce the means needed for common food collection, to build his house on the site apportioned by the community and to harmonize his demands and behaviour with the views of the majority. Each case of indiscipline and independent action must have had as its consequence the exclusion of the refractory individual from all communal activities. Moreover, at Lepenski Vir isolation meant death; between the forest, the rocks and the water the individual was powerless and lost. Only self-discipline and total assimilation into the community provided the means for survival. However, by the sacrifice of individual freedom and the dedication of all forces to the common aims, human energies developed to a remarkable degree and a strong social organization and a powerful, expressly masculine, culture was created.[24]

When confronted with such Marxist propaganda and such a paranoid vision of a fishing community with enough time on its hands that it can create "Europe's first monumental sculpture," it is hard for the cultural historian not to despair. It is hard not to give in and accept the verdicts of Voltaire that "history is the lie commonly agreed upon" and of Henry Ford that "history is bunk." When faced with the Marxist fantasies of Srejovic or Childe, or with the psychohistorical hallucinations of Julian Jaynes,[25] I realize that history is never a science and rarely an art, and the historian who pretends to the former loses the latter.

However we wish to see these new sedentary villages, we do need to understand that they arise long before the appearance of agriculture. Even by the time agriculture has been well established, villages of hunters and gatherers still persist. An example of just such an entity is Suberde in Turkey of 6600 B.C.

> Suberde is functionally a sedentary village of hunters, dependent entirely upon the taking of wild game. The site was occupied year-round, not seasonally, and there is evidence that the presence of the village had a marked effect on the local game populations . . .
>
> The prehistoric levels at Suberde show poorly preserved remains of mud-brick walls, fragments of plastered floors, and burned remnants of wattle-and-daub, either from roofs or upper walls. There are grinding stones and large clay storage bins but no pottery.[26]

Although Suberde is described as a village of hunters, the grindng stones and clay storage bins tell us that it is also a village of gatherers. Once again, we see the anthropological bias against women (perhaps related to the fact that meat-eating Europeans and Americans cannot take grains seriously as a source of complete nourishment and so feel a need to stress meat eating and hunting). The cartoon image of prehistoric woman being dragged by the hair by her caveman-husband probably conditions the perceptions of archaeologists far more than they realize. As Childe expressed it: "Probably at first cultivation was an incidental activity of the women while their lords and masters were engaged in the really serious business of the chase."[27] There may have been a mother's brother in 8000 B.C., but I doubt if there was any such animal as a husband, and certainly not "a lord and master."

The period from 9000 to 7000 B.C. in the Near East is a period in which gathering is being transformed into gardening. The collection of wild cereals has enabled the sedentary villagers to keep more livestock, and the very process of gathering the grains has served to stimulate the crosses which produce the new varieties of domesticated cereals. Step by step each accidental discovery leads to the formation of an entirely new way of life. By 6500 B.C. agriculture is so well established that Neolithic society can enjoy a renaissance of the thought and religion of the Upper Paleolithic. Just as Renaissance Florence, through the banking wealth of the Medicis, could enjoy a revival of the old Platonic and Neo-Pythagorean religion of the Hellenistic world, so the great

Anatolian ceremonial center of Çatal Hüyük could become not only the center of the prosperous obsidian trade, but an academy for the expression of the old universal religion of the Great Mother.

It is possible that there had never been a decline of religion in the Mesolithic, that there had only been a decline in art. At all events, in religion, art, and technology, Çatal Hüyük stands as a cultural entity far richer and more complex than its neighbor, Suberde.

> The wealth of material produced by Çatal Hüyük is unrivalled by any other Neolithic site. Moreover, not being a village but a town or a city, its products have a definitely metropolitan air: Çatal Hüyük could afford luxuries such as obsidian mirrors, ceremonial daggers, and trinkets of metal beyond the reach of most of its known contemporaries. Copper and lead were smelted and worked into beads, tubes and possibly small tools, thus taking the beginnings of metallurgy back into the seventh millennium. Its stone industry in local obsidian and imported flint is the most elegant of the period; its wooden vessels are varied and sophisticated, its woolen textile industry fully developed. At Çatal Hüyük we can actually study the transition from an aceramic Neolithic with baskets and wooden vessels to a ceramic Neolithic with the first pottery.[28]

James Mellaart's discovery of Çatal Hüyük is as exciting and important as Schliemann's discovery of Troy, and for similar reasons; both sites help the historian to connect myth and prehistory. The continuity of tradition from the Upper Paleolithic to the Neolithic is uninterrupted in Anatolia. An *art mobilier* from the south at Antalya has the naturalistic and the geometric styles of the Upper Paleolithic, and in the Neolithic art forms of Çatal Hüyük to the north, we can see the movement from cave painting to wall painting. The iconography of these murals looks forward to Minoan and Mycenean times, as well as backward to the religious imagery of the Upper Paleolithic. Like the paintings of Bellini which look back to the iconography of the Middle Ages and forward to the physical examination of nature in the rise of science, the paintings of Çatal Hüyük are a bridge between two worlds. As in the case of Renaissance Italy, it is precisely the presence of the archaistic in the modern that is so fascinating to the cultural historian.

In contrast to other contemporary Neolithic cultures, Çatal Hüyük preserved a number of traditions that seem archaic in a fully developed Neolithic society. The art of wall-painting, the reliefs modelled in clay or cut out of the wall plaster, the naturalistic representations of animals, human figures, and dieties, the occasional use of finger-impressed clay designs like "macaroni," the developed use of geometric ornament including spirals and meanders, incised on seals or transfered to a new medium of weaving; the modelling of animals wounded in hunting rites, the practice of red-ochre burials, the archaic amulets in the form of a bird-like steatopygous goddess, and finally certain types of stone tools and the preference for dentalium shells in jewelry, all preserve remains of an Upper Paleolithic heritage.[29]

What is implicit at Lascaux is explicit at Çatal Hüyük. At Lascaux we must infer that the cave is the body of the Great Mother and that the images in the central chamber are beings in the womb of Mother Nature. At Çatal Hüyük we are given a literal representation of the Great Goddess with her legs spread widely apart to show the horns of the great bulls emerging from her womb (see Figure 10). Although most of the houses were entered from an

Figure 10. Shrine VI. A. 10, Çatal Hüyük.

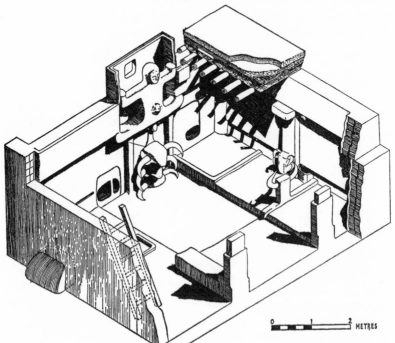

opening in the roof, some of the shrines have small passageways on the ground level, so that the worshipper must crawl in on her or his hands and knees. Clearly, in the imagery, in the darkness, and in the kinesthesia, the builders have gone to some effort to re-create the atmosphere of the cave.

All these similarities are immediately obvious, but what has not been noticed is that the placement of the animal images seems to give corroboration to Leroi-Gourhan's theories about Paleolithic cave art. Some rooms are decidedly female in imagery, with pictures of the twin goddess (see Figure 11); other rooms are decidedly masculine and filled with bulls' horns; others still seem to be shrines pairing male and female icons, for on one wall we see the twin goddess, whereas on the other we see the bull over the waters. The entire system of iconography seems to represent the Paleolithic cosmology explicated by Leroi-Gourhan as a pairing of male and female forces. Because the imagery of Çatal Hüyük is more literal than that of Lascaux, the site can serve as a kind of Rosetta Stone which gives us a few known words to crack the code for the unknown.

It is not only the internal decoration of the architecture of the town which is interesting, but the external forms as well. The houses are built close together and share common walls, express-ing a close and intimate sense of community. There are no external doors, since the people entered the rooms from the roof. Mellaart interprets this feature as an architecture of defense, but it may be a feminine architecture of containment, the architecture of the female body. The nineteenth-century theorist J. J. Bachoven's brilliantly intuitive insight about the prehistoric matriarchy would seem to be born out in Çatal Hüyük.

> The origin not only of customs and laws, but also of cities, may be traced back to Demeter. Cities were founded amid Demetrian rites, the walls arose from the womb of the earth, and their inviolability was rooted precisely in this relation to maternal matter.[30]

The walls may be there to keep out not the invader but the ritually unclean. With its thirty-two acres and its population of several thousand, Çatal Hüyük would be threatened by few hunting bands. The walls and towers of Neolithic Jericho certainly seem to suggest the architecture of defense, but Çatal Hüyük was most likely large enough and important enough as a ceremonial center where traders could stop and safely exchange their goods—outside, but not inside, the ceremonial walls—to obviate the need for defensive structures.

Only a part of the mound of Çatal Hüyük has been excavated, and so Professor Mellaart does not know whether the rest of the site is filled with shrines or craft and industry workships. My own conjecture is that the entire site is filled with shrines, and that the ceremonial center, as has been described by Jane Jacobs, spun off

Figure 11.
The Twin Goddess,
Çatal Hüyük.

its crafts to the suburbs. Its amazing wealth argues that the town was important not only for the Konya Plain, but for all of Anatolia and the Near East.

As a ceremonial center of the old universal religion, Çatal Hüyük provided a cross-cultural atmosphere in which traders of different tribes could come together. It would seem that even as far back as the Neolithic, religion was good for business. If obsidian was looked upon as a dark, chthonic milk which flowed out of the great breast of the volcano, Hasan Dag, then the relationship between Neolithic religion and economics might have been as intimate as the more familiar "Protestant Ethic and the Spirit of Capitalism." One of the murals in the shrine (see Figure 12) seems to be a bird's-eye view of the town and the volcano; perhaps this mural is just such a celebration.

Another wall relief which holds an equal fascination is the image of the twin goddess. Mellaart interprets this icon to be the two women of Greek and Mycenean times, the Demeter and Kore of the grain mysteries of Eleusis. The woman with breasts is the mother, the young maiden by her side, her daughter. The bull on the opposite wall of the shrine room suggests the masculine principle, the underworld that opens up to steal the daughter away. Not just Greece but Minoan Crete seems to be suggested by Çatal Hüyük. The very city plan looks like the floor plan for the labyrinthine Palace of Knossos. The juxtaposition of goddesses and bulls recalls the bull-baiting paintings of Minoan times. If one compares murals of Crete to the similar scenes from Çatal Hüyük, one can begin to understand how strongly conservative the power of religion is. One can begin to understand, also, that the religion of the Great Mother is indeed the world's first universal religion.

In the images of Çatal Hüyük the Great Mother herself seems to have three distinct sides. One is the familiar version of the obese Great Mother with wide hips, enormous stomach, and pendulous breasts. Childbirth was only suggested by these features in the Solutrean culture, but now all is made definite and explicit as she is shown seated upon the leopard throne with the divine child emerging between her legs (see Figure 13). In other versions the Goddess is shown in a more stylized version with the bull's horns emerging from her womb. In this epiphany, she is not so much the mother of the divine child as the old Paleolithic "Mistress of the

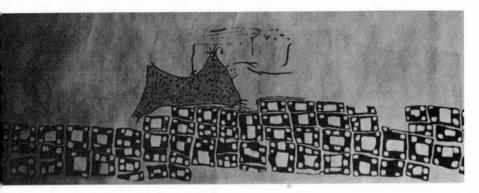

Figure 12. Wall painting from Çatal Hüyük.

Figure 13. Clay figurine, the Goddess on the leopard throne giving birth, Çatal Hüyük.

Animals." In her next epiphany we see her as the Twin Goddess, the Mother and the Maiden, the Neolithic version of Demeter and Persephone. And finally there is the old crone of death, the steatopygous figure with pointed feet, that goes all the way back to the Paleolithic settlement of Dolne Vestonice. At that time the daggerlike figurines of the crone were stuck into the earth on a shelf near the hearth, but this statue (Figure 14) was found in the vulture shrine with an offering of human skulls. Vultures seem to have been used for a funeral practice of excarnation: after the flesh had been cleaned from the bones, the bones were interred in the shrines. The vulture shrine seems especially devoted to

Figure 14.
Goddess figurine
from Çatal Hüyük.

funeral rites, and in one of his books Mellaart has tried imaginatively to reconstruct a ceremony.[31] One side of the shrine features images of headless men with vultures aloft; the skulls were laid before these paintings. On the opposite wall there is a huge bull's head, and within the shrine was found the old crone with a statue of the young man, the son-lover of the Great Mother. This shrine is presumably devoted to that part of the mythological narrative that tells of the death of the male god, a version of the old story of rise and fall. As Adonis was brought down by the boar, or Osiris slain by the Mother's brother, Set, so the vulture shrine probably tells the earlier version of the life and death of the young god.

The three images of the goddess—maiden, matron, and old crone—present us with the three archetypal relationships of the female to the male: she is huge and calls us from her womb; she is beautiful and calls us to her bed; she is old and ugly and calls us to the tomb. Womb and tomb rhyme in the unconscious as well as in the English language. Nothing bears this out more strongly than the actual burial practices.

The dead were buried within the houses at Çatal Hüyük, directly under the platforms where the living slept. The living literally made love on the graves of their ancestors. Women were buried in the large and central platform; sometimes they were buried with children, and most often with the best luxury items of the community—the jewelry and the obsidian mirrors. The men, by contrast, were buried in the corner in a much smaller space; they were never buried with children or with the luxury items attending the death of a female. They were instead buried with the Stone Age weapons of the hunt. Such preferential treatment for the women in death argues for some sort of preferential treatment in life, since the meaning of a funeral rite is to create a continuity between life and death. Mellaart speaks of the burial of the "master" and the "mistress" of the house, but I think that if we stop to consider the voluminous ethnographic material brought together by Briffault in *The Mothers*, we can see that the fellow shunted off to the corner is more likely to be the mother's brother than a husband. The dwelling at Çatal Hüyük is not a cozy English bungalow with the missus making tea for her lord and master. The wall paintings, the statuary, the burial practices, the close and intimate architecture of the town: all say rather clearly that at Çatal Hüyük we are dealing with a matrilineal society.

One truly remarkable statue says it all, for it is like a Henry Moore sculptured vision of the archetypal family. This greenish-gray schist statue is really two Figures in one (see figure 15). On one side we see the Great Mother with her infant, on the other we see the Great Mother in embrace with her lover. The two females are back to back and are really a single body, and in each case, the female is larger than the male.

The statue is a vision of the son-lover of the Great Mother. Another remarkable vision of this relationship comes from near-by Hacilar (see Figure 16). Here the son nurses at the breast but lies with his genitals over the groin of the Mother. Here it is worthwhile recalling Hockett and Ascher's speculations on the significance of the hominid shift from dorsal to frontal sexual intercourse.

> Our guess is that it changed, for the adult female, the relative roles of the adult male and of the infant, since after the innovation there is a much closer similarity for her between her reception of an infant and of a lover.[32]

In Neumann's discussion of the Great Mother he notes that at this early stage of the adolescent son-lover, the phallus belongs to the Goddess; like all life, it is her property, not his. The offering or return of the phallus is thus simply a reparation, in Anaximander's words, "according to the arrangement of time." The statues of the male gods, and they are few and far between when compared with the female statuary, represent the stages in the career of the male, stages in the mystery of time. First he is the infant emerging from the womb of the Great Mother, then he is the adolescent son-lover sporting with bulls, and finally, before his death, he is the bearded figure seated on top the bull (see Figure 17). The seated figure is the one found with the old crone in the vulture shrine (see Figure 14). Mellaart's analysis of this placement is an interesting performance of the archetype itself.

> Male deities, though not as prominent as their female counterpart, are still a feature of neolithic Çatal Hüyük. The proud adolescent

Figure 15. Statue from Çatal Hüyük.

figure, [see Figure 14], found with the Death Goddess and her
vulture in shrine VI A.25, seems characteristic of the confidence,
pride, and virility of the male at Çatal Hüyük, still a figure to be
reckoned with and not yet entirely subservient to the wiles of
women, as at Hacilar.[33]

That there are no statues of men at the nearby Anatolian village of
Hacilar, which dates to about 5400 B.C., causes Mellaart to
conclude that the women, in the late Neolithic, have taken over
completely. Hacilar is a peasant village; Çatal Hüyük is a complex
town. A richer, more complex, and complete iconography would
be expected, whereas a peasant village would concentrate on the
major figure of the Great Mother. The priests or priestesses at a
ceremonial center, however, might be interested in the male and

*Figure 16. Baked
clay statuette
from Hacilar.*

Figure 17. Clay statue from Çatal Hüyük.

the metaphysical subtleties in which the phallic male is seen as a symbol of time and its vanishing. The absence of male statues does not argue that Hacilar is a matriarchy and Çatal Hüyük not, but the art forms of both communities do raise the important question: are these cultures matriarchal?

V

THE QUESTION of the existence of a historical matriarchy is difficult, because the subject is so connected to the emotions of archaeologists and historians that it is impossible to discuss it without encountering castration anxieties in men and shouts of triumphant Amazon joy in feminist scholars. Marvin Harris, who gives evidence of never having read or understood Bachoven, speaks for the fraternity of anthropologists when he says:

> Among non-anthropologists this has led to a resurrection of mystical theories about a golden age of matriarchy when women reigned supreme over men. Anthropologists themselves have found

nothing that justifies the exhumation of this nineteenth-century corpse.[34]

And for the sorority of nonanthropologists, Elizabeth Davis speaks out:

> Of supreme importance in the archaeological revelations of Anatolia has been the confirmation of the myth of female authority in the golden and silver ages of man—the proof that woman domination was a fact not only of Paleolithic and Neolithic life but that it endured into the highly civilized Bronze Age of historical times.[35]

The difficulty is that when a man thinks of matriarchy, he thinks of a patriarchy with women in the place of men; he does not stop to consider that matriarchy may be a complete mirror-image. Where patriarchy establishes law, matriarchy establishes custom; where patriarchy establishes military power, matriarchy establishes religious authority; where patriarchy encourages the *aresteia* of the individual warrior, matriarchy encourages the tradition-bound cohesion of the collective. When, therefore, one envisions a matriarchy, one should not conjure up visions of a gang of Amazons lopping off breasts and testicles to rule by force of arms. Bachoven was right on that score: Amazons are not prehistoric creatures, but historical figures from the Dark Ages of 1200 B.C. In some Aegean community in which a raid had killed the men and carried off the young virgins, only the middle-aged matrons, not considered beautiful enough to be carried off or respectable enough to be killed, were left behind. If only *once* in Aegean prehistory such a band of women gathered themselves into a force, imitated the warring ways of their attackers, and wiped out with bow and arrow a band of outlaws and plunderers, the incident would become a legend. It would survive as a legend because it would become layered over the old racial memories of the days of the prehistoric matriarchy—to the eternal confusion of us all ever since.

I do believe that Çatal Hüyük was a matriarchy, but I do not see a matriarchy as an "Amazon state." City-states and standing armies are to come later; what we see at Çatal Hüyük is a ceremonial center, a matrilineal culture in which exists an organized class of priestesses and priests because it is a center for the old Paleolithic religion. At Çatal Hüyük we have moved from the diffused spirituality of hunters and gatherers to the beginnings of organized religion and the emergence of a priesthood. The rule in this Neolithic town of shrines is not by force and masculine law, but by custom. One should remember that as late as the twentieth century, custom could rule without a police force. In the *Aran Islands,* J. M. Synge remarks with astonishment that when a fisherman had done wrong, he took the boat over to Galway alone to put himself in jail.[36] Custom, the collective, and a religion of some twenty thousand years of tradition is the force that holds Çatal Hüyük together. It is a question not of masculine political power, but of feminine cultural authority.

The women as gatherers had slowly, in the years from 9000 to 6500 B.C., transformed gathering into gardening and agriculture. The vast storages of grains produced the economic surplus that enabled the men to turn hunting into a nostalgiac sport and atavistic ritual, and trade into their major economic activity. As a ceremonial center situated near the routes of the obsidian trade, Çatal Hüyük was an important cultural force, for as a religious center it could exert an influence to keep trade open and peaceable. Like a Hong Kong, a Geneva, or a Zurich, Çatal Hüyük did not have to defend itself because the need for it was recognized by all concerned in Anatolia and the Near East. But, of course, that kind of religious influence can be cashed in for economic power. As cities grow, they become too large for the intimate rule of custom and maternal authority, and the balance of power between religion and trade begins to shift. We can see the beginnings of just such an internal contradiction if we take a much closer look at the wall paintings concerned with hunting.

The wall paintings of the hunt, or what more properly should be termed bull and deer baiting, do not come from the lower levels of the mound of around 6500 B.C. but are found in those closer to the end of the settlement at around 5400 B.C.; they therefore do not express the culture of the period of the transition from hunting to agriculture (see Figure 18). With the men dressed in valuable leopard skins and accompanied by musicians, the paintings seem to present a scene from a ritual, a nostalgic expression of the good old days of the hunt. In fact, what the paintings may represent is the first expression in history of the phenomenon of

Figure 18. Wall painting from Çatal Hüyük.

"a nativistic movement."[37] The anthropologist A.F.C. Wallace has explained how a culture at the edge of extinction explodes into a ritualistic "revitalization movement." The Ghost Dance of the American Indians is an example of this phenomenon. The movement at Çatal Hüyük seems to have been as unsuccessful as the Ghost Dance, for the murals were later whitewashed with plaster and replaced with vulva patterns from the *kilim* designs taken from the women's weaving. Wall paintings as a genre of art disappear from the walls and are transferred to pottery designs. For a while the animals are still recognizable, but then with each successive generation of pots, the designs become more stylized and abstract until finally they lose all contact with their source. Since pottery is most decidedly part of woman's mysteries, this loss of contact with the source may be expected; the woman, not caught up in male subculture and the mystique of the hunt, would be expected to evidence interest in design over loving portraiture of the animals.

The attempt on the part of the men to avoid the drift to agriculture and urbanization and return to the good old days was not successful. The community did not dissolve and take to the woods. With each step in the transition from gathering to gardening, the old division of labor between the sexes was disturbed. Some men were able to make the shift from hunters to traders, but such a way of life would not satisfy the needs of those who hungered for the old religious connection with the animals.

The mystique of the hunt had millions of years of tradition behind it; it was obviously not going to quit overnight simply because agriculture had created a new way of life.

The power of the hunting mystique can be seen even today. Many men have a deep religious need to get away from women, join with a group of men, engage in a ritual drinking of whiskey (recall that in Gaelic *uiskebaugh* means the water of life—a decidedly masculine substance), and re-enact the ancient ways of the hunt.[38] The fact that hunting took too much time for too little return and could not support large, settled populations was irrelevant to the meaning of hunting. In fact, as hunting came into clear economic contradiction with gardening, the difference between the two would most likely encourage the rise of a ritual in a hunting nativistic movement. Leon Festinger has described a theory of "cognitive dissonance" in which the follower of a religion, when confronted with contrary evidence, does not abandon his faith but goes out to seek converts to ease his own growing anxieties, doubts, and insecurities.[39] So hunting as a ritual is not likely to develop until it is threatened by agriculture. Economically, hunting would not stand a chance in competition with gathering, much less gardening. The more the cognitive dissonance of the conflict between hunting and economics built up, the more the men would need to join the nativistic movement. But the whitewashing of the wall paintings seems to indicate that the nostalgic ritual was indeed a Ghost Dance. There was no going back.

And so the men went forward into trade and warfare. The hunting band turned on the spiral of history and became the trading band and the militaristic force. Woman stayed close to home, as gardener, potter, and perhaps even architect; the Neolithic settlement was her creation and her triumph. It was also to become her undoing. Woman chose to stay close to home in the sisterhood of women's mysteries, the old Great Goddess religion, and the priesthood. If a ceremonial center like Çatal Hüyük was a conservative Vatican of the old universal religion, the new economic surplus of grain was enabling the men to escape the tight and close horizons of the religious ceremonial center to participate in the larger and more open world of cross-cultural trade. As a new economic order was developing and as the nexus of trade began to create a lattice-work across the Near East, new forms of association between specialists were going to develop. The technical order was about to break away from the moral order.[40] As happened in our Industrial Revolution, a new class of economic specialists and technicians was going to break the power of the old Holy Mother Church.

Trade was to encourage the rise of new specializations, like metallurgy, and the more these specializations contributed to the growth of wealth, the more the new specialization of the military class would grow.

Women created agriculture and produced the economic surplus that required new forms of human settlement and new forms of storage. As the walled town and the cereal bin are containers, so is religion: an organized religion with a class of supported specialists is a form of cultural storage. It is not surprising, then, that the art and iconography of Çatal Hüyük is so conservative and Paleolithic. The spirituality of hunters and gatherers is a sacralization of everyday life, but once we move to maintain a formal priesthood, we also move to split experience into the sacred and the profane. Agriculture and organized religion are intimately related to one another; in the storage of grains and in the storage of the past, Çatal Hüyük was the containment of the first universal religion, the religion of the Great Goddess.

Every form of culture, in its vanishing, receives its most elaborate and intense expression. Çatal Hüyük was the supernova of the old religion, for the agricultural surplus not only supported a conservative priesthood of women, it also enabled the hunting band of men to shift their activities to trade and warfare. As the process of military development grew, the contradiction would grow, until eventually the conservative religion of the Great Goddess would be surrounded by a new culture.

Çatal Hüyük was a brilliant achievement, but it also represents the maximum development of traditional, matrilineal society. The obsidian trade was drawing people from far and wide to the town. Just how cosmopolitan the town was is clear from the fact that two different races are found buried in the graves: the dolichocephalic Eurafrican, and the brachycephalic Proto-Mediterranean. As a town becomes a cosmopolitan city it grows too complex to be ruled by the close and intimate mores and custom of matrilineal society.

In Elise Boulding's analysis, the conservative qualities of woman's mysteries chose not to keep pace with the complexification of urban life.

> The instability of matrilineal systems can be explained entirely in structural terms. Had women given more attention to spin-off activities with which they were not directly concerned, and adapted their communication patterns to encompass a wider range of happenings, matriliny might have adapted to a new scale of social operation. The fact that women did not do so should not be put in primarily biological terms, although their triple producer-breeder-feeder role may have put them at a disadvantage. An inspection of their daily work load compared with that of the earlier hunting-and-gathering era suggests that they were probably suffering from work overload and information overload, and did not stand back to get the larger picture.[41]

With the rise of trade and the accumulation of wealth, warfare and raids became more common. Hacilar II of 5250 B.C. is a fortress settlement that shows evidence of having been burned and invaded by newcomers with different traditions of building, statuary, and pottery.[42] As warfare grows more common in the late Neolithic, a new culture comes into existence, the culture of the pastoral nomads. In Jane Jacobs's analysis, these pastoralists are not an evolution from Mesolithic hunting, but a degeneration from Neolithic cities.

> If fatal misfortune dealt either by men or by nature befell a parent city, then its farming villages—if they managed to survive the disaster—would be cast loose with their incomplete fragments of a rounded economic life. These orphaned villages would of course continue to specialize—do the work they could do—but now only for their subsistence. They would not develop further because there would be no parent city economy from which they might receive new technology. Again and again during prehistoric times, villages must have been orphaned by the destruction of cities.
>
> When those villages lost some part of their own economic life, they would have no way to retrieve or reformulate it. I suspect this explains the origins of nomadic herding peoples. Neolithic villagers who lost their seed grains after their parent city had been destroyed would have no place to get more. All that would be left to them would be animal husbandry and the practice of a relatively few subsistence crafts based on materials derived for the most part from

the animals. Such people would have to become nomadic herds-men.[43]

Just as the collection of grains triggered a runaway positive feedback system that transformed hunting and gathering bands into sedentary farmers, so the establishment of trading and raiding bands triggered a runaway positive feedback system in which matrilineal, gardening societies were transformed into patriarchal, agricultural, militaristic cities. The debris spun off by such a cyclone of a transformation was indeed the nomadic herdsman.

> The growth of private ownership derived a powerful impetus from the domestication of cattle. Game is perishable and land is immova-ble, but wealth in the form of cattle is durable and easy to steal or to exchange. Being necessarily nomadic, pastoral tribes are quick to increase their wealth by cattle raids and war; and since warfare, which had grown out of hunting, was waged by the men, it reinforced the tendency, already inherent in pastoral society, for wealth to accumulate in their hands. Constantly on the move, these turbulent tribes plunder one district after another. The male captives are killed, the women are carried off as chattels, their skill at the loom being measured in terms of cattle. But warfare requires unity of leadership, and consequently these tribes develop a type of kingship which is primarily not magical, but military. In reward for their successful leadership, the kings receive the lion's share of the spoils, and the wealth thus amassed promotes social inequalities which shake the whole fabric of tribal society, beginning at the top.[44]

Women had been at the top of traditional, Neolithic society, but with the shift from religious, magical authority to masculine, military power, their influence collapsed and they became private property in the new trading and raiding society. Mesolithic society may have seen the domestication of animals, and Neolithic society may have seen the domestication of plants, but what the age after the Neolithic sees is the domestication of women by men.

The period 6000–4000 B.C. is the *Magnus Annus* of the Neolithic Great Goddess, but by 4000 B.C. the Near Eastern world is so criss-crossed with trade routes that the lattice-work itself begins to be a new cultural entity, the entity of civilization. Civilization involves not simply the rise of one city, but rather the rise of an urban nexus in which the specializations of civilization are supportable. By 4000 B.C. the new world of trade, of craft specializations like metallurgy and militarism, have created a whole new world, a decidedly masculine world.

Biological paternity had probably been discovered in the Mesolithic and, perhaps, even as early as the Upper Paleolithic, but in the conservative, matrilineal society of the old universal religion, there was little room for the husband or the father to rise to any prominence. In matrilineal societies it is the mother's brother, and not the father, who is the important male figure. But with the rise of a new economic order through trade and the appearance of skills and specialties associated with the rise of a military class, the social conditions were created in which biological paternity and the inheritance of private property could become culturally recognized and socially institutionalized.

It may not have happened overnight, but it was a revolution nonetheless. For hundreds of thousands of years the culture of women and women's mysteries had been the dominant ideology of humanity. The hominization of the primates in the shift from estrus was a feminine transformation. The rise of a lunar notation and the beginnings of an observed periodicity upon which all human knowledge is based was a feminine creation. Agriculture and the rise of sedentary villages and towns were feminine creations. But civilization and warfare were not; they spelled the end for the Great Mother. The father had appeared on the historical scene and was going to do battle with the mother's brother, and in that revolutionary struggle the most long-lived tradition on the face of this earth was overthrown. So recent and so revolutionary is that struggle that to this day men have not forgotten, and the slightest stirring of the ancient mother can send them running for their swords and guns. Women may look back to a golden age of close, intimate, and peaceful village life, but men tremble in visions of asphyxiation and extinction in the herd. As C. S. Lewis has expressed the male nightmare:

> You may add that in the hive and the ant-hill we see fully realized the two things that some of us most dread for our own species—the dominance of the female and the dominance of the collective.[45]

Man cut the umbilical cord to the Great Mother with a sword, and the sword has been hanging over his head ever since.

PART THREE

Western Civilization and the Displacement of the Feminine

CHAPTER FOUR

Civilization and Alienation in Ancient Sumer

IT WOULD BE uplifting to think that the ziggurat was the first expression of Near Eastern civilization, for then one could speak about humanity's fascination with the heavens, of the human quest for communion with the infinite. Whether one saw the temple as a table-topped mountain where the flying saucers of the gods touched down (after the theories of Erich von Däniken), or as the home of a cult statue which spoke to the hallucinating members of a humanity whose right brain hemisphere was as cut off from the left as Heaven was from earth (after the theories of Julian Jaynes), would not matter: whatever the ziggurat was, religion wuld be seen to be primary, for the temple would be there first. Unfortunately, it was not. The fortress was.

We cannot tell whether the walls of Çatal Hüyük were raised in Demeterian rites, as the architecture of the womb, or whether they were raised in martial orders, as the architecture of defense. It would appear that the town was never sacked from the time of the seventh millennium into the sixth, but the fifth millennium B.C. was no such quiet period.

At Çatal Hüyük the architecture of residence and the architecture of worship are one and the same; there are no temples, only shrines; a home of the god is quite literally a home, much like any other. At Hacilar II, however, a greater collective effort would be needed to construct, all at once, a great wall to protect the settlement. Hacilar II is, in fact, as Mellaart describes it, a fortress. The period of Çatal Hüyük's greatness ended around 5400 B.C., and with it, seemingly, a period of peaceful Neolithic trade and worship of the Great Goddess. By 5200 B.C., the time of Hacilar II, Anatolia had become a theatre of war. Hacilar II was destroyed, as were nearby Mersin and Can Hasan.

With the fortress came a new weapon, the sling. Perhaps in the treeless Konya plain, wood was too precious to be squandered in arrows. Both sling and walled fortress seem to be Anatolia's contribution in the period of 5000–4000 B.C. As Mellaart notes:

> Compared with the Hacilar I fortress, that of Mersin shows considerable advance in military architecture combined with older principles, such as one might expect to have developed during almost a millennium that separates these two earliest examples of Anatolian fortresses. It should be emphasized that this type of architecture appears to have originated in Anatolia and probably on the plateau.[1]

In spite of warfare, or perhaps because of it, the influence of Anatolia spread widely. According to Mellaart,[2] the Halafian culture on the shores of the Euphrates in the mid-sixth millennium B.C. seems to have been greatly influenced by Anatolia; this would bring the Anatolian culture down from what is now modern Turkey into North Syria and Iraq.

The period of warfare seems to have placed a heavy burden on the development of human culture. Some settlements in Palestine and South Syria experienced a return to nomadic life, and no known great settlement like Çatal Hüyük seems to have exerted an influence on the growth of urban life. If Jane Jacobs is right in her contention that the pastoral nomads are the remnants of destroyed cities and towns, then the period 6000–4000 B.C. seems to be one of the fall of fortresses and the rise of pastoral nomadism. This shift from stable and developing urban conditions to unstable and nomadic ones would indicate a shift of emphasis from settled agriculture to herding and raiding, both of which are activities likely to stimulate the growth of the male subculture into the dominant culture. Such a shift in emphasis could, in fact, be described as a revolution in which the feminine activities of pottery and gardening become the subculture in a new militaristic and nomadic way of life.

With the spread of Anatolian culture down to the banks of the Euphrates at Tel Halaf, we approach the period before the rise of cities. Like the Mesolithic age of 10,000–8000 B.C., the period 6000–4000 B.C. seems to have been a painful period of transition. Innovations like metallurgy were not lost, and clay figurines of the Great Goddess are still found, but no culture was able to blend religion and technology into the brilliant synthesis of a Çatal Hüyük. The sign of Gemini does not seem to have exerted a beneficent influence on the growth of human culture, but as the *Magnus Annus* of Taurus came round, things seem to have grown more stable and solid. The transitional period of raiding and warfare, which seems to have disrupted the life of villages in the Chalcolithic period, stimulated the growth of larger and larger defensive settlements. As more and more people moved behind the increasingly larger walls, the fortress settlement evolved into the walled city. And from the implosive force of such concentrations of people, culture itself began to change. Like organelles within a single cell, whole new specializations began to develop. The simplicity of village life was gone, and with the appearance of writing a new relationship was created between literate elite and illiterate peasant. The archaeologists have called this configuration of irrigation farming, specialization, and literacy "civilization," and they have further credited the Sumerians with creating the world's first civilization. As the archaeologist S. N. Kramer has said: "History begins at Sumer."

> Although it was once believed that the Sumerians made their entry into Sumer from some highland area only in the Uruk period, scholars now tend to agree that they were there before, at least during the 'Ubaid period; and as 'Ubaid is the cultural culmination of two previous phases of development, Haji Muhammad and Eridu, it would be difficult to deny that the Sumerians were the first settlers of lower Mesopotamia. The discoveries of Seton Lloyd and Fuad Safar have thus traced the beginnings of Sumerian civilization back to the middle of the sixth millennium B.C. in the alluvial plain of ancient Sumer. . . .
>
> If the earliest inhabitants of Eridu were Sumerians, as we also believe, then it must be accepted that they made their homes in the plain only after having mastered irrigation techniques in their former abodes at the foot of the Zagros mountains, probably in Khuzistan. Heirs of nearly a thousand years in Iran of simple village life, of primitive agriculture, herding and hunting and the production of pottery, they were at last fully equipped to deal with a new and challenging environment. Sheltered from invasions by the lakes and marshes, they were gradually able to develop a civilization that was to have few equals.[3]

When we come to the period of civilization, we come to the period of history and written records. At Lascaux and Çatal Hüyük we have to infer a mythology from the iconography on the walls, but with the culture of Sumer we can read the mythology directly from the translations of the clay tablets. What we encounter there are the remains of a revolution, a shift from the dominant female gods of the Neolithic village to the organizing and controlling male gods of the literate city. In one myth, known by the title "Enki and the World Order," the changes in the new male culture are openly celebrated in what is for all intents and purposes an ode to the phallus.

> After he had cast his eye from that spot,
> After father Enki had lifted it over the Euphrates,
> He stood up proudly like a rampant bull,
> He lifts the penis, ejaculates,
> Filled the Tigris with sparkling water.
> The wild cow mooing for its young in the pastures,
> The scorpion [infested] stall,
> The Tigris surrendered to him, as to a rampant bull.
> He lifted the penis, brought the bridal gift,
> Brought joy to the Tigris, like a big wild bull,
> rejoiced in its giving birth.
> The water he brought is sparkling water,
> its "wine" tastes sweet,
> The grain he brought, its checkered grain,
> the people eat it,
> He filled the Ekur, the house of Enlil, with possessions.
> With Enki, Enlil rejoices, Nippur [is lighted].[4]

In the Sumerian language the word for water also means semen, and since Enki is the god of water, he is therefore the god of semen. In this ode to the Great Father, the land of the Sumerians is literally awash with semen. The landscape of Sumer, with its marshes, dikes, and canals, is, therefore, a male landscape of irrigation technology, military societal organization, and male fertilizing power. Just how revolutionary this transformation is can be seen in another myth in which Enki, the god of water, and Ninhursag, the goddess of earth, are pitted against one another. As water, Enki flows everywhere. In this myth the ability of water to overflow all boundaries is expressed in the narrative by the fact that Enki inseminates his daughters and the daughters of his daughters. This union of earth and water, of course, creates plant life, but the mother of the stony ground, Ninhursag, finds Enki to be a nuisance; after Enki has seduced her daughter, Utu, she removes Enki's semen from her body, and from this semen eight plants grow up. After a while, Enki comes upon these plants, eats them, and finds himself pregnant with eight gods lodged in different parts of his body. However, since Enki is obviously not built for pregnancy, he becomes very ill. Ninhursag takes pity on Enki and comes to his aid by placing him in her vagina, where he is then able to give birth to eight goddesses, all named for various parts of his body.[5]

The story is a profoundly ambiguous one, dramatizing the conflict of the sexes which has arisen in the shift from the Neolithic matrilineal order to the civilized patriarchal one. On the one hand, the myth shows the power of the male god, Enki, who is able to move about unchecked by Mother Earth; it shows the male going beyond natural limits in trying to take over the power of the old childbirth mysteries from women. But the image of the auto-inseminating Enki is not a healthy one, and so the myth expresses the need for a mediation of the opposites of male and female. The infant on the lap of the Great Mother is a Neolithic image; Enki inside the vagina of the Great Mother, but himself giving birth to goddesses, is the civilized image of the stand-off between the sexes. Enki is clearly brought back to the ancient icon, the vulva, but even in the heart of the female body, he is himself trying to give birth. This effort to displace the female seems to be the archetypal foundation for civilization, for mankind has been at it ever since; whether he is challenging Mother Nature in flying away from her in rockets, or in changing her on earth through genetic engineering, man has not given up in the attempt to take away the mystery of life from the Great Mother and the conservative feminine religion.

This uneasy relationship between male and female, Enki and Ninhursag, water and stony ground, is the alluvial mud upon which Sumerian life is based. The instrument which has enabled man to change his relationship to the earth is the plow. A new technology has enabled man to take gardening away from women and turn it into agriculture; the plow is the great phallus that separates the labia majora of the furrows of earth, and the plow is under the majesty of Enki.

> He directed the plow and the yoke,
> The great prince Enki put the "horned oxen" in the . . . ,
> Opened the holy furrows,
> Made grow the grain in the cultivated field.[6]

Gardening had been women's work; the domestication of animals
had been the work of man the hunter. When man led his animals
into the fields for plowing, he surrounded the old culture with a
new technology. Women's work became a content in a new larger
structure. When to that relationship of ox and plow was added the
complex social organization represented by dikes, canals, walls,
storehouses, and recordkeeping, civilization was crystallized out of
the liquid solution of Chalcolithic village life.

In the movement from village to city the old order of woman
becomes seen as simple and primitive, possessing none of the
great technological wonders of male civilization. A woman is a
gardener, but a man is a serious farmer. A woman is a generalist,
but a man is a specialist. In a foreshadowing of the contemporary
male view that a woman as a cook is a mere housewife but a man as
a cook is a professional, a chef, Enki himself declares in the face of
Inanna's complaints about the new order: "Enki perfected greatly
that which is woman's task."[7]

What is to become of woman in this new order of civilization?
The goddess Inanna, the Queen of Heaven, feels left out of this
new masculine world, and so she comes to Enki as a humble
suppliant to ask for her fair share. Behind this plea of the young
maid we can hear the complaint of the Neolithic Great Goddess,
lamenting the passage of her era.

> Then all by her[self], having abandoned the royal scepter,
> The woman, . . . , the maid Inanna having abandoned the royal
>   scepter,
> Inanna, to her [father] Enki,
> Enters the house, (and) [humbly] weeping, utters a plaint:
> "The Annunaki, the great gods—their fate
> Enlil placed firmly in your [hand],
> Me, the woman, [wh]y do you treat differently?
> I, the holy Inanna,—where are my prerogatives?[8]

The sisters of Inanna have been given tasks by Enki, but Inanna
has been forgotten. This queen of love and battle, this goddess of

the morning star whom the Akaddians will later name Ishtar, will prove herself to be a fierce woman whom it does not pay to forget. Enki tries to calm Inanna, and he recites a litany of the spheres of influences she has been given: the staff of shepherdship, onslaughts and battles, the twisting of the thread. But all this seems merely the leftovers from the main course taken by mankind. Even in the midst of this recitation of the grants to Inanna, Enki breaks off, for the revelation of male power and fertility, the inundation of the rivers, has come to the land.

> Maid Inanna, you who know not the distant wells,
> the fastening ropes (?)
> "Lo, the inundation has come, the Land is restored."
> "The inundation of Enlil has come, the Land is restored."[9]

The remaining nineteen lines of the tablet have been destroyed, but it would seem that this hymn to Enki was chanted at the season when all awaited the overflowing of the Tigris and Euphrates. And so Inanna's complaint must be put aside; the flood of male power pushes it to the side of history. The great god Enki is too busy to deal with a maid who feels slighted.

II

WHEN WOMAN'S POWER is taken from her, and when the old sisterhood of the matrilineal order is displaced, the power of woman can no longer be direct and open, for direct military power is precisely the force which has displaced the feminine for the masculine order. The feminine compensation for this shift in the natural balance of things is a shift in sexual emphasis from fertility—that is, reproductive power—to erotic power—that is, power not over the child but over the lover. Gone is the obese Great Goddess; come is the sleek young maid, the Queen of Heaven. What we now encounter in the male order of civilization is "sexiness," the erotic power of the beautiful woman to lure the powerful man to his own destruction. Inanna becomes the archetype for all the Cleopatras to come; she is "the bitch goddess" who from her first appearance in Sumerian civilization will live on in all other civilizations—in myth and legend, novel and poem, Shakespearean play and Hollywood film. The first of all the thousands of stories that are to follow is the love story of Inanna and the shepherd-king, Dumuzi. Leroi-Gourhan speculated on "the wounded-man theme" in Paleolithic art, and Mellaart conjectured about the death of the son-lover of the Mother Goddess at Çatal Hüyük, but at Sumer we no longer have to speculate or conjecture; we can read the tragic story of the rise and fall of the shepherd who became a king straight from the tablets of clay.

Thorkild Jacobsen describes the Dumuzi story as part of a fertility cult and sees this myth of the dying corn god as the central metaphor of Sumerian religion in the fourth millennium B.C. But myth as a written document is always much younger than its parent, oral legend. One can see the older, oral quality of the stories and songs in the confusion of identities for Dumuzi. In some songs he is a shepherd; in others he is identified with the date palm, and in still others with cattle herding and dairy farming. In village times, before the growth of the great cities, these activities would not be separate and distant from one another; they would only be separated by time. Just as in Christianity there is a Virgin Mary for the farmer and another for the fisherman, but in the litany of the names and attributes of Mary all the characteristics are still merely aspects of one Virgin Mary, so are there many Dumuzis, but all are facets of one great story, the dying god of the dying year.

The central focus of the myth is the sacred marriage of Dumuzi to Inanna. In the consummation of their marriage is seen the prosperity, fertility, and abundance of all the varieties of food producing in the land. Inanna is the Queen of Heaven, the morning star, but on earth she is the goddess of the storehouse.

> Correspondingly, the bridegroom, Amaushumgalanna, represents what is to be stored in the storehouse. As indicated by his name, which means "the one great source of the date clusters," he is the personified power in the one enormous bud which the date palm sprouts each year, and from which issue the new leaves, flowers, and fruits. Dumuzi-Amaushumgalanna is thus a personification of the power behind the yearly burgeoning of the palm and its producing its yield of dates; he is, in fact, the power in and behind the date harvest.
>
> That these two powers are wed means that the power for fertility and yield has been captured by the numen of the storehouse—and

so by the community—and has become its trusty provider for all time.[10]

The copulation of Dumuzi and Inanna is thus the placing of male fertility inside the storehouse. This vision of the *cornu coepia,* the womb from which all life comes, has undergone a transformation in urban society to become, not the cave from which the animals of the hunt appear, but the storehouse in which the grain is kept. We should recall that the statues of the Great Mother at Çatal Hüyük were found inside the cereal bins, but what is most fascinating about this transformation of the image is that it is associated with the transformation of the obese Great Goddess into the sleek and erotic young maid. Woman has assented to the new militarist order of civilization, but in the home, the storehouse, the marriage bed, she has found a new compensatory erotic power. The masculine militarization of culture has led to a feminine eroticization. It is no accident that Inanna, the goddess of love, is also the goddess of the battlefield, for the rise and fall of the phallic principle is most dramatically countered in bed and battlefield by the enduring power of woman.

The love-cycle of poems about Inanna and Dumuzi contain songs which come from different times, and perhaps from different classes within society. But in keeping with Lévi-Strauss's advice that one should not get caught in the futile search for the original and true version of the myth but should treat all versions, early and late, as parts of the one true myth, I consider the songs as parts of a single mythological cycle of seasonal work songs much older than the versions which are finally copied onto the clay tablets. As seasonal work songs, the poems punctuate the mystery of time, the first flush of spring, the full burgeoning of the dates, the tall erection of the stalks of grain, the final withering and dying of the year. Because the poems are an investigation into the nature of time, it is important to be aware of the overall temporal architectonic of the love-cycle. As I see it, there are six movements to the cycle, which can be blocked out as follows:

I. *Introduction.*
    The lovers' first sighting of one another and the arousal of their mutual passion.

II. *Frustration and Sublimation.*
The eagerness of Dumuzi is checked as his wild passion is directed into the societal form of marriage.

III. *Consummation.*
The sexual intercourse of the lovers, the union of natural fertility and the cultural container of the storehouse, and thus the wedding of nature and culture.

IV. *Preservation.*
The period of post-coital warm after-glow, the autumnal prosperity of the full storehouse.

V. *Disintegration.*
The warm after-glow leads to *hubris,* a false sense of confidence; the mistake of thinking that the food can last forever, that there will always be enough of it to make it through the winter. The time of the solstice.

VI. *Destruction.*
The death of Dumuzi. The time of late winter, before the critical turning and the birth of the new year.

In the texts as we have them on tablets from different cities, there is no such order as I have indicated above. No poet, as was the case with the cycle of poems about Gilgamesh, wove the songs into a single great work. And so in different recensions, different poems will appear in different places. For example, the Sumerologist Jacobsen places the poem in which the young Inanna, still a maiden in puberty, asks a court musician to help her compose a poem to her vulva, in the middle of the cycle, at a point in time when she is recalling the early days when she first chose Dumuzi as her spouse; yet in the poem she is clearly inquiring who will become her lover, and so I place it as part of the beginning: a poem about the virginal Inanna in meditation on the mysteries of her own vulva.

> Inanna exa[lts] him,
> [Composes (?)] a song about her vulva:
> The vulva, it is . . . ,
> Like a horn it . . . at the large wagon,
> It is the "Boat of Heaven," fastening ropes . . . ,
> Like the new crescent, passion . . . ,
>
> As for me (?), my vulva is a hillock,—for (?) me (?),
> I, the maid, who will be its plower?

> My vulva is . . . wet ground for (?) me (?)
> I, the queen, who will station there the ox?
> "Lady, the king will plow it for you,
> Dumuzi, the king will plow it for you."
> "Plow my vulva, my sweetheart." [11]

In the opening poems of the cycle Dumuzi's sister, Gestinanna, tells her brother how smitten with love for him Inanna is, and how she pines away for him at home alone, "smiting her hips" in love pains for him. In another poem of the early phase of courtship, the lovers have met and Dumuzi is trying to tell Inanna how to lie about her whereabouts so that they can become lovers, but Inanna hesitates; she prefers marriage to clandestine trysts. Then we have a poem concerning Dumuzi's lineage which shows he is a suitable spouse for Inanna. The marriage is arranged: there are poems that deal with the brother's preparations, the purchasing of bridal sheets, and finally the wedding. In one of the poems concerning the wedding, a great deal of attention is paid to the ceremonial robing of Inanna with jewelry for the various parts of her body; this robing is parallel to the disrobing of Inanna in the poem "Inanna's Descent into the Nether World," and so we should be aware that the jewels probably had a strong symbolic dimension that is lost to us.

The ceremonial robing of Inanna is the preparation for the bride's opening the door to the bridegroom, the central rite which precedes the consummation of the marriage.

> The king goes with lifted head to the holy loins,
> goes with lifted head to the loins of Inanna . . .
> After he on the holy bed in the holy loins
> has made the queen rejoice,
> After he on the bed, in the holy loins
> has made the holy Inanna rejoice,
> she in return soothes the heart for him
> there on the bed:
> "Verily, I will be a constant prolonger of Iddin-Dagan's days of
> life." [12]

The marriage of the goddess to the shepherd makes him the shepherd-king; Heaven and earth are wed in their embrace. Long before the appearance of the biblical shepherd-king, King David, the Near Eastern pattern was set by Dumuzi. And long before the Hebrew *prothalamion,* "the Song of Songs which is Solomon's," the style and tone for erotic poetry was set by the love-cycle of Inanna and Dumuzi.

> As I . . . the beloved of my eye,
> My beloved met me,
> Took his pleasure of me, rejoiced together (?) with me.[13]

In the warm afterglow of the lovers' night, the land fills with contentment, security, and the continuation of life through sexuality and food. In a quite explicit poem the oral nature of sexuality and the orality of food are joined in a *participation mystique.*

> At the lap of the king, the high-standing cedar . . . ,
> The plants stood high by (his) side, the grain stood high by his side.
> The garden flourished luxuriant by his side.
> In the house of life, the house of the king,
> His wife dwelt by (his) side in joy,
> In the house of life, the house of the king,
> Inanna dwelt by his side in joy.
> Inanna rejoicing in his house,
> Utters a plea to the king:
> "Make yellow the milk for me, my bridegroom, make yellow [for me]
> My bridegroom, I will [drink with you] the fresh milk.
> Wild bull Dumuzi, make yellow the milk for me,
> My bridegroom, I will [drink with you] the fresh milk.
> The milk of the goat [make flow (?) in] the sheepfold for me,
> With the cheese fill (?) my holy churn,
> Dumuzi, the milk . . . the "cheese of heaven,"
> Of the "cheese of heaven" its milk . . . ,
> Its cream is good beer . . . ,
> Lord Dumuzi, I will [drink] with you the fresh (?) milk.
> My husband, the goodly storehouse, the sheepfold (?)
> I, Inanna, will preserve for you,
> I will [watch] over your house of life.
> The brilliant place which enraptures the Land,
> The house where the fate of all the lands is decreed,
> Where the breath of life is ordained for the people,
> I, Ninegal, will preserve it for you,
> I will watch over your house of life.
> The house of life, the storehouse which gives long life.[14]

In Sumerian, the word "sheepfold" also means vulva, and from the poem it is clear that "house of life" also means scrotum. Thus the stored grain in the storehouse and the stored seed in the scrotum are both signs of security and the perpetuation of life. What we have in this poem is a work song, sung by the dairy maids as they churn the cream to thicken it, or make it yellow, to become butter. Churn and stick, and the agitation needed to make the butter, would obviously suggest sexual intercourse, and so the work song becomes an occasion for a series of *double entendres* in which the dairy maids could tease the men working in the vicinity and thus enact the courtship of Inanna and Dumuzi to make their work sacred.

Many people tend to think that oral sexuality is the recent invention of decadent intellectuals raised on the works of Joyce or D. H. Lawrence or on an alien French literature; still others seem to think such practices are characteristic of decadent courts from the time of medieval Khajuraho in India or Hellenistic Greece. This celebration of oral sexuality, coming as it does from the oldest literature of the world, challenges these notions.

Another old-wive's tale demolished here is the idea, lingering on in the twentieth century from its expression in Victorian medical textbooks, that intense sexual passion is male, that the woman endures it for the sake of childbearing. In Sumerian literature, it is the female who is made to rejoice at the bridal gift of the penis; it is in gratitude for the satisfaction of her sexual desires that the female blesses the male, promises to look after him and watch over his "house of life." In being a good lover to the goddess Inanna, Dumuzi is ensuring that his people will prosper, for prosperity is the bestowal of the goddess. In Paleolithic and Neolithic times, this bestowal of life would be expressed in terms of the Great Mother, but in civilized times the outer appearance of the Great Goddess has changed to become the slender young lover, the goddess of love. Her ancient role, however, has not been forgotten; the Sumerians still know that the Great Mother is the mistress of life and death, and they express this recognition by describing Inanna as the goddess of love and war.

In other work songs of the love-cycle of Inanna and Dumuzi, it is not milk and cheese that are celebrated, but beer and wine. In one poem Dumuzi is the power in the grain which is transformed into beer and then stored underground. The cutting of the grain in late spring and early summer becomes a symbol of Dumuzi's death, but the storing of the grain underground becomes a symbol of his descent into the netherworld. His death helps to ensure the community's life. Dumuzi's sister, Geshtinanna, becomes the spirit of the grape, which is harvested in autumn.[15] The grain becomes beer, the grape becomes wine; thus brother and sister become spirits of transformation of nature into culture.

In the Middle Ages certain work guilds were under the patronage of certain saints or the Virgin Mary. The religious quality of this consecration of work turned what we would know as a labor union into a mystery guild. Something like this blending of religion and economics was obviously going on in ancient Sumer. The workers in the dairy, the vineyard, or the brewery would come together in celebration of the festivals which marked the important times of the year. In consecrating their works to the gods, and in singing their songs of sexuality and food, they hoped to ensure that their work would help the community live on. The harvesters of dates would have their songs, the dairy maids theirs, but as the village grew into a city, these festivals of different times of year would be organized into a priestly calendar.

III

ONE OF THE MOST COMPLEX of all the poems in the mythological cycle is "Inanna's Descent into the Nether World." This work does not have the air of a dairymaid's song but rather seems to be an expression of priestcraft, astrology, and an investigation into the nature of time.

> More difficult is the myth about Inanna and her descent. Tentatively we would suggest that it deals with the time of year when food supplies are at their most critical point, which is late winter when the stores in the storehouse dwindle and finally come to an end. In the humanizing terms of myth that becomes the death of the storehouse and the power in it to function, Inanna; its subsequent replenishment from the pastures in spring correspondingly becomes a revival of its power. If this is true, Inanna's intention in the myth of taking

over the netherworld will reflect the way that the underground storeroom looks roomier as it becomes more empty and seems to vie with that other underground space familiar to the ancients, the grave vault.[16]

"Inanna's Descent into the Nether World" may have begun its life as a work song of the storehouse in winter, but in the complex form in which we have the poem, it seems to have become elaborated by a caste of priests into something much more metaphysical than a peasant's song. There is another dimension to myth that scholars like Jacobsen and Kramer ignore; to appreciate this dimension, we should take in the theories of Professor Hertha von Dechend. Von Dechend has argued that the astronomy of the most ancient civilizations is far more complicated than we have hitherto realized. She sees myth as the technical language of a scientific and priestly elite;[17] when, therefore, a myth seems to be most concrete, even gross, it is often using figurative language to describe astronomical happenings, such as the entry of a planet into a lunar mansion. Thus when Saturn is said to be devouring his children, or when Marduk is described as slaying the Great Mother, something more is going on. Sometimes these goings-on can become quite complex, as when the figure which Mercury makes going back and forth in the sky is traced and then turned into a glyph. The caduceus of Mercury or the serpent face of the Mexican rain god, Tlaloc, von Dechend would claim, are hieroglyphs for the movements of the planet Mercury.[18]

Von Dechend's thesis that there is an astronomical dimension to myth that is not understood by the conventional archaeologists of myth is, I believe, quite correct. The amount of information she has gathered from myths all over the world is impressive, but like Freud or Lévi-Strauss she overgeneralizes her thesis. What should be one dimension among many becomes the *only* way to look at myth, and thus a complex mythology is flattened by a scholarly steam roller into a very thin sheet. But though Professor von Dechend has not created the *oeuvre* of Freud, Jung, or Lévi-Strauss, she is very much like them. After we have read Jung or Lévi-Strauss we can never look at myth in the old way, and so it is with von Dechend: once she has made us aware that there is an astronomical dimension to mythic narratives, we can never again look at the subject in the same way.

Had professors Kramer or Jacobsen read von Dechend, their understanding of their own areas of specialization might have been increased. Professor G. S. Kirk has attempted to write the definitive explanation of myth,[19] but he too has overlooked von Dechend and, therefore, cannot make much sense concerning "Inanna's Descent into the Nether World." But when from von Dechend's tutelage we realize that Inanna is identified with the planet Venus, then we understand that there is more going on in the myth than a dramatization of the empty storehouse in winter.

> From the "great above" she set her mind toward
>   "the great below,"
> The goddess, from the "great above" she set her mind
>   toward the great below.[20]

The opening of the poem announces that we are dealing with the sinking under the horizon of the evening star. Venus appears as the evening star, sinks under the horizon for eight days, and then reappears as the morning star. To the ancients in Mesopotamia as well as in Mexico this movement was poeticized as a journey through the underworld. As Inanna prepares to descend she fastens the seven divine laws to her side, and as she walks toward the netherworld she speaks to her vizier, Ninshubur. When she is in the netherworld, Ninshubur is to set up a lament and go to the assembly of the gods. He is to go to Enlil (the god of air); if Enlil will not help her, then he is to go to Enki (the god of water). Now, if you imagine this poem being chanted in the temple at the time of the winter solstice, you should also imagine the priests and the chanters moving ritually to various windows to observe the position of the heavenly bodies. When, therefore, the text says that Enlil does not respond to the vizier's supplication, we should understand that this means that one planet does not appear or move; when, by contrast, the chanters move to another window and find night after night that this other planet has indeed moved, then this would signify that this planet is being dramatized as coming to her aid. Since Enki is described as the tricky and fast god, I would imagine that he is associated with the planet

Mercury. The movements of Mercury and Venus around the winter solstice would then be the astronomical backdrop for the myth. It is, of course, difficult to know what is truly going on here, but from von Dechend's insights, we can become more sensitive to the sky and its role in the myth. Jacobsen's theory about the empty storehouse is still valid, for a myth never has one meaning only; a myth is a polyphonic fugue of many voices. This is one reason why a myth can become the receptacle for many different interpretations. To the usual Freudian, Jungian, and structuralist interpretations, we must add a fourth, the astronomical interpretations of Professor von Dechend.

The drama of the storehouse on earth has its counterpart in Heaven, and if we accept the insights of both Jacobsen and von Dechend, we can see that the myth is bodying forth a principle which will later be expressed in the Hermetic axiom, "As above, so below." In fact, it is precisely this relationship between above and below that the myth explores. By the raising of a lowly shepherd to become a consort of the goddess, the mediating institution of human kingship is created. In descending into a mortal's embrace and in stealing the laws of civilization, the *me's*, away from the gods to bring them to the city of men, Inanna has brought Heaven and earth together in ways that make civilization possible. Civilization is, through the numinosity of divine kingship, the mediation between the impossible heights of the gods and the terrifying depths of the underworld. But as such a mediation of opposites, civilization is a threat to the position of both extremes, and so what Inanna's descent sets out to discover is just how above and below can be articulated into a human cosmos.

The marriage of Inanna, the Queen of Heaven, with the shepherd-king, Dumuzi, has brought man up and the gods down to create civilization. When, therefore, Inanna withdraws from human society and descends into the netherworld, the entire civilization is threatened. The myth describes the dangerous moment of the nadir, the dead of winter, the moment when it is not known whether the world will be re-created and another cycle will bring on another spring. When Inanna descends into the netherworld she is ceremonially robed with all her power, the seven divine laws. The cabbalism of the number seven is emphasized, for in hell seven judges at each of seven gates take one of these divine laws away from her. The number mysticism would seem to indicate that there is an esoteric dimension to the myth, the dimension of initiation. As with the opening of the seven seals in the book of Revelation of St. John, we are dealing not merely with the physical body, but with the subtle body as well.

The opening of the seals, or the opening of the *chakras* in the yogic tradition, is the process of initiation, the descent into the subconscious as the necessary prelude to the ascent to a higher consciousness. To be an initiate one cannot rest in the normal consciousness of the shopkeeper; one must go both lower, into the subconscious, the repressed, the functions of the autonomic nervous system excluded from consciousness, the instinctive; and higher into the superconscious, the realm beyond subject and object, into *samadhi*. This form of initiation means that at least one human being, the shaman, can connect the human realm of consciousness with the divine and thereby preserve the integrity of the human world. The yogi or shaman is a transformer who takes in powerful energies, steps them down, and turns them into a weaker alternating current that can be used in all the homes of the ordinary folk. The civilizational process depends on society's having someone who can connect the two worlds; that person can be a god, or the agent of a god.

To the great mass of Sumerian society, the psychological and astronomical dimensions of the myth would not be known. Theirs would be a simple peasant religion concerned with the mysteries only as they affect their bellies; for them the myth is about the storehouse at midwinter. The ordinary man might feel the terror of the winter solstice, but he would have no sense of the esoteric process of initiation. It is no different for our own civilization.

If one takes a closer look at the seven laws that are taken from Inanna in the underworld, one can begin to see a faint pattern emerge.

> Upon her entering
> the shugurra, the corns of the plain of her head,
> was removed.[21]

The removal of the corns of the plain, the removal of agriculture, would spell a reversion from civilization to barbarism. In the terror of the winter solstice, time seems to be moving backward to what Milton would call "Chaos and Old Night." The very foundation of civilization is being taken away. This is the social dimension of the myth; the esoteric dimension is that the golden grains surrounding her head express what the Christians knew as the halo. This ring of golden energy in the subtle body of an initiate is the *prima facie* evidence of the awakened *kundalini*; in the myth, Inanna is not only reversing cultural evolution, she is reversing the evolution of consciousness: and this makes it a very terrifying myth indeed.

This reversal of time is made even clearer when Inanna enters the second gate, for then "the measuring rod and line of lapis lazuli was removed." The standardization of weights and measures is the system upon which a city depends; take away this small and simple thing, and chaos would result in any city. The esoteric significance of this is difficult to decipher; it could be (depending on the shape of the lapis lazuli rod, a symbol for the spinal cord) that slender line that holds the physical and subtle bodies together.

The donning of the seven laws and their removal by the seven judges at the seven gates does seem to be parallel to the seven seals and the seven chakras, but the symbolism for the third, fourth, fifth, and sixth laws are unclear to me. At the third gate, the small lapis lazuli stones at Inanna's neck are removed; since the throat chakra governs speech and normal rational intelligence, this could symbolize the loss of language ability, but I don't wish to strain this esoteric interpretation. If the reader wishes to avoid esoteric speculations on the significance of these jewels, he can hold with the more modest interpretation that the subtraction of the corns of the plain and the measuring line of lapis lazuli do clearly indicate that in the descent into the netherworld time is being reversed, and that the terror of the winter solstice is being presented as a reversion of civilization to barbarism.

At the fourth gate the twin nunuz stones at Inanna's breast are removed; at the fifth gate, the gold ring of her hand; at the sixth gate, the breast plate which says "Come, man, Come"; and finally, at the seventh gate, the "pala garment" of her ladyship is removed. Naked in hell, Inanna is brought before the goddess Ereshkigal and her seven judges. Exoterically, the removal of the garment of her ladyship would indicate that in death all social distinctions are obliterated, and that death rules all in an ultimate equality. Esoterically, if indeed the seven laws are the seven chakras, then the untying of the knots which bind the physical body to the subtle would remove the etheric and astral body to wander in hell in the out-of-the-body state. This removal of the etheric or subtle physical body from the physical body would place consciousness in such a profound state of concentration that the outward appearance of the physical body would be comatose. Just such a state descends on Inanna, for Ereshkigal fastens the look of death on her and then hangs her up as a corpse on a nail. Inanna hangs for three days and three nights; this period of time is not arbitrarily chosen. As in other myths, like Christ's harrowing of hell, the initiate descends into the netherworld for the magical three days. Three days seems to be the maximum time the etheric body can be separated from the physical body without permanent deterioration. In the experience of initiation, the individual moves into a tomb, goes into a deep trance in which he separates his etheric and astral bodies from the physical body, and then in this *bardo* state goes through a series of confrontations and trials. Since the physical body is really a filter which shuts out the psychic realms, when one is out of the body one is out of the protection of the wall: whatever one thinks is immediately experienced—nightmare or beatific vision. If the journey through the subconscious is successful, the initiate can return to his physical body; if the confrontation with terror is too much, then the individual becomes psychotic, dies, or is rescued but is refused admission to the mysteries.

Agnostic or atheistic scholars in the universities try to interpret these myths in ways that are in harmony with their own worldviews, but a religious myth has to be interpreted with the intuition and with a sensitivity and understanding of the nature of religious experiences. "Inanna's Descent into the Nether World" cannot be fully understood in only sociological terms. The rituals of the season, the empty storehouse, and the astronomical backdrop are all important parts of the myth, but they are parts that are under the domination of the esoteric whole.

As Inanna hangs on a nail in hell, her vizier goes to the gods in search of help. But "Father Enlil stood not by her," and "Father

Nanna (the moon god) stood not by her." Presumably, this would mean that neither Jupiter nor the moon appear in the dark night of Inanna's terror. But Father Enki is troubled, and he moves. The planet Mercury moves closer to Venus and brings the magical water of life that can revive Inanna. From the dirt under his fingernails, Enki fashions two messengers and gives to one the food of life; to the other, the water of life. They go to the netherworld, and, as the magical substances are sprinkled on Inanna, she is resurrected. I would interpret the water of life sent by Enki to be the male semen, and the food of life to be the female blood that feeds the embryo when the woman does not menstruate during pregnancy. What Enki is offering to Inanna in her *bardo* state is really incarnation: a way out of the psychic plane of the netherworld back up into life.

In the marriage of Inanna and Dumuzi we saw a commensurate relationship between the two, a marriage of Heaven and earth, but now in the fall of Inanna into hell, the relationship becomes incommensurate. Each one "lives the other's death, dies the other's life," in the esoteric words of Heraclitus so favored by Yeats. Like the twin gyres of Yeats, or the twin souls of Gnostic mythology, when one half of the soul is incarnate, the other half remains above.[22] Therefore, as Inanna is resurrected and rises, Dumuzi is doomed and must descend into hell.

What is going on in all this religious mumbo-jumbo that is so foreign to the positivism of contemporary scholarship is a re-enactment of the history of the soul before the beginning of terrestrial evolution. The ritual of initiation in the *bardo* realm is just such a re-enactment which seeks to awaken the deeper memory of the soul and thus enable the initiate to become enlightened to the truth of existence. To remember, the initiate must overcome the racial amnesia, the illusory history which locks him into a local time and place.

As the water of life revives Inanna, Ereshkigal is enraged and cannot stand to see her realm violated, and so she demands a substitute. She sends her demons along with Inanna to make certain that she does send back a substitute from the upper world. When Inanna returns she finds that Dumuzi has not been lamenting her but has been acting high and mighty in his seat of kingship. Such is the story of the soul: as the *anima* moves in the world of psyche, the normal *ego* forgets all about her and busies himself with the "real" facts of amassing wealth and exercising power. The ego thinks that his local time and space is all there is to reality, and that the busy affairs of state and trade are more important than a lot of obscurantist hocus-pocus. Enraged at Dumuzi's overweening pride, Inanna becomes the fierce *anima* figure and tells the demons that they can have Dumuzi as her substitute in hell. The days of the Elysian marriage of Heaven and earth are over; kingship, as the mediation of the opposite realms, is shattered. Man has forgotten the soul and thus doomed his civilization to apocalypse.

With the demons in pursuit, Dumuzi flees to his father-in-law, Utu, the sun. Utu turns Dumuzi into a snake so that he may escape the demons, but even this solar awakening of *kundalini* cannot reverse the condition of incarnate history. All Dumuzi's transformations are in vain; neither Utu nor his sister Geshtinana can save him. The shepherd-king flees to the country; in his end is his beginning, and Dumuzi finds himself once more inside the sheepfold. His days of kingship are over, he is a humble shepherd once more. The demons enter the sheepfold and one by one the five demons strike him down. When one realizes that "sheepfold" in Sumerian means "vulva," one can see that in death the Great Mother is taking him back. Inanna as the erotic maiden had only been a civilized disguise for the ancient Great Goddess, the Great Mother. If civilized life had covered over the ancient verities, Dumuzi learns in his tragic death that the sheepfold is still there to reclaim him. His brief career as a king of a civilization was only a momentary forgetting.

And so the pattern remains: the female dies but is reborn; the phallic male rises to greatness and then falls. In "Enki and the World Order," we see the confident male god in charge of the universe, directing the plow and telling the female gods what their prerogatives should be. In the older mythic cycle of Inanna and Dumuzi, we are further back in time at the transition from village to urban life, the transition from the Neolithic religion of the Goddess to the civilized religion of the god. In the later work, "Inanna's Descent into the Nether World," we are at a time of priestcraft and temple astronomy and associated rites of initiation. The period of a fully developed civilization is a time in which individuals and institutions have forgotten their origins; it is a time of great divorce between the ego and the soul, between man and gods, between Heaven and earth. Ultimately, "Inanna's Descent" embodies the tragic vision that humanity in a civilization can only be awakened by a violent apocalypse, a tearing of the veil, the rending of the very fabric of reality. All civilizations are founded on a vision, and all civilizations in their late development forget their founding visions, and so the mighty throne becomes a sheepfold and the ego and civilization are sent back for another reincarnation. W. B. Yeats understood these ancient mysteries better than any modern:

> Another Troy must rise and set,
> Another lineage feed the crow,
> Another Argo's painted prow
> Drive to a flashier bauble yet.
> The Roman Empire stood appalled:
> It dropped the reigns of peace and war
> When that fierce virgin and her Star
> Out of the fabulous darkness called.[23]

IV

IF DUMUZI is the shepherd-king of a city who forgets that he owes his power to the Goddess, the later poems about Gilgamesh show a quite different relationship between the sexes in the culture of cities and civilization.

Lévi-Strauss has said that the search for the true and authentic version of a myth is not to the point, that one should take every variant into consideration. Again with this point in mind, I would like to begin my discussion of the Akkadian Epic of Gilgamesh with the earlier fragment, the Sumerian "Gilgamesh and the Huluppu Tree."[24] The story goes like this. Once upon a time there was a huluppu tree (perhaps a willow) which grew along the banks of the Euphrates, but the place of its origin was not good, for the South Wind tore at it from root to crown and the Euphrates flooded it. The Goddess Inanna, the Queen of Heaven, came upon it one day, took the tree in hand, and transplanted it to the holy garden in her main sanctuary in Erech. There she took good care of the tree, for when it was larger she planned to make from its wood a chair and a couch for herself.

The tree grew, but when the time came for Inanna to cut it down to make her couch, she was unable to do it, for at the base of the tree the "snake who knows no charm" had built its nest, while at the crown of the tree, the Imdugud bird had placed its young, and in the middle, Lilith, the maid of desolation, had built her own house. Inanna wept bitterly and complained to her brother, Utu, the sun god.

Gilgamesh, the great hero of Sumer, the legendary king of Erech (Uruk), heard Inanna's weeping complaint and decided to come to her aid. He donned his armor and took his great axe in hand, his axe of the road, and slew the snake at the base of the tree. Seeing this, the Imdugud bird fled with his young to the mountains, and Lilith tore down her house and fled to the desolate places she was wont to haunt. The men of Erech who had accompanied Gilgamesh now cut down the tree and presented it to Inanna for her chair and couch.

There is disagreement among the translators as to what happened next. Kramer says that Inanna took the wood and built a drum and drumstick, but Jacobsen maintains that the *pukku* and *mikku* are the puck and hockey stick of a game the men of Erech played in celebration of Gilgamesh's victory.[25] It would seem that the men became too celebrative, for a poor little girl who had been left out recited the magical and fearful name of the sun god, "I-Utu," and the god heard her; the ground cracked open and the puck and stick fell into the netherworld. Gilgamesh was unhappy and greatly disturbed, and so his beloved companion, Enkidu, rashly offered to descend into the netherworld to fetch them back. Gilgamesh gave Enkidu elaborate instructions on how to carry himself in the netherworld so that he would be able to return: to be quiet, not to wear fine clothes, not to show any emotions to those he loved or hated in life. But Enkidu disregards the wisdom of this advice and so becomes trapped below. Only his ghost is able to come up through a crack in the earth to speak to Gilgamesh and tell him of the miseries of the lower realm. Gilgamesh asks how certain people are being treated below, and it seems that some are treated "as one close to the gods," while others are shades who find no rest.

Accepting Jacobsen's translation of *pukku* and *mikku* as puck and hockey stick, I would venture to interpret this myth as follows. The story is a myth of origins, in this case the story of the origins of a sacred sodality of men in the city of Erech. It begins with a description of the landscape of their world before civilization, when the southern Euphrates at the Persian Gulf was a wild swamp beaten by the South Wind, no fit place for a tree to grow. The Goddess Inanna, whose main sanctuary was at Erech and who therefore was most likely the patron deity of this religious sodality of Gilgamesh and the men of Erech, found something that could not grow in its wild state but could prosper in her beloved Erech. So we can see that the myth celebrates not only the founding of the sodality but also the special qualities of Inanna's city. The tree which cannot prosper in the wild grows well in the city. The city, and civilization in general, do leave themselves open to certain problems. The tree in the holy garden of Inanna is the symbol of the human body; here again we encounter the familiar structure of bird-tree-snake, a symbolism which goes back to the Upper Paleolithic religion. The snake who knows no charm, coiled at the base of the tree, is the familiar *kundalini* coiled at the base of the spine. The Imdugud bird, the mischievous thunder bird, is consciousness, and Lilith, the mirror-opposite of Inanna, the patroness of the city, is the patron deity of ruins; she inhabits the middle region around the spine which connects the snake and the bird. Esoterically, three realms are represented: the physical plane of the snake, the astral or psychic plane of Lilith, and the spiritual plane of the thunder bird. The body, through a proper transformation by the Goddess, can be turned into a divine bed.

> Inanna tended the tree with her hand, placed it by her foot,
> "When will it be a fruitful throne for me to sit on," she said,
> "When will it be a fruitful bed for me to lie on," she said.[26]

The poem thus focuses on the process of transformation of wild nature into the realm of human culture, the natural tree into the couch of the Goddess. In Christianity, the world is called the footstool of Christ; in this Sumerian vision, the awakened body would be called the bed of the Queen of Heaven. Inanna takes nature and turns it into culture in her holy garden in her city, and so the body must be prepared. But the body can also attract lesser entities, and so the demons must be chased away, if the process of transformation is to be completed.

With the help of the great hero, the king of Erech, the male and female principles, the human and the divine, come together in a mediation of opposites which create the sacred game. As in the love-cycle of Inanna and Dumuzi, the institution of kingship is presented as a realm which raises man up to the gods and lowers divinity into human society. Through the offices of the king, Heaven and earth can come together. Out of the wild tree comes the wood used for a sacred game, and this game, like the sacred ball game of the Maya, should be seen as a ritual sport with cosmological dimensions to its performance, and not simply physical recreation. Unfortunately, the men of Erech, the men of the sacred sodality, forget the wild feminine principle; the little girl who has been left out is obviously a mask for Lilith, the maid of desolation. In the later Hebrew *midrash* Lilith is presented as the woman who knows how to recite the fearful name of God to work calamity; that this little girl cries out the fearful name of the sun god and thereby causes an earthquake would indicate that this girl is linked in the structure of the myth with Lilith.

The game itself, though played by men, was probably meant to enact a mediation of the opposites of male and female, with a circular puck being the feminine symbol and the phallic hockey stick being the masculine symbol. But clearly in the sodality of men, and in the male bonding of Gilgamesh and Enkidu, the feminine principle is not powerfully present and balanced with the masculine, and so the little girl is able to stop the game. But the game itself should also be seen to be a mediation between the upper world and the netherworld; the fact that the men play upon the thin crust of life that separates them from the world of death is yet another symbol of the relationship between death in the wild realm of nature and life in the realm of human culture.

The instructions which Gilgamesh gives to Enkidu in preparation for his descent into the netherworld are, to me, clear indications that the poem, like *The Tibetan Book of the Dead,* is a manual of initiation, a series of instructions by the initiate to the candidate for initiation on what he must remember to do in the out-of-the-body or *bardo* state. In fact, Gilgamesh's instructions are still-valid directions from the *guru* to the *chela.* One must not identify with what he sees; he must not show the normal attachments of the ego, the love for the lost wife, the anger for the disobedient child, the attachment to fine clothes or to the sense of one's own pride and self-importance. One is counseled not even to carry on as if he were a powerful magician and initiate, for such a thought would simply attract more powerful demons.

> Do not throw the throw-stick in the nether world,
> Lest they who were struck down by the throw-stick
> will surround thee . . .
> Kiss not thy beloved wife,
> Kiss not thy beloved son,
> Strike not thy hated wife,
> Strike not thy hated son.[27]

Only if the candidate for initiation can master his emotions, that astral plane where the goddess Lilith dwells, can he become a true initiate and a member of the sodality of Inanna and the men of Gilgamesh's Erech. But Enkidu fails and is caught in the nether-world; he only returns as a specter to warn the living to be good so they will have better treatment in the afterlife. Initiation by the priest is turned into a lesson on social morality; the poem itself dramatizes the societal stage when initiation is becoming impossible and the priests are turning from esoteric transformation to exoteric morality. For the men of the sodality, who like Enkidu cannot possibly master their attachments to the things of this world, the best hope is to be good in this life and wish for a better place in the life to come.

The story of Gilgamesh and the huluppu tree was not included in the Akkadian Gilgamesh Epic, perhaps because the cultural meaning of the Sumerian tale was lost on the later Akkadians. No doubt the court poets did not include many tales in the final recension of the Gilgamesh cycle, but it is hard to fault them since the epic as we have it is an incredibly fine work. Just as Faust's story was the medieval legend which became the myth of modern scientific man and was given such different artistic renderings by Marlowe, Goethe, and Mann, so Gilgamesh is the central legend of ancient civilized humanity that becomes *the* myth of humanity and civilization.

Gilgamesh, as far as one can judge, was a historial figure, the ruler of the city of Uruk (the biblical Erekh) around 2600 B.C. It stands to reason that stories about him would have been current long after his

death, but they only became graspable to us around 2100 B.C. when
they were taken up by the court poets of the Third Dynasty of Ur.
The kings of that dynasty counted Gilgamesh as their ancestor. We
possess a number of short epical compositions in Sumerian, the
originals of which must date to the revival of interest, but the
Gilgamesh Epic proper, with which we are here concerned, dates
from around 1600 B.C., at the end of the Old Babylonian period,
and was composed in Akkadian.[28]

The poem opens with a celebration of the great hero. Gilgamesh,
he who traveled far, knew the secret things and brought knowledge of the days before the flood.

> He built the wall of Uruk, the enclosure,
> Of holy Eanna, the sacred storehouse.
> Behold its outer wall, whose brightness is like copper!
> Yea, look upon its inner wall, which none can equal!
> Take hold of the threshold, which is from of old!
> Approach Eanna, the dwelling of Ishtar,
> Which no later king, no man, can equal!
> Climb upon the wall of Uruk and walk about;
> Inspect the foundation terrace and examine the brickwork,
> If its brickwork be not of burnt bricks
> And if the seven wise men did not lay the foundation.[29]

The seven sages are the legendary wise men who brought
knowledge to the seven oldest cities of Mesopotamia, and the wall
which is built by these initiates is more than a heap of rubble that
stands between city and desert; it is a piece of sacred geometry
whose measure and canons of proportion are celebrations of
universal law. The city did not evolve up from the ground, it
descended from Heaven; the *me's*, the divine laws which constitute
the program for civilization, were carried by Inanna from the seat
of Enki at Eridu to her beloved Erech (Uruk); without these divine
laws, no city can hold together, no wall can stand against the
disintegrating wind of the desert. In the Sumerian vision, civilization does not evolve upward from village life, it develops downward from the gods. Kingship descends from Heaven.

Gilgamesh is himself a man, two-thirds god, one-third mortal.
He is the place where the devolution from Heaven and the
evolution from earth meet. The divinity in Gilgamesh gives him

more sexual energy than any normal man, and as king he demands the *jus primer noctis* of all the brides in the city. The men of the city groaned under the weight of his arrogance and unbridled lust and prayed to the gods for an equal to Gilgamesh so that the two giants could contend with one another and leave Uruk in peace.

When the goddess Aruru heard the prayers of the townsmen she conceived within herself a double of the god Anu; she pinched a piece of clay and then cast it out on the steppe. Thus Enkidu was created, the wild man of the steppes, a man completely covered with long and shaggy hair. Enkidu runs with the animals of the steppes, drinks with them at their watering holes, and feeds on grass. If Gilgamesh is the half-immortal who descends from Heaven, Enkidu is the wild man of nature who approaches the city from the ground up. One represents an evolution upward from nature to culture; the other represents a devolution downward from divinity to humanity.

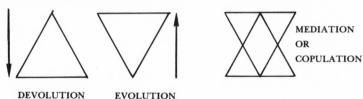

DEVOLUTION   EVOLUTION   MEDIATION OR COPULATION

In the love cycle of Inanna and Dumuzi, the sexual intercourse of the lovers was the mediation of the opposites of Heaven and earth, which produced the city as the place where nature (fertility) and divinity could be mediated in culture, in civilization. Here, interestingly enough, the mediation of the opposites is seen in the male pair bonding of Gilgamesh and Enkidu. The Platonic soul love of the two men creates a bond that transcends the ordinary shopkeeping world of the city folk.

As a pair, Gilgamesh and Enkidu constellate an archetypal pattern. In the turning spirals of human history, one pattern turns round and moves back, close but still above an older version of the pattern. In our myths and history we seem to be fond of this vision of two kinds of man: there are Australopithecus gracile and robustus, and recent research seems to indicate that Homo erectus and Homo sapiens coexisted in Central Europe during the penultimate interglacial period;[30] later, the pattern would turn on the spiral to express itself in the coexistence of Neanderthal and Cromagnon. Perhaps this prehistoric pattern is one reason we are so fond, in myth and literature, of pairs like Gilgamesh and Enkidu, Jacob and Esau, Robinson Crusoe and Friday, Natty Bumpo and Chingachgook, Ishmael and Queequeeg. In our religious myths we say that we have fallen from Heaven to earth, and in our scientific myths we say that we have evolved up from the animals; perhaps we have need of stories that speak of the two races, the brothers of two different mothers, or the loving friendship of the wild man and the white man.

When patterns line up on the spiral, they become like music on the different lines of the staff, a synchronic unity, an archetypal pattern. We can visualize them thus:

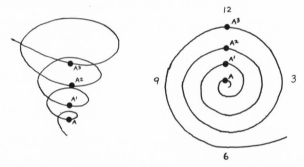

If we see the top of the spiral as the face of a clock, then all those turnings that are in the position of one of the hours, six o'clock or twelve, are harmonic with one another. Thus Gilgamesh and Enkidu as a dyad express a Wagnerian *leitmotif* that plays upon themes from racial memories of the two different races at the dawn of hominization. We can think of them as Cromagnon and Neanderthal, Australopithecus gracile and robustus, or man and the sons of god. A story, a science fiction film, or, in fact, a scientific theory, can thus be positioned at a higher and later turning of the spiral, diachronically, but synchronically it can be a performance of a pattern or theme. This synchronic harmony, this metastructure that is beyond mere chronology, is what I mean by an archetype. Gilgamesh and Enkidu become an archetypal male pair because the theme they establish points backward in time to a much larger context. The Fall, as I have presented it in the Prologue, is precisely one of these archetypal patterns that keeps repeating itself with each turn of the spiral. If we visualize the spiral from the top and place the Fall at the dark midnight of twelve o'clock, then all the twelve o'clocks at whatever level of the spiral are recapitulations of the initial Fall into time, the beginning of the spiral of human history.

In fact, we see just such a performance of the mythic pattern of the Fall in the story of Enkidu's socialization. As Enkidu runs wild on the steppes and drinks with the animals at the water hole, he is discovered by a trapper. The trapper is amazed and disturbed because he sees that this wild man has been freeing all the animals from his traps. He goes home to complain to his father, and the two of them decide on a plan to entrap Enkidu. The father tells the son to go to Gilgamesh in Uruk to ask for a harlot from the temple, for a woman's power will be able to tame the wild man. The son obeys the father's instructions, goes to Uruk to see Gilgamesh, and returns to the steppe to set the trap with the harlot. Trapper and harlot go to the watering hole and wait; when the trapper sights Enkidu, he pleads with the harlot to take off her clothes, "laying bare her ripeness."

Enkidu sees the harlot with her bare breasts and open ripeness, and for six days and seven nights he makes love to her. After he has had his fill of her, he returns to his beloved companions, the wild beasts, but now the gazelles run off and draw away from him. Sexual intercourse with woman has taken away Enkidu's wild innocence and simple communion with the animals of nature. Enkidu has fallen, and sexuality has been the condition of his fall. Here we see the yogic pattern, "Loss of semen equals loss of soul." But there are two turnings of the spiral here. First there is the fall of the soul into the body. The father and son here talking about ways to entrap Enkidu are like the Archons of Gnosticism trying to find ways to entrap the soul into a body. The second turning of the spiral is the fact that the pink blush of the female genitalia is what lures Enkidu away from his wild companions into what becomes the beginning of his movement into human society. On this turn of the spiral, we see a recapitulation of the time when the female shift away from estrus, the blushing of the genitals and the filling out of the breasts, lures the male away from his companions into the new social group of the hominid band. In one turn of the spiral is the Fall of the soul into the body, or the descent of consciousness into the emerging form of the cooling planet; in the next turn of the spiral, consciousness is focused into a more specific form as it descends into the upwardly evolving body of the hominid. First is the Fall into time, then is the Fall from animal innocence into human culture. A third turn of the spiral would be expressed in the life cycle of the individual, when the filling out of the genitals takes the human from the innocence of childhood and animals into adulthood. In unconscious memory of this relationship of animals and innocence, children's rooms are traditionally filled with stuffed animals. As the virginal girl prepares psychologically to take a lover to her bed, she must put the stuffed animals away.

Enkidu cannot return to his animals; there is no going back, but the harlot comforts him and says: "Thou art wise, Enkidu; thou art become like a god." The words of the serpent to Eve were similar, for the Hebrews recognized that in offering the red apple to Adam, Eve was like the harlot who offered her ripeness to Enkidu. The harlot consoles Enkidu and offers to take him back to her city of Uruk. "His heart enlightened, he yearns for a friend." Splitting her clothes in two, the harlot gives him the outer garment, while she puts on the inner; clothed now in a sexual body by the sacred harlot of the temple of Inanna, Enkidu walks out of nature into culture, into the great city of the king Gilgamesh.

But before Enkidu is fit to walk into the city, he stops at a halfway house, the sheepfold where the shepherds gather at the outskirts of the city. Since "sheepfold" in Sumerian also means vulva, we can see that in his passage here Enkidu is being reborn. He cannot go directly from the wild animals of the steppes to the city of men, and so Enkidu passes through the place of the domesticated animals, and there he becomes civilized by taking in human food and drink. Lévi-Strauss has discussed cooking as a symbol for the transformation of raw nature into culture;[31] it makes sense that food as well as sexuality would be the physical means for Enkidu's transformation. At first Enkidu gags on the food, but then he grows to like the strong drink and takes seven goblets, until his face glows. Having taken in the food and drink of men, Enkidu has passed over to the other side, and now, rather than using his strength to free the wild animals from the traps, he captures the wolves and lions that had been attacking the shepherd's flocks.

While Enkidu is staying with the shepherds a weary traveler stops with them; during his rest he speaks about life in the great city and tells of the excesses of the King Gilgamesh, of how the king intrudes into the popular assembly, of how he demands the *jus primer noctis,* an archaic custom which had evidentally fallen into disuse for the Sumerians but which the lustful Gilgamesh had revived. Enkidu is appalled at such goings-on and rises immediately to go to Uruk.

As the great Enkidu walks through the streets, the people gather around him and exclaim how like the great Gilgamesh he is. Finally it seems as if their prayers have been answered and that an equal to Gilgamesh has appeared. The wild man of nature is seen as the champion of the people against the celestial king. As Gilgamesh walks through the city to exercise his *droit de seigneur,* he finds Enkidu barring the door with his foot. The wild man of the steppes who has emerged from the vulva/sheepfold now stands at the vulva/bridal door, forbidding entry to the king himself. In this confrontation between the earth man and the sky god, another ancient battle is implied: Enkidu has become the mother's brother, the protector of the matriliny, and therefore the defender of the bride. In barring the way, he is enacting a ritual which demands that the new way of patrilocal marriage pay its respect to the more ancient way of matrilocal marriage. Thus this story of urban life plays upon ancient themes, and in expressing the struggle of the forces of Enkidu and Gilgamesh against one another, it sets up the opposition of one complex against another. Enkidu expresses the values of nature, matrilineal conservatism, and the populism of the assembly, the assembly of village elders from the days before military dictatorship. Gilgamesh expresses the values of the gods who bring culture down from the heavens, patrilineal succession and patrilocal marriage, the charisma of the military hero and its institutionalization in monarchy. The battle of the giants at the bridal door thus recalls the whole painful transformation in which Neolithic village culture was transformed into urban civilization.

The battle of the titans at the bridal door explodes into the marketplace; and wall and doorpost shatter as they fight with the fury of bulls. But Enkidu is able to get the better of Gilgamesh and forces his knee to the ground. Amazed at his own unbelievable defeat, Gilgamesh accepts his new condition in a quiet and chastened mood, but as he turns to go, he hears the noble words of Enkidu: "As one alone thy mother bore thee . . . kingship over the people Enlil has granted thee." Touched as much by his opponent's nobility as by his recognition of his kingship, Gilgamesh befriends Enkidu.

The two who have no equals become friends without equal. At another historical moment it would probably not be necessary to explain something as simple as friendship and to distinguish it from homosexual love; but we live in a time when homosexuality is being turned into a political ideology, and so it is necessary to look at the friendship of Gilgamesh and Enkidu very closely. Both Gilgamesh and Enkidu are presented as men with an enormous sexual appetite for women; in fact, their erotic drives dwarf the passions of common men. If they are heroes, their sexuality is also expressed on a heroic scale. There is no blockage in their instinctive life, and when the two men fight the physical closeness is not a substitute for a thwarted sexual life. Precisely because both men are consumed with a sexual drive that is gigantic, both long for something that is beyond sexuality; they hunger for a complete freedom, an escape from the body of sexuality and death. The two men long for a freedom of soul which is not restricted in bondage to the body, and to the degree that women express the life of the body, they long to be free of women.

In the hominization of the primates in the Pliocene, the female shift from estrus pulled the males away from their pair bonding and their freedom into the demands of a new social structure. Females, therefore, express the pressure of the collective will, the social demands for protection for the infants in their unusually long period of dependency. From the hominid band to the Neolithic village, women express the power of the collective in the conservative religion of the Great Mother. But in trade, in warfare, and in sports, men break away from the close, asphyxiating controls of the village to assert the subculture of the male. The archetypal pair bonding of males is thus an effort to escape into the old freedom. In countless Hollywood movies we see the story of two soldiers or sailors on leave; for them the pursuit of women is simply a way of relieving a genital pressure. Women are seen as mere objects of exchange, incapable of the true understanding and companionship of men. Now, of course, in many cases such a relationship between men is homosexual, and the man who seeks to share the same woman with another man is really seeking a sexual relationship with his beloved friend. And in many cases the man who hates women, marriage, and the bourgeois household-ing life and desires the freedom of the bohemian artist or the outcast at the margins of society is a man for whom homosexual love is a celebration of escape from the incarnate bondage of the female body and the demands of the collective. I am not in any way trying to deny the reality, complexity, or varieties of homosex-uality, but I am denying that what we see in the Gilgamesh epic is a portrait of two homosexual lovers.

What we do see celebrated in the epic is the "higher" soul-love that is later praised and developed by Plato and Ficino in their all-male academies of Athens and Florence. For these transcendental mystics, both homosexual and heterosexual eroticism are forms of bondage. The homosexual dismisses heterosexual love as a dis-tasteful bondage to normalcy and bourgeois domestication, but the Platonic lover of the soul is dismissing all sexuality as bondage to the physical world. It is not by accident that the desire of Gilgamesh and Enkidu to escape the bondage of sexuality and death brings them into face-to-face conflict with the goddess of sex and death, Inanna. In the linkage of sex and death in sexual reproduction, one cannot encounter one and not the other. The desire of the two men to make a name for themselves and defy death is an out-and-out affront, not simply to the good housewives of the village, but to the Great Goddess herself.

The archaic heritage of the male is freedom and lack of responsibility. The burden of infancy and child care is none of his business and is only forced upon him. Although the ethological studies of chimpanzees cannot present us with a picture of the life of the protohominids, they can give us some insights into what these conditions may have been like. When Jane van Lawick-Goodall describes a way of life in which the mother and infant comprise the family, with the males left free to make lasting friendships and to roam through the forest, playing and feeding

with the food readily at hand, she is also describing the aboriginal
life before Eve offered Adam the red apple and lured him out of
the garden and away from the trees. Precisely because the human
infant is so dependent for so long a time, the human female
instinctively and unconsciously exercised an attractive pull on the
male. The ambivalence of the males' attention and repulsion for
the female is played out in the division between soul and body.
The body is under the dominance of the female, and no male can
resist the pull of mother and lover, but in his mind and soul the
male longs for the old freedom, the freedom of the forest before
the savannah, the freedom of the soul before its incarnation in the
planetary stream of evolution. Once the male has relieved himself
at the body of the female, he longs to return to that old freedom in
the companionship of men. Whether the boy runs from the food
of the mother to rejoin his playmates, or whether the man runs
from the responsibilities of society to go to the bar, the club, the
hunting camp, or the philosophical Academy of Plato or Ficino, he
longs to escape incarnation into the absolute and unconditioned
freedom of the soul.

Just such a division between body and soul is what we see in the
Gilgamesh epic. The two supremely potent men are drawn to
women, but they long for some greater, transcendent love. The
love of Inanna and Dumuzi was not personal and romantic love; it
was impersonal and elemental, a metaphor for natural processes
and cultural needs: the marriage of fertility and the storehouse.
Man does not want to see himself as simply the phallic tool owned
by the Great Mother; that may be all right for the eunuch-priests
who place their testicles on the altar of the Great Goddess, but the
hero longs for something more from existence. (This and the
following excerpts of the Gilgamesh epic are taken from the same
source; see note 29.)

> Gilgamesh opened his mouth,
> Saying to [Enkidu]:
> "Who, my friend, can scale heaven?
> Only the gods [live] forever under the sun.
> As for mankind, numbered are their days;
> Whatever they achieve is but the wind![32]

Together inside the city, Gilgamesh and Enkidu can only grow old
and soft and lose their powers. A life amid the pleasures of food

and sex is a life of imprisonment inside a system of limitations. The mind of the partly divine Gilgamesh cannot accept these limitations, for his divided nature torments him. If he were not partly divine, perhaps he could relax and accept the shopkeeper's lot, but he is two-thirds god and one-third man, and so the limitations gall him, just as later the same limitations would gall the partly divine Achilles. In history, the revolutionary or the prophet is often the divided man, the being of two cultures in whom the opposites are at war and in their conflict generate an energy that is beyond the level of the normal man. Moses, half-Egyptian and half-Hebrew, is the archetypal example for such revolutionary prophets as Louis Riel, Padraic Pearse, and Malcolm X. The leader is the man who knows the way of the overlords but identifies with the life of the oppressed. As king and child of the gods, Gilgamesh knows the ways of the gods, but as a mortal he knows that his lot is cast with humanity, and the indignity and affront of death galls him.

And so the hero proposes a sacred quest, a journey into the depths of the Cedar Forest to slay its guardian demon, Huwawa. Here the tragic paradox of the epic is most clear: man is limited, and a man's name, his ego, is the very label of limitation, for the name is the label of the thing which dies. When Gilgamesh proposes to Enkidu that they go out to slay the guardian spirit of the forest to make a name for themselves, a name that can live on after them, he is proposing to set up a monument to the ego. Contrary to the theories of Julian Jaynes stating that consciousness only rose in the sixth century B.C., it is absolutely clear that with this great work of art we have entered into the world of self-consciousness, for the dilemma of consciousness is what the Gilgamesh epic is all about.[33]

The name is the label of egohood. The heroes have achieved egohood and consciousness and now they are painfully aware that they are no longer part of the cyclical eternal round of the Great Mother. They live a life, a linear phallic extension, a life with a beginning and end. Precisely because they are cut off from the eternal return to the bosom of the Great Mother, they cannot accept the natural life of death. The ego has definitely arrived on the scene of history, and it is screaming out against its cosmic isolation. It is not in the sixth century B.C. that consciousness and egohood are born; it is in that century that the lament sounded by

Gilgamesh is heard and answered by the Buddha, Lao Tzu, Pythagoras, and the Second Isaiah. Egohood dawned with civilization, and no doubt the rise of warfare associated with it gave many a man an occasion to meditate on the meaning of death. The hunter prays to the guardian spirit of the herd; he justifies his kill by saying that he takes only what he needs. Like the wolf, man the hunter in killing the weak and unfit, actually works to maintain the health of the herd. But civilized man is quite a different animal, and when he wipes out an entire city or levels a forest, he is no longer working within the natural balance of things. In warfare one is cut off from nature in cutting down his enemy; in warfare the *nature* of death takes on an entirely new cultural dimension.

Conscious egohood is intensified in the civilizational process. The walls that rise up to isolate the city from nature also rise up to isolate the citizen from nature. The continuum is broken, and the rise of writing helps to break up as well the continuum of the sensorium, to locate consciousness in the written word. What the written word is to the sensorium, the ego is to the entire consciousness, and the city is to the entire encirclement of nature. Writing, individuation, and civilization are all parts of one larger cultural phenomenology. Because civilization is at a moment of overripeness in the Third Dynasty of Ur, the whole civilization process is being lifted up into consciousness in the Gilgamesh epic. "The owl of Minerva flies at dusk."

The walls of the city define Uruk; the name of a person defines the individual, but what is shut out by both city wall and personal name is the spiritual dimension, the connecting nature that unites unique and universal. To a civilized man anxious to make a name for himself the guardian deity of the forest is a monster and a demon. Gilgamesh, the king of the city, the man who most exemplifies personality and civilization, therefore takes it as his project to go forth from the city to slay the spirit of the forest. Here are the roots of the ecological crisis of our civilization. The furniture of civilization comes from the death of forests, not merely of trees. Men no longer ask permission of the guardian spirit to take the minimum for their needs; they march in pomp and glory and level the entire forest. Gilgamesh does not realize, though, that when he slays the spirit of the forest and cuts off the city from nature, he gives a new life to death. Before, all the processes of culture were connected with the cycles of nature; in death, tribal man simply returned to the Great Mother. But when civilized man sets up walls between himself and the forest, and when he sets up his personal name against the stars, he ensures that the now-isolated ego will cry out in painful recognition of its complete alienation in the fear of death.

As the great Gilgamesh polishes his armor and weapons in preparation for the great expedition, he attracts the attention of the goddess of love and war, Ishtar (Inanna), and she asks to become his lover. Ishtar displays all her beauty and makes great promises to Gilgamesh, but the hero focuses on his heroic ideal and rejects Ishtar in what amounts to a curse. Here the conflict between male bonding and the companionship of the transcendent quest versus sexual love and involvement in the immanence of bodily life comes right out into the open. Gilgamesh recites an entire litany which unfolds all the treacheries of Ishtar; he recites the list of all her past lovers who have come to ruin. When Ishtar hears this she is enraged and mounts to the realm of the sky god, Anu, and demands that the Bull of Heaven be sent to earth to destroy Gilgamesh. Threatening to create famine and raise the dead unless she has her way, Ishtar is able to compel Anu to grant her the demand. Anu relents and sends down the Bull of Heaven (a comet?) to attack Gilgamesh. But the goddess has forgotten that bulls and oxen are the province of man, the domesticator of animals, and so the two cowboys, Gilgamesh and Enkidu, make short work of the Bull. Ishtar is again enraged and mounts the walls of Uruk and cries out: "Woe unto Gilgamesh because he insulted me." When Enkidu hears Ishtar's threat, he tears loose the right thigh of the Bull of Heaven and flings it at her. No doubt, "right thigh" is a euphemism for the genitals of the bull, and by flinging the phallus into the face of the goddess Enkidu is mocking her role as the goddess of love *and* war and parodying the old rituals of appeasement of the Great Goddess in rites of castration. That we are witnessing the parody of an ancient ritual becomes clearer when Ishtar responds to Enkidu's taunt by setting up the old lament for the torn god.

> Ishtar assembled the girl-devotees,
> The prostitutes, and the courtesans;
> Over the right thigh of the bull of heaven
> she set up a lamentation.

But Gilgamesh called the craftsmen, the armorers,
all of them.
The artisans admired the size of the horns . . .
He brought (them) into the room of his rulership (?)
and hung (them) up (therein).

While the women wail over the severed phallus of the torn god, the craftsmen go to work, and Gilgamesh places the more durable horns in his room, a room that would thus have the appearance of the male bull shrine at Çatal Hüyük. By placing an old ritual in a new context, the men are mocking the old religion in which the women lament the death of Dumuzi; in this new context, the old conservative religion of the women is being mocked in a celebration of male ambition. The battle between the sexes could not be clearer.

In the ancient rituals the bull was slain to honor the Great Goddess, but now these two men have affirmed their independence, their egos, their desire for transcendence from the downward pull of the collective, by making a sacrilege out of a sacrament. And here we need to remember that Uruk is the city of Inanna; it is the city into which were transferred the very arts of civilization, the *me's* from Eridu; it is the city which contains the Eanna, the holy precinct of Inanna. Gilgamesh is, therefore, mounting a quite radical challenge to traditional authority. If we read between the lines of the epic, we can see that this incident describes not only the conflict between the sexes, but also the conflict between the political and secular forms of authority in kingship and the old traditional forms of conservative religious authority in the temple. Contained in the conflict between Ishtar and Gilgamesh is the conflict between the institutions of temple and militaristic monarchy, the conflict between the civilized remnants of the old neolithic religion and the new masculine order of civilization.

The action of the two men is nothing short of cosmic revolt. Something has happened, for now men are not only intent on attacking the old elemental spirits of nature, but they are also bent on defying the gods. The pattern of overweaning pride associated with tragedy here makes its first appearance in literature. In celebration of himself, Gilgamesh sings to the lyre maids:

Who is most splendid among heroes?
Who is most glorious among men?
Gilgamesh is most splendid among heroes,
Gilgamesh is most glorious among men.

The epic of Gilgamesh is the very foundation of Western literature, for what we are witnessing here is to set the pattern for all Hebrew and Greek literature to come. The two heroes are awe-inspiring, exciting, and terrifying, but like Achilles, or Patroklos at the wall of the Achaeans, or King David, they are men who have gone too far. The ego, in establishing an individual consciousness by cutting itself off from the gods of Heaven and the spirits of nature, has screamed out its "name" in an "I am!" to the horizon, but the echo which will rebound from sky and earth will be a single word, the sentence of death.

The expedition to slay Huwawa, the spirit of the forest, is doomed from the start. Perhaps because he is the wild man of the steppes, it is Enkidu who hesitates when they finally come to the house of Huwawa. Enkidu had barred the way to Gilgamesh when he wished to cross the threshold to the bride; now he tries once again to hold Gilgamesh back at the gate of the guardian of the forest. But Gilgamesh entreats him not to speak like a coward, and the two thrust beyond all limits into the spirit's realm.

Huwawa is slain; the victors triumph, but the victory is to be a pyrrhic one for Gilgamesh, for the gods have met in counsel and decreed that Enkidu should die. The consciousness of death is to be rubbed in Gilgamesh's face, for he will live on to spend his life brooding over the death of his beloved friend. There is to be no heroic death for Enkidu; he is not to die in battle but is to decay slowly from a degenerative disease. And all that the great and powerful Gilgamesh can do is look on in utter helplessness.

As Enkidu is lying on his deathbed, he looks back over his life and curses the harlot who ensnared him on the steppes. He asks that the street be her dwelling place and that the drunken may strike her. When the god Shamash hears Enkidu's curse, he stops him and asks how can he curse the woman who taught him to eat bread fit for divinity and who brought him to his beloved friend, Gilgamesh. Looking on the other side of his fate, Enkidu relents and blesses the prostitute and says that for the love of her the man will leave the wife and mother of seven. In the curse and blessing of the prostitute, we see the ambivalence of man's perception of woman. He is drawn to her and repelled; he sees both the beautiful courtesan for whom empires will fall, and the wretched streetwalker plying her trade in taverns in the shadows of the city walls.

In man's perception of the prostitute is a progression of four stages that recall the stages of the Viconian cycle of history: the Age of Gods, the Age of Heroes, the Age of Men, and the Age of Chaos. The first age is the age of the Great Goddess; next comes the age of the temple priestess, then of the sacred temple prostitute, and finally of the entirely secular street walker. As the power of man gains in ascendency, the religious power of woman declines. First there was a *hieros gamos,* a sacred intercourse of fertility and the storehouse in which a woman played the role of the goddess. Then there were sacred temple prostitutes who spread the ritual from the one to the many, but in that routinization of charisma the sacred meaning was lost, and the common prostitute became the totally secular figure who haunted the subculture of men. In the *diminuendo* of the movement from priestess to prostitute we see described a process of increasing urbanization and secularization in a new world in which the old universal religion of the Great Goddess is forgotten.

With a curse and a blessing for the harlot who had trapped him and brought him into society, Enkidu dies, and Gilgamesh takes up his wild lament. The man who slew the spirit of the forest has now to confront death and the meaning of his act. He who would separate an ego from the universe to make a name for himself must learn that the very definition of individuality is limitation; the form of a thing is described by its edge, and the edge of being is death.

Because Gilgamesh is a hero, two-thirds god and only one-third man, death is more of an affront to him than it would be to an ordinary mortal. He cannot rest content with the limitations of being human but must always press on to the outermost limits of all things. His refusal to accept death causes him to go on a journey to the outermost edge of the world. He goes to the edge of space to look behind the edges of time, to gaze into the mystery of the time before the Flood, the time before this world epoch began.

At one of the way-stations on his long journey a barmaid at a tavern speaks to Gilgamesh and tries to give him common sense on the human condition.

> Gilgamesh, whither runnest thou?
> The life which thou seekest thou wilt not find;
> (For) when the gods created mankind,
> They allotted death to mankind,
> (But) life they retained in their keeping.
> Thou, O Gilgamesh, let thy belly be full;
> Day and night be thou merry;
> Make every day (a day of) rejoicing.
> Day and night do thou dance and play.
> Let they raiment be clean,
> Thy head be washed, (and) thyself bathed in water.
> Cherish the little one holding thy hand,
> (And) let the wife rejoice in thy bosom.
> This is the lot of [mankind . . .].

But the common sense of mankind is not for Gilgamesh, and so he continues on his journey until he comes to the dangerous sea at the edge of the world. He has crossed over the steppes, passed through the Scorpion Gate, climbed over the mountains, and gone through the long darkness of a tunnel where he was without light for the twelve double hours of the day. When finally Gilgamesh comes to the edge of the waters of death, he searches for the boatman of Utnapishtim who can alone carry him across the treacherous waters. He cannot find the fabled boatman, but he does come across the two stone images that belong to the boatman, and in rage and frustration, the great heroic extrovert, the man who is used to acting out whatever he feels inside, smashes the stones.

Scholars regard the two idol stones used by the boatman as a magic talisman to help him cross the treacherous sea, but there may be another meaning. In the *midrash* about Noah it says that Noah had a stone which, when held up in the darkness of the ark, would change color when the sun was shining outside.[34] The

Vikings also used certain polarizing crystals to help them navigate on foggy and overcast days. It is likely that the stones of the boatman are not mere fetishes, but probably a kind of ancient navigating crystal. In fact, the boatman, when he returns to his boat, tells Gilgamesh that he has destroyed the very things which would enable him to cross the sea.

Without the magic stones, the boatman seeks another way back and instructs Gilgamesh to cut down one hundred twenty trees to make punting poles for the waters that are so deadly that they corrode the poles with every push. Once he has accomplished his task, the boatman accomplishes his, and after great lengths, Gilgamesh finally arrives at the home of Utnapishtim. At this point of the story we encounter a new set of oppositions. Enkidu was the hairy man of the wild steppes, and Gilgamesh was the hero of civilization; but now the contrast is between Gilgamesh, the king, the man of political power, the heroic man of action, the extrovert, and Utnapishtim, the man of religious authority, the introvert, the sage. Beyond the edge of the world, and far beyond anything anyone knows about history, Gilgamesh sits at the feet of the sage, the great old man of the mountains, and hears the story of the Flood, and how the gods themselves warned Utnapishtim and told him to build an ark. The boat which the gods tell Utnapishtim to build is no ordinary boat but a perfect cube with seven levels; the ark resembles more a Platonic solid from the *Timaeus* than a seaworthy craft. The cube is the traditional Hermetic and alchemical symbol for the earth; it would seem that what is being described is the creation of a new body for the earth for the newly emerging world epoch. The seven levels would, therefore, correspond to the various vibratory planes of the subtle bodies of the world. To save oneself from the catastrophes that always come at the end of a world cycle, one cannot simply escape; one has to be attuned to the newly emerging subtle body of the planet: not to a hideaway in the physical body, but to the forms of the etheric body. The ark is therefore not a boat, but a crystalline cube in which the new forms of life are contained.[35]

The story of the Flood and the boatman who is warned by a god is, of course, familiar to us from the story of Noah, a story which has borrowed much from its Sumerian predecessor. Although there are many similarities between the two stories of the Flood,—

the ark, the rescue of the animals, and the sending out of the raven in search of dry land after the rains have stopped—the differences are also striking. The Sumerian version is more esoteric; sacred geometry and numerology are associated with the structure of the ark, and Utnapishtim becomes an initiatic sage and guru. The epithet of Utnapishtim is "Atrahasis," or "the exceedingly wise," but his wisdom is not the simple folklore of an old man. Utnapishtim is much more of a yogi than was Noah. His instructions to Gilgamesh are deceptively simple, but there is a hidden knowledge to his words:

> But now as for thee, who will assemble the gods unto thee,
> That thou mayest find the life which thou seekest?
> Come, do not sleep for six days and seven nights.

What this introvert is saying to the great extrovert is, in effect, "You have slain lions, O great hero, but can you slay your own mind?" Only the most advanced practitioner of meditation could pass Utnapishtim's test to watch the mind for six days and seven nights without falling asleep. What Utnapishtim has given Gilgamesh is an exercise from *yoga nidra*, the yoga of sleep. The advanced yogi watches his mind go into the hypnagogic state, then into the dreaming state, then out of the dreaming state to "wake up" in a clearer mind in the astral plane in which he can look down and see his physical body at rest on the bed. From there the yogi can go through various *bardo* experiences in the astral plane, until the astral body itself is put aside, and the being rises to the higher planes of the spiritual realms. Eventually, as the Vedic *Unpanishads* teach, the individual goes to the feet of the Braham, beyond any planes of manifest form to a realm of pure Divine consciousness. A night of sleep is a microcosm of the entire cosmic cycle of the creation and reabsorption of the universe. When Utnapishtim slyly asks the great hero to watch his mind and not fall asleep, he is in effect asking him to become a yogi. The test set for Gilgamesh is deceptively simple, but it is in reality the most difficult test of all.

Not surprisingly, the great hero is snoring within a few seconds. As Utnapishtim regards Gilgamesh, he remarks to his wife: "Look at the strong man who wants life (everlasting)." The contrast between the man of political power and the man of religious authority, the extrovert and the introvert, could not be more intense, and one can only marvel at the greatness of the court singer of the Third Dynasty of Ur who put the episodes of the mythic cycle of Gilgamesh together, for the epic is no longer simply a myth expressing the collective unconscious; it has become a work of art expressing the artist's individual consciousness. Through the greatness of art the unique consciousness of the individual artist and the universal consciousness of the culture have achieved unity.

Gilgamesh falls asleep and sleeps for as many days as Enkidu had made love to the harlot on the steppes. When he finally awakes, he claims that he had only nodded off for a second, but the wife of Utnapishtim had baked a loaf of bread every day and set it before the sleeping king. The mold on the old bread tells Gilgamesh that he had not been sleeping for merely a few seconds. Now the great hero realizes that his quest for personal immortality has been in vain; in despair Gilgamesh realizes that he must accept as his own fate the common lot of humanity. In pity for him, Utnapishtim tells his boatman, Ursunabi, to take Gilgamesh to the place of washing so that Gilgamesh can erase the marks of his long and fruitless journey. As a slight consolation Utnapishtim gives him a special garment which will last for the entire journey back to Uruk.

Bathed and freshly attired, Gilgamesh climbs back into the boat of Ursunabi, but as they all make their farewells, Utnapishtim's wife tells her husband that Gilgamesh should receive some parting gift. Utnapishtim hears his wife's plea and tells Gilgamesh where he can find a miraculous plant of invigoration and rejuvenation. The miraculous plant grows in the deep and to fetch it Gilgamesh must tie weights to his belt in order to be able to sink to the bottom of the underground waters. In this quest which requires heroic action and daring, Gilgamesh is in his element, and so he is able to discover the plant and carry it up with him. Now with his parting gift from the sage in hand, Gilgamesh sets off on his return journey, but when Gilgamesh and Ursunabi stop for the night, Gilgamesh goes to bathe in a pool, and from the depths of a pool there comes a serpent which seizes the plant. Immediately upon eating the magic plant, the serpent sloughs off its skin and rejuvenates itself. Gilgamesh sees what the serpent has done, but it is too late to prevent the theft. Realizing his loss, the great king sits down to weep. It seems that the only thing the hero will be able to bring back from this expedition is what can be carried by the heart and mind—the wisdom of the journey.

The snake that lives at the depths of the pool and rises to take the plant of rejuvenation is a familiar emblem of the serpent of *kundalini* which, when it rises, releases a power of great vigor and a new youth. But the fact that the snake returns to the depths of the well after seizing the plant indicates that Gilgamesh has not become an initiate. The old yogi, Utnapishtim, had given Gilgamesh a chance, but Gilgamesh did not take it; instead he tried to store the plant away, to hold it for the old men of the city and for his own old age. Wisdom, however, is not a commodity that can be stored; it has to be used immediately, or it slips away. (The medieval vision of this spiritual truth is expressed in the history of the Holy Grail; when Perceval sees the Grail in the castle of the Fisher King but neglects to ask about it, he loses his opportunity and damages his fate.) Spiritual transformation is not an object that can be hoarded; its energy must be used immediately, or else one becomes worse, not better: stasis leads to degeneration. The image of the sleeping serpent at the bottom of the pool, with its mouth closing over the plant of rejuvenation, is an image of the subtle body of an unawakened human being. Gilgamesh may have been two-thirds god, but the end of all his wandering is that he must return to Uruk as one who is fully human and is defined by the limitations that are upon all men.

Gilgamesh returns to his city, and in an *aria da capo* the court singer brings his audience back to a meditation on the walls of the city; the great epic ends with an acceptance of limitation and a celebration of that form of delimitation, the walls. The man who has slain the spirit of the forest has not slain the monster of death; the walls of the city may rise up against the desert, but for how long no man can say and no poet sing.

V

THE COURT POET who put the legends of Gilgamesh into the form of the epic was a servant of kings; he was a man kept to the side who could watch the power struggles, the wars, and the greed. The Third Dynasty of Ur was a time when in the royal graves seventy servants were killed and buried with the dead king amid a whole ceremonial procession of luxury, gold chariots, fine clothes and jewelry. Perhaps the kings thought that they could take all this gold with them beyond death, and perhaps the court singer was one of the servants put to death to accompany the great king and descendant of Gilgamesh on his journey to the netherworld. The poet, however, left behind a monument greater than the gold of the tombs or the great wall of Uruk, for in his meditation on death and the limits of heroic action in the pursuit of power, he gave us a portrait of the wise old sage who lives beyond civilization and its walls, and knows the folly of it all. The pattern set down by this anonymous court poet of the Third Dynasty of Ur was to become the foundation for all the later stories about the opposition of power and authority, from Lao Tzu who would not come to the Emperor, or William Faulkner who would not come to the fashionable dinners of President Kennedy. When both sage and artist refused to dance in attendance at the royal court, they followed the path of the wise old man far beyond the centers of power.

For all its power and wealth, the Third Dynasty of Ur was not to last very long. The court singer may have chanted the epic around 2150 B.C., but by 1950 B.C. another poet is chanting the "Lamentation for the Destruction of Ur."

> The people mourn.
> Its people's (corpses), not potsherds
> littered the approaches.
> The walls were gaping;
> the high gates, the roads,
> were piled with dead.
> In the wide streets,
>   where feasting crowds (once) gathered,
> jumbled they lay.
>
> In all the streets and roadways bodies lay.
> In open fields that used to fill with dancers,
> the people lay in heaps.
>
> The country's blood now filled its holes,
>   like metal in a mold;
> bodies dissolved—like butter left in the sun.[36]

* * *

The walls of the city had surrounded the storehouse and the treasury, and both attracted the wild men of the mountains, the Elamites. In humanity's "rise to civilization," the human race had been split into the civilized and the barbarian, and the pattern of barbarians against the city had been set. In China, in Mohenjo Daro in India, in Sumer, in Mycennae, in Troy, in Rome, in Teotihaucan, in ancient Mexico, cities would rise with their walls, ziggurats and pyramids, and then after a little season of glory, the barbarians would pour through, and the spirit of Lilith would once again come to dance in the ruins. Whether the barbarian was Elamite, Hun, or Chichimec, the story of wild men against the city was the same.

But even in its death Sumerian civilization would take hold of the imagination of the ancient world. The Sumerian language, like Greek in the days of the Roman Empire, ruled as the classical language of art and scholarship; its cultural patterns continued on in the lives of the Semitic people who came after. Sumerian civilization lasted for an entire Platonic month from 4000 to 2000 B.C. Many civilizations cannot claim as much. As the zodiac turned and history moved into the second millennium before Christ, a new period of instability appeared. Ur is destroyed in 1950 B.C. By 1900 the Greek people are established in Macedonia, by 1850 the Indo-European Hittites have settled in Anatolia, around 1750 Stonehenge is abandoned, and at that time other Indo-European tribes are beginning to push down from the steppes of Eurasia, first into Iran, and later into India. Wherever these tribal people go, they carry with them a highly mobile warrior society.

> It is reasonable to conclude that the Indo-Europeans had a pa-
> triarchal social organization. There is considerable common vo-
> cabulary of terms for agnatic relations, and hardly any for kindred
> on the mother's side. This accords with the strongly patriarchal
> character of society among the Romans, the Aryas, and the early
> Celts and Germans . . .
> The Indo-Europeans also appear to have developed a kind of
> tribal society which made for effective leadership in war.[37]

The indigenous villages of the Deccan may have prayed to the Great Mother, but the tribal warriors who swept into India to

establish Vedic civilization were patriarchal and militaristic societies. Whether in India, Anatolia, or Mesopotamia, the shift
from small and comparatively peaceful Neolithic village life to the
stage of civilization is a shift from the Great Mother to the Great
Father.

Neumann would see a psychological evolution of consciousness
in this development,[38] but there are other explanations as well.
Whether one lives in a wandering tribal band or a settled
civilization, warfare is the nature of social reality, and warfare is a
subculture constellated around the figure of the tribal warrior-
chieftan or king. Village matriarchy simply cannot hold up to the
threat of full-scale invasion.

Helmut Wilhelm, who participated in Jung's annual Eranos
conferences, would concur with Neumann in seeing a psychological shift in archetypes in the shift from village life to civilization,
but Wilhelm also recognized an external, historical dimension to
this transformation of consciousness. Whether we are talking
about India, Anatolia, Mesopotamia, or China, we seem to be
talking about a shift from matriarchy to patriarchy.

> The totemistic matriarchal religion of the Shang, which controlled
> its believers through fear, was alien to the early Chou rulers. Equally
> alien was that indefinable twilight which permits the sway of dark
> forces of the human psyche and provides them with a sanctioned
> outlet in blood sacrifices.[39]

From Neolithic villages to organized state, from gardening to
irrigation farming, from inconography to writing, from disor-
ganized raids to institutionalized warfare, from custom to law,
from matriarchal religious authority to patriarchal political power,
from mystery to history: the transformation was so complete that
the past itself was reinvented to create a new foundation for a
radically altered present. Now that we ourselves are moving into a
radically altered present, it is small wonder that the patriarchal
image of prehistory is disintegrating. The movement into the
future always involves the *revision*ing of the past.

CHAPTER FIVE

Civilization and Initiation in Ancient Egypt

I F A HISTORIAN were to look at Çatal Hüyük in the seventh
millennium B.C. and at Uruk in the fourth millennium and
then ask himself whether or not there were some mythological
painting or story that could express the transitional stage of
culture from the matriarchy of the Neolithic village to the
patriarchy of the urban civilization, the myth of Isis and Osiris
would be his answer. In this legend of ancient Egypt we find a
clear expression of the conflict between the mother's brother and
the son over the legitimacy of so novel a historical character as
"the father."

Unfortunately, though we have many hymns which sing the
praises of Isis, Osiris, and their divine child, Horus, we do not
have a complete narration of the myth from a time earlier than
Plutarch's retelling of the story. The Egyptian myth in Plutarch's
Roman hands is like a fossil in the marble slabs that decorate the
foyers of Manhattan skyscrapers. When you look at a Precambrian
trilobite in the lobby of a New York bank, it is difficult to speculate
about its primeval environment. But if we again take heart from
Lévi-Strauss's advice that every variant of a myth should be taken
into consideration, then perhaps the late Roman preservation of
an ancient Egyptian myth is not worthless. Since a myth always has
a certain archetypal structure, it is hard for a teller of the story to
twist it wholly out of shape. You cannot tell the story of Jesus, for
example, without talking about his birth, death, and resurrection.
So it is with Osiris. We can tell from Plutarch's narration that he
does not understand what he is passing on, but the very fact that
what he is passing on is so alien to him indicates that it is not
original with him. Whatever accretions have attached themselves
to the story were part of the culture for which the myth of Isis and

Osiris was important, and therefore they become part of the whole. A myth is not so much an expression of one particular time as it is an expression of time. What is ancient for us was in its own time a reworking of what was ancient for the ancients. A myth is always about the old days. Specialized, scientific knowledge is about pieces, but mythology is about the whole, the beginning and ending of things. An astronaut circles the moon and recites Genesis, but the writers of Genesis were themselves putting together old stories in a new landscape. So it is with Plutarch: his story of Isis and Osiris is not simply a fossil; it is a fossil within a box within a box within a box. The mystery cult of Isis in Roman Egypt was an attempt to harken back to the religion of the New Kingdom, which itself was trying to harken back to the religion of the Old Kingdom. And the religion of the Old Kingdom was a civilized consummation of a process of change going back to prehistoric times.

> There is no definitive evidence as yet that Osiris was worshipped in the prehistoric period. Even if he were, that would not imply that the primitive figure had much in common with the highly developed god we encounter in historical times. A symbol of Osiris has recently been found that dates from the beginning of historical times, about 3000 B.C., otherwise there is no specific proof of his existence until he appears in the Pyramid Texts which were inscribed between 2400 and 2200 B.C. In these texts he is already fully developed, not only already provided with a complete mythology but a carefully thought-out theology as well.[1]

History turns on a spiral, and with each turn it comes back on a new level to the initial position, from the Freemasonry of Mozart's *Magic Flute* to the Hermeticism of the Renaissance to the syncretism of Plutarch's Roman Empire to the New Kingdom and the reformation of Egyptian religion to the Old Kingdom and the founding of the civilization. But as this book has tried to show, the birth of civilization in the Near East is far from the beginning of things. And so I turn back on the spiral to Plutarch, who himself is turning back.

> They say that when Nut [the sky] had intercourse with Geb [the earth], Ra [the sun] came to know about it and set on her a curse that she should not give birth in any month or year. Then Thoth,

falling in love with the goddess, became intimate with her, and then played draughts against the moon-goddess [Selene]. He won the seventieth part of each of her illuminations, and having put together five days out of the whole of his gains, he added them to the three hundred and sixty [days of the year]; these five the Egyptians now call the "additional days" [epagomenai] and on them they celebrate the gods' birthday. For they say that on the first day Osiris was born and that as he was delivered a voice cried out that the Lord of All was coming to the light of day. . . . On the second day, it is said, Haroeris was born, whom some call Apollo and the elder Horus; and on the third day Seth was born, not in the right time or place, but bursting through with a blow he leapt from his mother's side. On the fourth day Isis was born near very moist places and on the fifth Nephthys . . . They say that Osiris and Haroeris were the offspring of Ra, Isis of Thoth, and Seth and Nephthys from Geb. For this reason kings used to regard the third of the epagomenal days as unlucky and on it they did no public business nor did they attend to their own persons until night. They say that Nephthys married Seth and that Isis and Osiris, being in love with each other even before they were born, were united in the darkness of the womb.[2]

The myth opens with a discussion of the formation of the calendar and the five extra days of the year, because the myth is about the nature of time. The gods are immortal and therefore they are not born *in* the human social time of the year; they are born "outside" in the larger frame of the epagomenal days. Since the formation of the calendar is basic to the formation of a civilization, the origins of society are being used as a metaphor for the formation of everything—in particular, the origin of the solar system.

We must remember, as von Dechend warns, that when we are dealing with seemingly absurd mythological narratives, we should not be patronizing, but we should realize that we are dealing with the technical language of an elite caste of astronomer-priests. A thousand years from now another culture might come along to make fun of us by saying that in those days it was thought a wind blew from the sun to the end of the solar system, not appreciating that when we say "the solar wind" we are using the term "wind" as a metaphor for an activity. So it is with the ancient Egyptians: when they place an animal's head on the body of a god or color Osiris's body green, they do not mean that gods literally have animal heads or that Osiris had green skin. Rather an activity or quality characteristic of the animal can metaphorically describe the activity of the god. Since Osiris was considered to be intimately related to the power which animated vegetation, he was painted green. It would take an Egyptologist, an astronomer, and a psychologist to decipher the specifics of this ancient cosmology, but nevertheless we can, at least, alert ourselves to the idea that what is being presented in this myth of origins is not merely superstitious gibberish but a poetic and intuitive recollection of the formation of the solar system.

Geb is not so much the earth as he is a metaphor for the cosmic dust cloud before the separation into the sun and distinct planets. In other Egyptian myths, Shu, with the aid of the wind-spirits, helps to lift the sky to separate Nut from Geb. In Sumerian cosmology, Enlil, the god of air, expands to separate Heaven and earth, An and Ki. Thus when the Egyptians or Sumerians talk about air or wind, they are talking about the expansion of gases and using the wind, as we still do, as a poetic metaphor. As the primordial gases change, the indistinct cosmic dust of Geb and Nut is transformed, and from these primeval parents new off-spring begin to appear, the planets. Isis, a mother-goddess figure up to even Roman times, is most probably the planet earth, and Osiris, known to have been originally a moon-god,[3] is her accompanying lunar orb. When the myth says that Isis and Osiris were making love in the womb, we should understand that this represents a conviction that at one time the moon and earth were one and had not separated.[4] And so when the myth speaks of the intercourse of other gods, we can suspect that the formation of the distinct planets and their later astrological conjunctions are being discussed. Since Seth cuts up the body of Osiris into fourteen pieces and later becomes the prow of the sun god, Ra, I would guess that Seth was associated with Venus. When Venus is close to the moon, it is the time of the dismemberment, and when Venus is the morning star, rising ahead of the sun in the dawn sky, Seth is the prow of the ship of Ra, leading the sun.

The movements of the planets are dramatized as stories that, like all great myths, can have one meaning for children, and another for the adult telling the story to the child. In a hierarchi-cal society, the myth would have one meaning for the astronomer-priests, and another for the peasants.

To understand how a myth about the origins of the calendar can also be about the origins of the solar system, we need to understand that a myth is not a linear code, but a polyphonic fugue. One single myth can be a narrative about the formation of the solar system, the seasonal movement of planets and stars, the formation of civilization in the shift from Neolithic matriarchy to the patriarchal state, the development of consciousness in the emergence from the Great Mother to the fully individuated being, and, finally, the transformation of the central nervous system in the yogic achievement of illumination. A mythic narrative works through a system of correspondences, so a god is at once a principle of order, a number, a geometrical figure, a dancing measure, a mantram, a special planet, and a heavenly body. If one puts together the analyses of Jung, Lévi-Strauss, von Dechend, Neumann, and myself, one would still not have all the dimensions of the myth drawn out.

> The Lunar Mansions—spell them inns,—and the planets stopping off at these inns, made up "celestial writing," the sky was understood as a book; which might explain to you, why several ancient alphabets do not write the vowels: they are "planets," wanderers among the letters, and it would not be proper to pin them down.
>
> But every planet has not only a corresponding vowel, and element, and a metal, a jewel, a tree, certain animals—they have dancing steps, and meters.
>
> All this, and more, can be done when *number* is the only recognized reality . . .
>
> Difficult as this sounds, and really is: there you have it in a nutshell: *words* are likenesses, or copies of numbers, and number is the intelligible order of the kosmos. We remind you of the Babylonian "gods," written with pure numbers.[5]

In the old days of the scholarship of F. M. Cornford and Henri Frankfort,[6] the expressions of mythopoeic thought were seen as products of a prelogical mentality, because Aristotle's law of the excluded middle was ignored, and one thing could be two things, or more, at the same time. Had the Platonic tradition in Western thought triumphed over the Aristotelian, then the linear misunderstandings of the polyphonic thought of myth might not have led us astray.

Now many different sorts of attempts have been made to revive the Platonic or Pythagorean tradition, but they are all so different that they have not formed into a single and focused image.[7] Von Dechend stresses that "number is the only recognized reality" and thereby reduces a god to "nothing but" a number, and so she becomes too much like the very scholars she opposes. I have argued elsewhere that there are four levels to myth or hieroglyphic thought: (1) a melodic line, (2) a geometrical figure, (3) an equation or numerical relation, and (4) an archetypal image.[8] To regard a myth as only an expression of number is to hear only one line in a four-voice fugue. In the system of correspondences characteristic of an esoteric cosmology, there are four levels to mythic thought because there are four levels to manifest existence: the causal, astral, etheric, and physical planes of vibration. If one is talking about the physical plane, the god can be a planet; if one is talking about the etheric or astral plane, then that god becomes an animating force; if one is talking about the causal plane, the archetypal world of forms that mediate between the manifest world and the transcendental realm, then the god is a formative principle, an archangel, a crystal, or a number that is all four of the levels at once; it is a "seed" for manifestation. Each of the four levels "prehends" the other, and so in the punning of words so frequent in hieroglyphic writing, we encounter a richer and more inclusive mode of thought than we are accustomed to.

> This strange proceeding is no longer part of our conscious thinking, but the psychologists have shown that similar verbal exercises underly the free association of ideas. It is, of course, the technique of James Joyce in *Finnegans' Wake*. The Egyptians lived closer to the forces of their unconscious minds than we do. If two words had similar sounds, what they expressed must have something in common.
>
> The addiction to punning was related to a reverence for the "Word."[9]

In a pun or a hieroglyphic figure, several lines come together in what Whitehead would call "a prehension"; in the comprehension of an event, that sympathetic resonance between the observor and the "thing" observed, there is a correspondence between the cosmic word of the gods (the Logos of St. John) and the inner words of the human mind, for each shares existence because it is a manifestation of divine laws and harmony. In this comprehensive mode of thought what is important is not the discrete "thing" or "number," but the pattern, the total configuration of meaning. In this patterning there is a principle of recapitulation, for a recent historical event can be used as an analog for a more ancient prehistoric or cosmological event. Thus the formation of the calendar and the establishment of civilization can be used as vehicles to describe the origins, not merely of the calendar, but of time itself. Thus the stereotype is overlighted by the archetype, just as in conventional Egyptian statuary the historical pharoah is often shown standing under the god, the wings of Horus. (This and the following quotations from Plutarch are taken from the same source; see note 10.)

> It is said that Osiris when he was king at once freed the Egyptians from their primitive and brutish manner of life; he showed them how to grow crops, established laws for them, and taught them to worship gods. Later he civilized the whole world as he traversed through it, having little need of arms, but winning over most of the peoples by beguiling them with persuasive speech together with all manner of song and poetry. That is why the Greeks thought he was the same as Dionysus.[10]

Here we see Osiris presented as the familiar figure of the "culture hero," the bringer of the arts of civilization to humanity. The shift from hunting to agriculture is a peaceful revolution, and no conquest of arms is responsible for its adoption. The god associated with the crescent moon is the mysterious force that helps things to grow, *crescere*. (This ancient mode of thought exists to this day in the mystical biodynamic gardening practices of Rudolph Steiner, which call for planting only when the moon is in a favorable position for the variety of plant chosen.) Osiris is the hero of civilization, but he is also an old Paleolithic god of the moon who is the spirit of growth; he is not the earth, but the imagined relationship of the moon with vegetation. He is a spirit of growth and transformation, expressing the transformation of barbarism into civilization. As the moon calls secretly to the plant to blossom, Osiris calls humanity away from savagery, cannibalism, and human sacrifice to a new age of agriculture and the arts of poetry and music. As such an avatar of a new epoch, he is naturally pitted against the protector of the old nomadic life of Africa, Seth. Flint tools, the wild boar, Africa to the south of Egypt, and the constellation of the Great Bear are all associated with this reactionary figure. Seth is the embodiment of mother-right, warfare, terror, human sacrifice; he is an elemental deity who deals in the fundamental reality of blood.

> When he [Osiris] was away Seth conspired in no way against him since Isis was well on guard and kept careful watch. But on his return he devised a plot against him, making seventy-two men his fellow conspirators and having as helper a queen from Ethiopia, whom they name Aso. Seth secretly measured the body of Osiris and got made to the corresponding size a beautiful chest which was exquisitely decorated. This he brought to the banqueting hall, and when the guests showed pleasure and admiration at the sight of it, Seth promised playfully that whoever would lie down in it and show that he fitted it should have the chest as a gift. They all tried one by one, and since no one fitted into it, Osiris went in and lay down. Then the conspirators ran and slammed the lid on, and after securing it with bolts from the outside and also with molten lead poured on, they took it out to the river and let it go to the sea by way of the Tanitic mouth, which the Egyptians still call, because of this, hateful and abominable. They say that all these events occurred on the seventeenth day of the month of Athyr, when the sun passes through the scorpion, in the twenty-eighth year of the reign of Osiris. But some state that this was the period of his life rather than his reign.

With the description of the chest which entraps Osiris, becomes his coffin, and sends him floating down the river, an esoteric note is sounded. The myth is here moving from descriptions of the formation of the solar system and the distinct emergence of the earth as a planetary body to the formation of the human body and the fall of the soul into time. Seth is the principle of limitation, of numbering the One into the many; because he learns the numbers of Osiris's body, he learns about its inmost nature, for to know the secret name of something, or to know its vibratory signature in numbers, is to know how to gain power over it. The beautiful chest with all its external bolts is the Causal Body, and the river on which Seth casts the body is the river of time. Seth is what, deriving from this ancient Egyptian tradition, the Gnostics know as the evil Archon who creates the human body and traps the soul into generation. The age of this Egyptian myth is the astrological age of Scorpio, the constellation said to rule the realm of sexuality and the loins; the cosmic stage is appropriately set for the entrapment into the world of generation. Only if Osiris can redeem this fallen world of generation can he rise to become the god of growing and generated things.

That we are at the beginning of time and generation becomes clearer when we stop to consider that there are seventy-two conspirators with Seth. The Platonic Great Year, the time it takes to make a complete circuit through the twelve astrological signs, is 25,920 years; $\frac{1}{360}$ of that circle, or one degree, is seventy-two.[11] With the entrapment into time the great clock of the heavens begins its round. The Sumerians also saw this number as significant, for it is the number of the lesser gods, the Annunaki, who are generally seen to be the major stars.

Seth takes the measure of Osiris; this act of measurement indicates that Seth is not simply evil but is the principle of limitation. To the soul, used to wandering freely in the spiritual realms, limitation is experienced as extreme imprisonment. But from another point of view there is no growth without the limitation of form; the myth can be seen to be speaking about the origin of form—the distinct forms of the planets from the cosmic dust clouds, the distinct form of the human body in its journey into time. The lunar quality of Osiris's body is emphasized by his age of twenty-eight, the number of the phases of the moon.

Osiris is the husband of Isis. The figure of Osiris harkens back to the old Neolithic religion in which Isis would be the Great Mother and Osiris her son-lover consort. But in this civilized myth we are witnessing a transformation, what Erich Neumann would call a myth of individuation,[12] for the mother-son relationship is becoming the husband-wife, brother-sister relationship. A new generation has appeared, and the universal feminine is expressed not so much as Hathor, the cow-mother, but as Isis, the wife and consort. Osiris is still the dying male god of prehistory, but he too has moved into a new role, for he is to become the father of the divine child, Horus, who becomes the worldly king.

The first to hear of the misfortune and to spread the news of its occurrence were the Pans and Satyrs who lived near Chemmis, and because of this, the sudden disturbance and excitement of a crowd is still refered to as "panic." When Isis heard of it she cut off there and then one of her locks and put on morning garment; accordingly the city is called Coptos to this day . . . Isis when she was wandering everywhere in a state of distress, passed by no one without accosting him, and even when she met children, she asked them about the chest. Some of these happened to see it, and they named the river mouth through which Seth's friends had pushed the box to sea. For this reason the Egyptians believe that children have the power of divination, and they take omens especially from children's shouts as they play near the temples and say whatever they happen to.

Here we encounter the earliest version of what will become an important motif for the Gnostics, both classical and modern (see the Prologue)—that as the soul is trapped into a body and falls down into matter, the female half, or double, is left above in the spiritual realms, lamenting and searching for its mate. Not all of the soul can incarnate into a body; the part which is left above is the psyche. The birth of a soul into a body is thus a death from the spiritual point of view; to go into a physical body for incarnation, one must climb into a spiritual coffin.

They say that she learned afterward that the chest had been cast up by the sea in the land of Byblos and that the surf had brought it gently to rest in a heath tree. Having shot up in a short time into a most lovely and tall young tree, the heath enfolded the chest and grew around it, hiding it within itself. Admiring the size of the tree the king [of Byblos] cut off the vaulted part of the trunk which encompassed the coffin, which was not visible, and used it as a pillar to support his roof.

When we come to the coffin that has become embedded in a tree, we are, as any student of yoga would recognize, clearly in the realm of the esoteric physiology of the central nervous system. As the great initiate William Blake would describe it in his poem, "The Human Abstract,"

> The Gods of the earth and the sea
> Sought through nature to find this Tree;
> But their search was all in vain:
> There grows one in the Human brain.

*   *   *

The coffin is the Causal Body; the movement down the river of time is the descent through the intermediate realms, the astral plane; and the beaching upon the earth where it becomes embedded in a tree is the final process of incarnation in a physical body. The trunk of the tree is the spinal column of the animal, physical form. To appreciate the differences between the physical body and the subtle bodies, which is admittedly rather difficult for someone not trained in yoga or such syncretic movements as Theosophy, one has to realize that for the esoteric physiology of the Egyptian priests, there is more than the single physical body of modern materialistic science.

> When an Egyptian was born he was believed to possess a physical body (Khat) and an immaterial Double (Ka), which lived inside the body and was associated closely with the Ba, which dwelt in the heart, and which appears to have been connected with the Shadow of the physical body. Somewhere in the body lived the Khu or Spirit-soul, the nature of which was unchangeable, incorruptible and immortal. When the body died there could be raised from it by means of words, holy or magical, and ceremonies performed by priests, a Spirit-body called Sahu, which the Khu (Spirit-soul) could inhabit at pleasure.[13]

This bizarre assemblage of bodies would be baffling to any modern scholar whose knowledge of these things is limited within the forms of university research. In our broken culture those who have experienced the training of the yogic ashram are often woefully ignorant in the ways of the university, and vice versa. In ancient Egypt all knowledge was held in the schools of the temples, and initiation and education were not separate. In our world the most respected Egyptologists loathe and ignore the esoteric, and most often for good reason, for the occult bookshops are filled with works of psychic trash and comic book fantasies, but, unfortunately, when these admirable scholars come to analyse the religion itself, they must find themselves cut off from their subject. Consider the plight of Henri Frankfort, trying to make sense of the Ba and the Ka:

> When we attempt to describe the Egyptian's view of the human personality, the differences between his mental processes and our

own become particularly disturbing. We meet a number of Egyptian terms which stand in one context for qualities while they appear in another as independent spiritual entities . . . The notions "Ka" and "Ba" are of somewhat the same order. They are traditionally translated as "spirit" and "soul," and the Egyptians use them sometimes in the familiar sense which makes them appear subordinate to a larger whole, the human personality. At other times, however, they endow them with a degree of independence which seems to us meaningless.[14]

Any ordinary person who has ever floated out of his body during a nap knows what a Ba is, but unfortunately the dogmas of our materialistic culture constrain the person to ignore and repress his experience. The average person is afraid that such a common experience means that he is "splitting off" and becoming schizophrenic. On the other hand, those who do not repress these experiences often become so fascinated with them that they start dabbling with them in the worst possible fashion, in an occult, magical lust for psychic powers that has been unanimously condemned by all the great esoteric schools of Judaism, Christianity, Buddhism, Islam, and Hinduism. But in an integral civilization the temple initiate would undergo the training that would give him the proper balance between psychic and intellectual experience. Perhaps, if we are lucky, the next culture after ours will be able to create institutions where wisdom and knowledge, initiation and education can be brought together. The first step toward creating the preconditions for the emergence of such a culture is to recover the meaning of these old myths of Egypt, as the Egyptologist Schwaller de Lubicz worked to do at the temple of Luxor.[15]

The Ba is the etheric body, the subtle physical body which is closely associated with the physiological processes of the ordinary physical body. Like a transformer which takes in a powerful energy and then steps it down to make it available for work at a lower level, the etheric body takes in the *prana* (energy) or *Chi* upon which the health of the physical body depends. All contemporary practioners of Hatha yoga, Tai Chi Chuan, Shiatsu, or acupunture are familiar with this subtle body that the ancient Egyptians called the Ba. The Ba is intimately connected to the heart, and so in deep meditational states or trances, one must still the heart or place the body in a comatose condition, to separate the etheric body from the physical, to separate the Ba from the Khat.

The Ka is what is known as the astral body. This is the spiritual body a person has between incarnations. The etheric body is constructed by the astral body during the development of the fetus, and the etheric body lasts beyond the life of the physical body for only the magical three and one-half days, discussed in so many myths, as in "Inanna's Descent into the Nether World." In traditional cultures, where "second sight" was more normal and accepted, the people could see the surviving etheric body of the newly dead; funeral customs, like the traditional Irish wake, in which the dead person is praised and encouraged to move on, were not intended only for the mourners; they were intended for the specter, which in its recently dead state was lost and disoriented. A proper funeral was a way of preventing the formation of a ghost, for if the soul was satisfied and released, and its last attachment was relinquished, the etheric body could dissolve, and the astral body could move on into the spiritual realm, or into a new incarnation.

In clairvoyant cultures, and in lingering clairvoyant individuals in our own materialist culture, parents can feel the presence of the astral body of a soul attracted to their karmic relationship and attracted to their physical act of intercourse. If the parents accept the presence of that soul in its astral form, then the soul incarnates and from the karmic pattern of the three of them, it begins to meditate on its life to come, and this meditation on its destiny takes the form of the construction of the new etheric body.[16]

The Sahu is the Causal Body or Daimon, the integral being of all one's incarnations, the being that descends into the round of birth and death. The Causal Plane is the first level coming down in the Fall from pure, undifferentiated Being into the manifest universe. The realm of the astral plane is an intermediate realm; below is the world of matter, above is the world of pure Being. The astral plane is the world of psyche, the domain of the collective unconscious, the world explored by Jung, but the higher realm of the Causal Plane is the archetypal world of Plato's forms; it is a world of angelic intelligences, or principles and laws, which are the seeds or causes of manifestation. The bodies of angels are more like music than matter; they are more singing crystals of complex geometry and a thousand eyes than men of flesh with pigeon's wings. The Causal Plane is much more "real" than the shifting world of psyche; it is the realm of the Gods, not the gods of the astral plane, which are projections from the unconscious, but what the Egyptians called the Neteru.

The highest level of consciousness is with the Khu; this is what the Indians would call Atman. At this level we are dealing with a Divine realm in which the Spirit and God are One. The lower realms are worlds of cause and effect, of opposites and distinctions, but in the world of the Khu we can no longer use language to any effect. If one persists in trying to use language then one must either speak in paradox and oxymoron or become ensnared in absurdities like the question of how many angels can dance on the head of a pin, or of who is "right"—the Hindus with their vision of Atman, or the Buddhists with their vision of no Atman, anatama. There is no Atman, and there is. Language is useless here; one must have the experience. Too often the doctrinal theologian is the man who does not *know* what he is talking about. At this level Atman and Brahman are like a Klein bottle or a Möbius strip: there is no edge where one can say that this is Atman, but this is Brahman. The whole is in the part; the universe is a holograph. The Hindu would say Atman and Brahman are one; the Buddhist would say, "Form is not different from Emptiness, Emptiness is not different from Form."

But Brahman can veil itself through *maya* (illusion) to allow the Atman to project a Daimon, or Causal Body, down into the manifest world. This is the Fall from the One into the many. In the Cabbala this notion is described as God withdrawing so that Creation can take place. In Gnostic mythology the Fall would be described as the work of the Archons, the archangels of evolution who create the planet, the coffin of Osiris, or what the Cabbalists would call the original body of Adam, and thus encase the Being into physical time and space. The coffin of Osiris is the Causal Body; its journey on the river is the descent through the intermediate and watery realm of the psyche, the astral plane, and its eventual washing ashore, where it becomes embedded in the tree, is the final process of incarnation in a physical, terrestrial body.

That the tree is the central nervous system of the physical body becomes obvious when we examine the two most important symbols of the god, the sceptre of Osiris, and the Djed or Tet pillar.

> One of the earliest things associated with the worship and cult of Osiris was the object which is usually represented by the sign ☒ , and which is called "Tet." Many theories have been formulated about it, and many explanations of it given, but none is satisfactory from all points of view. The object is, in my opinion, the *sacrum* of Osiris ☒ , which was confused with a portion of the backbone and was therefore drawn as ☒ . . .
> At a very early period Osiris was assimilated to the Tet, and the ceremony of "setting up" the Tet became the equivalent of the reconstitution of the backbone and the body of Osiris generally.[17]

The base of the spine is considered extremely important in yoga, for it is considered the seat of *kundalini,* the serpent force which seals the subtle bodies to the physical. In raising the serpent-force one is able to reverse the power of *kundalini* to untie the seven knots, the *chakras,* which bind the subtle bodies to the physical. This enables the initiate to move, or expand, his consciousness into the other worlds. In the descent of *kundalini,* the soul incarnates, or Osiris becomes encased in the tree; in illumination, *kundalini* is raised, or the Tet is set up, and the higher body is reconstituted. As I have noted earlier, a subtle etheric channel is said to connect the sacrum with the seminal vesicles in the male, so in the practice of *kundalini* yoga, the *chela* is counseled to be celibate so that the *prana* can reverse its outward flow in sexuality and the generation of *karma,* to flow inward and upward through the spinal column into the brain. As this etheric energy floods the brain, the subtle centers in the brain are awakened, the "third eye" opens, and the *chela* has visions of the spiritual realms.

We have all long since forgotten why we call the base of the spine sacred with the word "sacrum," but the terms and images of this ancient system lie all about us, like the stones of an ancient temple next to a McDonald's stand in Rome. In the fascination with Indian mysticism which became popular in the sixties, this esoteric knowledge became more widely known; in fact, it became vulgarized and commercialized, and with some gurus we came close to having McDonald's of mysticism. Since the ancient civilization of Egypt is dead, but the ashrams of yoga are still flourishing, most people tend to associate this esoteric physiology exclusively with India, but both India and Egypt derive from an earlier initiatic tradition. Since the schools of Egypt and Mexico are gone, and since the esoteric knowledge is available through the gifts of a living India, it is necessary to have studied or received initiation in one of these yogic traditions to have more than an academic understanding of what the religion of Osiris is all about.

For example, one of the other important symbols in ancient Egyptian religion is the sceptre of Osiris. Whereas the Tet symbol focuses on the relationship of sexuality and esoteric practice, on the necessity of maintaining celibacy if one is to impregnate Isis so that she may give birth to the divine child, the sceptre of Osiris focuses on the spinal column and its relationship to the midbrain bridge. Ϟ The two prongs at the lower end of the sceptre indicate the two nerve channels, known in Sanscrit as the *ida* and the *pingala;* the staff of the sceptre represents the central channel inside the spinal column, the *sushumna. Chelas* of yoga are taught that *prana* enters the physical body from the back of the head at a point in the medulla oblongata. This point, like the two poles of a magnet, has a twin point in the third eye, the pineal gland. The pineal gland, an ancient, supposedly vestigal organ for sensing pulsations of light in the early mammals, receives a great deal of attention from yogis. Although the pineal gland is in the center of the brain, it is experienced as forward when one rolls his eyes upward in yogic meditation. From its central position, we can see that it is at the point that the three brains meet.[18] (Recall that Oedipus met his destiny and discovered the generator of his *karma,* his father, at the place where three roads met.) In the practice of yoga certain functions which were previously subconscious become open to consciousness; this opening of the subconscious is well pictured in certain Tibetan *tankas,* or in Western art, in the *Temptation of St. Anthony* paintings by Bosch and Grünewald. In a trained student of yoga this experience, though frightening, does not generate a psychotic break; in a neurotic person taking LSD, the sudden opening to subconscious material can indeed, and often has, generated a psychotic disintegration of the personality. Because the brain is what Aldous

Huxley called "a reducing valve" for shutting out the million signals a second that we receive, the brain shuts us into the few signals a second that we prefer to call "reality." When that function of suppression is suddenly suspended, and the individual is flooded with sensory signals and repressed psychic contents, he is overwhelmed by the serpent.

> During the early stages of Osiris' Underworld development Nehaher [the serpent] keeps the god closely enfolded; but when Osiris begins to revive, the serpent is an opponent to his recovery as a positive, active force. If Osiris is to "rise up" the serpent must be straightened out or overcome and chained down. The serpent is both protective and retarding.[19]

The reptilian brain, the oldest brain of evolution, the spinal brain, is the brain of the subconscious, the repository of the entire record of evolution, but that snake must be lifted up into consciousness for initiation. If a person is developed merely in an intellectual, ratiocinative way, then he will be a contradictory mix of cleverness and savagery. Such a man is dangerous to himself and his culture. As a leader such a person could become the kind of doctor who does research on electrical forms of torture or genocidal weapons. If the individual is not to become a twisted monster, he must learn to straighten out the serpent to allow the force to rise up the central channel of the sceptre of Osiris, the spinal column.

Here again, I would like to emphasize that this esoteric knowledge was at one time universal. Whether one is an ancient Mexican initiate of Quetzalcoatl, teaching the serpent how to fly, or a disciple of Moses and Isaiah and knows how to raise the serpent in the wilderness and "make straight in the desert a highway for our God," he is an initiate of the One. In the future, after the period of exoteric religious warfare has subsided, and after our global implosion of all the world's cultures has effected the transformation to a planetary culture, this relationship of the One and the many will be better understood. In the meantime individuals who do not understand the true meaning of their own religion kill members of other religions, whether it be Catholic against Protestant in Ireland, Christian against Moslem in Lebanon, Jew against Moslem in Israel, Hindu against Moslem in Pakistan, or Communist against all religions everywhere. These violent passions afflict us precisely because we train people to live by and through machines, but we do not educate them about the inner workings of the human soul.

When the instinctive and subconscious world of the snake is confronted in initiation, the vital force of the snake rises and floods the second brain, the midbrain, the limbic ring. This second brain is the old mammalian brain of "fight or flight"; it is the brain of passions and elemental sensations like smell. At this stage of meditative practice, the male *chela* finds himself experiencing erection or spontaneous orgasm, sudden bursts of tears and high emotional sensitivity, and peculiar sensations like the "smelling" of auras. Extroverted people will experience this stage of the energizing of the emotions and passions as reflected in the outside world of their relationships, their *karma;* introverts will experience a dissolving of the barriers between the physical and the astral planes. In either case this major transitional state is a dangerous period of instability. If the *chela* does not watch his emotions dispassionately but becomes identified with them and caught in them, then he can generate even more *karma* and ensnare others in his fantasies. Many individuals in our culture who feel this energy rushing up their spines mistakenly think that they are illuminated beings entitled to take on disciples. This stage of inflated feelings of power often generates the formation of unstable cults which catch an entire group in a collective delusion. The most caricatured form of this stage of inflation and delusion was expressed in the Guyana massacre of the cult of the Reverend Jim Jones.

The elevation of *kundalini* is not illumination, it is simply the beginning of initiation, not the end of it. A Zen master understands this very well, and his strategy for avoiding the excesses of inflation is to avoid all talk of psychic powers and yogic terminology, to ground the student in physical work and the intensely religious discipline of the monastery. Such discipline is prudent, for this stage of initiation is dangerous. The individual in the throes of this energy can be very charismatic.

I remember talking to one Christian monk who felt that the *purpose* of meditation was to develop psychic powers, and when he compared his glorious visions to the prosaic demeanor of his abbot he felt that he alone knew what It was all about. A good abbot would send such a man to clean the toilets, but this man felt put down by a mere priest who did not understand "the secrets," and so the monk quit the monastery and tried to become a teacher on the workshop circuits of the Human Potential Movement. In a similar way, Gopi Krishna, working alone without a guru or abbot, felt that he alone in the world knew "the secret of yoga" and proclaimed to an audience of a thousand in New York that he was the only man in the world who had experienced the elevation of *kundalini.*[20] Such intense inflation and narcissistic concern for the uniqueness of one's own emotions is characteristic of this second stage of initiation. In a true stage of illumination, however, one feels the universal compassion of unity with all sentient beings; one does not separate oneself from the rest of humanity in inflated feelings of glory and divine election. Such a person may make a dynamic leader of a cult, but he will not make a good abbot of a monastery of one of the great universal religions. Legend has it that when Genghis Khan reached the energizing stage of initiation, he killed his teacher so that he alone would have power over men and could conquer the world. A good abbot or *roshi* couldn't care less about power, and a truly enlightened philosopher-prince like the emperor Asoka of ancient India would become more interested in compassion for the suffering of humanity than in power over the states of the world.[21]

At least for the period of its greatness, before the decadence of its tradition, ancient Egypt had a priesthood within its temple schools that could overlook the educational process of initiation. When the initiate reached the second stage of energizing the' limbic ring of the midbrain, there were temple initiates who knew what personality changes he would go through and could steady him along the path. The sceptre of Osiris was said to symbolize power. Before a candidate could wield this sceptre with safety and wisdom, he had to understand that, for all the seductive glories of the psychic and all the inflated feelings of power, he was not at the end of the road, but at the beginning.

The third stage of initiation had to do with the development of "the higher mind," the *intellectus spiritualis,* as it was called by Joachim of Fiore. Through the opening of the third eye, the initiate begins to feel a unification of the three brains, and realms of rational thought in the neocortex begin to be balanced with the psychic sensitivities of the inner brain. Here the *chela* begins to pass beyond the shifting and illusory world of the pyschic, the astral plane with all its seductive glories and psychic powers, to the mental plane, which is the lower reaches of the Causal Plane. Here he experiences the archetypal world of music, mathematics, "the music of the spheres," and the Platonic world of archetypal forms. He passes beyond the projections and thought forms of his own creation to the wholly other and independent world of the angelic intelligences. From the experience of this realm in meditation, he is then able to return to the world and work in a grounded way upon the mastery of the physical in sacred architecture, mathematics, astronomy, music, and poetry. We see the expression of this higher mind embodied in the temples of Egypt, in the pyramids of Teotihuacan, and in our own Cathedral of Chartres and the music of Guillaume de Machaut.

Unfortunately, in moving from the sacred culture of Christendom to the secular culture of a commercial civilization, we lost the awareness of "the higher mind." The modern university-trained intellectual is something like a competitive weightlifter who develops his muscles to the extreme. It is fascinating to see that such growth is possible, but weightlifters, like Japanese Sumo wrestlers, are an abnormality that expresses the width of the cultural range. To be out of touch with one's body and one's emotions, concentrating solely on ratiocination, does not lead to wisdom or the true *intellectus spiritualis*. To develop the higher mind one must first lower himself to raise the serpent, or set up the Tet pillar of Osiris. One must face the subconscious, dispassionately observe the passions, and work with intelligence, charity, and humility on the stones of the temple. When one has the unity of the three brains well in hand, then he does indeed wield the sceptre of Osiris. The Tet is said to have symbolized stability, and the sceptre was said to have symbolized power. We can appreciate the wisdom of Egyptian civilization when we stop to think, for all our Harvards and MIT's, just now unstable all our power is.

The power of Osiris is so strong that it can become the pillar of society, and here the myth is marvelously perceptive. When the king of Byblos takes the coffin inside the tree and uses it to prop up his roof, he is acting as the ego in its kingly domain, using the gifts of the spirit to build a roof and block out the stars. Osiris, dead in his coffin and encased in the tree, becomes also encased in a social structure: the divine god in every person, through the Fall, becomes encased in an ego and held in place in a society of other egos. When our better half, our divine goddess, Isis, comes down in search of us, we are so dead that we cannot recognize her or remember where we came from.

> They say that Isis heard of this through the divine breath of rumor and came to Byblos, where she sat down near a fountain, dejected and tearful. She spoke to no one except the Queen's maids, whom she greeted and welcomed, plaiting their hair and breathing upon their skin a wonderful fragrance which emanated from herself. When the Queen saw her maids she was struck with longing for the stranger whose hair and skin breathed ambrosia; and so Isis was sent for and became friendly with the Queen and was made nurse of her child. . . .

It is important to notice that Isis does not invade the country and demand to be taken to the leader; she does not enter time on the terms of the ego, but she enters inconspicuously and consorts with servants. It is not the obvious sense of sight which identifies Isis's divinity, but the subtler, more ancient and animal sense of smell. A smell is a direct and innocent perception. The mind gets in the way of seeing, for one has to *know* what one is seeing; but one can experience a smell without really knowing what one is experiencing. So much older than language is this animal sense that it is hard to categorize smells; they are impossible to remember, and impossible to forget. A *vision* can be explained away as a fantasy or a dream, but a smell cannot; it simply *is*. When the *kundalini* is awakened and flowing into the midbrain, there are times when human auras are not seen but are smelled. These subtle and etheric odors are far more compelling than the odors of the physical body.

Modern man *looks* out at the world and interprets what he sees as objective and what he feels as subjective. Jung has noted that the unconscious expresses itself with numinosity through the individual's inferior function: if the person is intuitive and transcendental in personality, then the unconscious will announce itself through the body and animal instinct; if the person is highly rational, then the feelings will become the theatre of revelation.

Another archetypal pattern is expressed in the narrative at this point. In the Old Testament, Isaac, Jacob, and Moses all enter new lands or towns by coming to wells where they meet servant girls fetching water. This motif is picked up again in the New Testament in the scene where Jesus talks to the Samaritan woman at the well. Naturally, travelers coming to a new place would seek to refresh themselves at a well or fountain, but in myth no story ends at the literal level; every motif is an analogy for the parallel stream of the supernatural. Many different myths play with this water motif. We should remember that water springs up from unknown depths to sustain normal life on the surface, and that lowly servant girls who are either ignored or taken for granted are the ones who must draw the water. The fountain or the well represents a point where invisible energies flow into a society; in geomancy these would be known as "power points." Where these energies are, elementals or *genii loci* or nature spirits congregate. These creatures transform energy at their level and make it available for life on the physical level. The entire life of an area depends on these "fairies," and so when an initiate enters a place, he does not go to see the king, the royal ego who thinks that he is in charge; rather, he pays his respect to the angel of the place, the *genius loci*.[22] These beings then can more easily attune the stranger to the nature of the place, and so the stranger flows into the life of the community. Since to be a stranger in a strange land in ancient days could be a most dangerous state, the ancients developed their own, more psychic forms of passports.

> They say that Isis nursed the child, putting her finger in its mouth instead of her breast, but that in the night she burned the mortal parts of its body, while she herself became a swallow flying around the pillar and making lament until the queen, who had been watching her, gave a shriek when she saw her child on fire, and so deprived it of immortality.

The incommensurate relationship between society and the world of the gods, between the ego and the Daimon, are here expressed in the way the gift of the goddess is interpreted to be an attack. The ego would preserve itself and its kingdom, but the spirit would consume it in a flash. Since the kingdom is not open for the gifts of the gods, there is little that Isis can do but take Osiris back with her.

> The goddess then revealed herself and demanded the pillar under the roof. She took it from beneath with the utmost ease and proceeded to cut away the heath tree. This she then covered with linen and poured sweet oil on it, after which she gave it into the keeping of the king and queen. To this day the people of Byblos venerate the wood, which is in the temple of Isis. The Goddess then fell upon the coffin and gave such a loud wail that the younger of the king's sons died. The elder son she took with her, and placing the coffin in a boat, she set sail . . . As soon as she happened on a deserted spot, there in solitude she opened the chest and pressing her face to that of Osiris, she embraced him and began to cry. She then noticed that the boy had approached from behind and had observed her, whereupon she turned round and full of anger gave him a terrible look. The boy was unable to bear the fright, and dropped dead. . . .

The offspring of the king, the ego, are various sons, or thought forms; they have little substantial reality in and of themselves, but if they were given possession of the throne they could certainly continue the lineage of the ego. When the Daimon turns its glance from on high down onto these beloved offspring, they perish instantly. What would have to be interpreted as cruelty in a literal reading of the incident is a metaphor for spiritual counseling. The Vedic philospopher Patanjali says: "Let the seer slay reality, then slay the slayer." And in the *Bhagavad-Gita,* Krishna tells Arjuna to slay his relatives, meaning his *karma,* his relatedness in time. When spiritual knowledge is lost, then literal-minded fools go around slaying relatives or cutting out hearts and lifting them up to the sun.

> Having journeyed to her son Horus who was being brought up in Buto, Isis put the box aside, and Seth, when he was hunting by night in the moonlight, came upon it. He recognized the body, and having cut it into fourteen parts he scattered them.

In Plutarch's version of the myth it seems as if Horus is already born before Isis finds the coffin, but it is clear from an earlier New Kingdom hymn that Plutarch has confused the order of events.

When Isis finds the coffin she is not able to bring Osiris back to life, but she is able to revive him to the point that she raises up his phallus and inseminates herself with the child, Horus. A bas-relief from Abydos depicts the mummy of Osiris with Isis hovering, in the form of a falcon, above the erect phallus of the prostrate god.[23]

> Beneficent Isis, who protected her brother
>   and sought for him, she would
> take no rest until she had found him.
> She shaded him with her feathers and gave him air
>   with her wings.
> She cried out for joy and brought her brother to land.
> She revived the weariness of the Listless One
>   and took his seed into her body,
> [thus] giving him an heir.
> She suckled the child in secret, the place where
>   he was being unknown.[24]

The union of Isis and Osiris, like the union of Shiva and Shakti in yoga, is not a normal sexual union. The mortal child is born out of physical sexuality, the sexuality that generates *karma,* but the divine child is born from the union of the polarities of the subtle bodies. The union of the Fallen side of the being, the astral body, with the higher side, the Daimon or Causal Body, can engender the illuminated being who can become not the simple ego, the king of Byblos, but the great Being in time, the king of Egypt, Horus. But since the ruler of this world, the Archon, is Seth, the divine child cannot announce himself openly in the world; he must be "suckled in secret" and await the final agon between good and evil. Upon the outcome of that contest depends the entire destiny of the world.

That Seth is an Archon and a power from the days before civilization is clear, for he is presented as a hunter in the night. In finding the body of Osiris and cutting it into fourteen pieces, he is dismembering the moon and its fourteen pieces from the full to the new moon. Seth not only kills the spirit by entrapping it in space and time, but he also dismembers it into the fragmentary bits that are the incarnations of little personalities that live their fragmentary life one after the other in the sublunary world. To gather up the bits and pieces of our lives on the astral plane and fuse them into one integral being who sees beyond the limits of the life of one ego is the task for both Isis and Osiris.

As the moon disintegrates in the sky, it becomes the pieces of the god. At later times the temple astronomers would associate Osiris with Orion,[25] but in the earlier version, with its roots in the Upper Paleolithic cosmology, Osiris was the moon, and the Great Mother looking for her dismembered son-lover was Isis.

> When she heard of this, Isis searched for them in a papyrus boat, sailing through the marshes. That is why people who sail in papyrus skiffs are not harmed by crocodiles, which show either fear or veneration because of the goddess. From this circumstance arises the fact that many tombs of Osiris are said to exist in Egypt, for the goddess, as she came upon each part, held a burial ceremony. Some deny this, saying that she fashioned images and distributed them to each city, as though they were the whole body, so that he might be honored by more people and that Seth, if he overcame Horus, when he sought for the true tomb, might be baffled in his search because many tombs would be mentioned and shown. The only part of Osiris which Isis did not find was his male member; for it had been instantly thrown into the river and the lepidotus, phragus, and oxyrhynchus had eaten of it, fish which they most of all abhor. In its place Isis fashioned a likeness of it and consecrated the phallus, in honor of which the Egyptians even today hold festival.

In this part of the story we encounter some elements which reveal the Upper Paleolithic origins of the myth. Marshack has tried to interpret the iconography of phallus-shaped batons with fish engraved upon them, coming to the conclusion that "Fish, phallus and water seem aspects of a larger myth which apparently also included the 'goddess.'"[26] Erich Neumann has argued that the phallus really belongs to the Great Mother,[27] and that in various rituals the phallus of the dying male god would be severed and returned to her, or kept for the fertilization of the fields in the next year. The eunuch priests of Diana of Ephesus would castrate themselves so that they could offer their genitals on the altar of the goddess as discussed earlier. It seems that we are in this part of the myth seeing a civilized sublimation of the ancient custom where the phallus is still emphasized in its association with the Great Goddess, but in the case of Isis it is she who tries to reconstitute the phallus in a sublimed form. The physical penis is consumed by despicable fish, animals of the turgid depths, but the higher phallus, the image of resurrection through the goddess, is fashioned as a sacred icon. To complicate the matter further, there is probably an astronomical dimension to this myth. Perhaps the fishes swallowing the phallus would have to do with the moon in the sign of Pisces or, perhaps, an association with the stars in Orion. To understand all the dimensions of the myth of Isis and Osiris, a scholar would have to be an Egyptologist, a cultural historian, a psychologist, an astronomer, and an initiate of one of the major esoteric schools. Since it is rather difficult to master all these fields within a single lifetime, the student has to take his knowledge, as Isis does, in the pieces strewn about the historical landscape. The final work on astronomy and ancient myth remains to be written. The best the student can do now is to remind himself that when a myth expresses a bizarre event, the strange language may be a technical language directed specifically to initiates.

> There were other versions of what Horus could do for his father, the chief of which was that he could "open his mouth." This was performed by touching the mouth of Osiris with an adze which represented the Great Bear—a constellation that belonged to Seth— and with which, in a lost myth, he "opened the mouths of the gods." [28]

The cosmology expressed in Seth's dismemberment of Osiris is most ancient, but, of course, we have no way of knowing what "fish, phallus and water" meant to the Paleolithic hunters and gatherers. If we can judge from the scene from the pit at Lascaux, the tragic death of the male and his return to the Great Mother were associated with a fish taking the phallus back to the deep waters of the Mother. The myth painted on the wall was also painted on the sky, and so the movement of the constellations would tell the story of the rise and fall of the male god. In Neolithic agricultural societies, the sacrificed male and his remains were transferred to the fields needing fecundation, and there the Great Mother becomes the soil receiving the fertilizing blood.

> The dismemberment of Osiris and the theft of his phallus, later attributed to Set, are the most ancient portions of the fertility ritual.

Isis compensates for this by replacing the missing member with a wooden phallus and is thereupon impregnated by the dead Osiris. We can reconstruct the ritual thus: While the torn limbs of Osiris, scattered over the fields, guarantee the year's fertility, the phallus is missing. For Osiris is robbed of his phallus, which is embalmed and preserved until the next resurrection feast of fertility. But it was from this embalmed phallus that Isis conceives the child Horus. Hence, for this Horus, as well as for Horus the sun-god, it is more significant that Isis was his mother than that Osiris was his father.[29]

In Neumann's Jungian interpretation of the myth, Isis is herself the Terrible Mother, the castrator of Osiris; at a later stage of culture the mother's brother, the muscular arm of matriliny, Seth, takes over the task of castration and dismemberment. There is, however, no indication anywhere that Horus was conceived after the dismemberment. Since the bas-relief at Abydos (see Figure 19) shows Isis as a falcon hovering over the erect phallus of the mummy of Osiris and thereby conceiving Horus, I assume that Isis conceived the child after she recovered the corpse from Byblos, but before the dismemberment by Seth. The first death and entombment in the chest would indicate the Fall into the Causal Body; the journey on the river would indicate the descent through the astral, psychic realms; and the encasement in the tree would indicate incarnation in a physical, animal body. When Isis takes Osiris out of the tree and then unites with him in intercourse to conceive the divine child, it would indicate the union of the higher and lower parts of the self to give birth to an illuminated being. But Osiris in the astral plane is still not free, for Seth finds him there and dismembers him, subjecting his soul to many fragmentary incarnations before liberation can be achieved and the soul can mount the heavens to become a star. Seth, who first bound Osiris in a coffin, is binding Osiris into the astral plane, the *bardo* realm of the disincarnate; before Osiris can become the Lord of the Dead, he must become the master of this astral plane. The Goddess again comes to his rescue and pieces him together, but she cannot find his phallus, for disincarnate specters on the astral do not possess the physical organs of generation. They are attracted to couples in intercourse for they are attracted to the world of generation; this attachment to sexuality binds them to the wheel of birth and death, and so they reincarnate. The Goddess

Figure 19. Isis as falcon conceiving Horus on Osiris's bier, from Abydos.

alone cannot save Osiris, for the astral plane is an intermediate
realm, one without the definiteness of the physical plane or the
spiritual power of the Causal Plane. Liberation from the wheel of
birth and death cannot take place on the astral plane: a soul must
incarnate into a physical body if it is to gain liberation or *moksha*.
In terms of the myth, this means that Osiris must look to his son,
his incarnate descendent on the physical plane, to overcome Seth.
The individual must accept incarnation and not toy with the
illusory, psychic realm of the astral plane. All the great universal
esoteric schools in Buddhism, Hinduism, Judaism, Christianity,
and Islam insist that the fascination with psychic powers that first
overtakes the student when he is free to project out of his body is a
dangerous trap; the yogi must not indulge himself by playing with
psychic powers but must realize that he has a work to do in the
physical body. Only Horus can defeat Seth. Osiris can come in his
astral body to counsel Horus, but only Horus in his definite
physical body can overcome the Seth of the Causal Plane and

redeem the Fall by turning spiritual death and the cycle of birth and death into resurrection and spiritual liberation.

> Afterward Osiris came to Horus, it is said, from the underworld, and equipped and trained him for battle. Then he questioned him as to what he considered to be the finest action, and Horus said, "To succor one's father and mother when they have suffered wrong."

There are many levels flowing at once here. At the sociological level, Horus is expressing very radical ideas, for he is creating a relationship to the father and not the mother's brother. But this sociological level is itself a metaphor for the esoteric; the maternal realm is the matter that binds the soul; to discover one's father is to discover the soul's history before it fell under the dominance of the Archon, Seth. The lunar dismemberment of Osiris is a motif that goes back to the Paleolithic; the resurrection of Osiris is a Neolithic, agricultural motif, but the battle of the father's son against the mother's brother is a motif from the time of transition from the Neolithic village to civilization. In the richness and complexity of the myth, no earlier level is abandoned; all are included. Each succeeding level of culture surrounds and incorporates the previous one; thus a myth about the evolution of culture becomes itself a performance of the evolution of culture.

In the training of the son by the father we have an exoteric and an esoteric narrative. The exoteric is concerned with the shift from mother-right to father-right; the esoteric is concerned with evolution to a heightened individuality, the creation of an incarnate being on the physical plane who can eliminate human bondage to the disincarnate realms of death. The process of individuation and the process of civilization are thus parallel constructions; the "setting up" of the Tet (Djed) pillar of stability is the creation of a spinal column for the individual body, and the body-politic. The passive being of Osiris, "the Listless One," the adolescent son-lover of the Great Mother of Neolithic religion, must be succeeded by the dynamic man of action, the warrior-hero of civilization, Horus. Horus is the only one who can challenge that Gnostic Archon who has entrapped the whole human race. Thus Seth, the ancient figure of human beginnings, and Seth, the arm of the Neolithic matriarchy, are telescopes into one single reactionary figure.

Osiris asked him again what he considered to be the most useful animal for those going out to battle. When Horus replied, "The horse," he was surprised and he queried why he did not name the lion rather than the horse. Horus answered that the lion was helpful to someone in need of aid, but that the horse routed the fugitive and so destroyed completely the force of the enemy. Osiris was pleased on hearing this, thinking that Horus had adequately prepared himself. When many were coming over, as they say, to the side of Horus, there came also Thoueris, Seth's concubine; and a snake which pursued her was cut in pieces by the followers of Horus, for which reason they now throw out a piece of rope in public and cut it up.

The lion had once been *the* symbol of ferocious power, and for the shepherds afraid for their flocks, the lion was a powerful image of terror. The episode of Gilgamesh wrestling with two lions speaks for the incredible power of the hero. Osiris, as a man of the past, the man of the transition from village to civilization, would naturally still hold on to that traditional image of power. But in the New Kingdom, after the invasion of the Hyksos in their horse-drawn chariots, the horse became a more powerful image. The technological superiority of the invading barbarians was stunning; the chariot became the tank of its day, and a far more potent image of force. In Figure 20 we see Ramses II in his chariot. There the smaller lion is framed in the mighty legs of the horse; the lion is running to escape, not to give battle. And so Horus's celebration of the horse over the lion is one of the details in Plutarch's narrative that shows how the accretions of the millennia have attached themselves to this Roman narrative.

The battle then lasted for many days and Horus won. When Isis received Seth tied in bonds, she did not kill him, but freed him and let him go. Horus did not take this at all calmly, but laying hands on his mother he ripped off the crown from her head. Thoth, however, put on her instead a cow-headed helmet. When Seth brought a charge of illegitimacy against Horus, Thoth helped Horus, and the latter was judged by the gods to be legitimate. Seth was defeated in two other battles, and Isis, having sexual union with Osiris after his death, bore Harpocrates, prematurely delivered and weak in his lower limbs.

In the conflict between Seth and Horus the antagonism between matrilineal and patrilineal succession comes clearly out in the open. As the mother's brother, Seth is the power and force of the old ways; he, not the father, is the important masculine figure in society. In a version of the trial, preserved in a text from 1150 B.C., Seth does not want to have a trial by law, but a trial by combat, for the mother's brother is at the height of his powers while the son is a mere adolescent. To wait for the prince to grow up is to enjoy a period of weakness; Seth is all for force and is impatient with this new evolution to a higher stage of individuality and a higher stage of civilization.

> Then Seth, the strong one, the son of Nut, said: "As for me, I am Seth, the strongest of the Divine Company. Every day I slay the enemy of Rê when I stand at the helm of the Barque of Millions of Years, which no other god dare do. I am therefore worthy to receive the office of Osiris."
>
> Then they said: "Seth, the son of Nut, is right." But Onuris and Thoth raised their voices, calling: "Should one give the office to the

Figure 20. Ramses II in his war chariot, from Abu Simel.

mother's brother, while the direct son of Osiris' body is at hand?"
    Then the Ram of Mendes cried out: "On the contrary, should the
office be given to a mere lad while Seth, his elder relative, is at
hand?"[30]

It is not surprising that in Plutarch's narrative Isis still feels loyalty
to Seth and unties him, for Seth is of her family. When she
releases Seth, however, she shows evidence of her old history as
the Mother Goddess. But Horus will have no part of the pull back
into the ancient ways; he is no son-lover of the Neolithic Great
Goddess; he is Horus, the son of the father. Therefore he rips the
crown from his mother's head. In a revelation of Isis's ancient role
as the mother goddess, Thoth places the cow's head on her as her
crown. Evidentally the ancient tidal pull of the blood is too much
for Isis and she cannot wholly side with Horus, and so the
patriarchal revolution is effected by Horus alone. The mother
goddess is demoted. True, the patriarchal revolution is not as
violent in ancient Egypt as in Sumer, for there is more of a balance
between Isis and Osiris than with either the female dominance of
Inanna over Dumuzi, or the male dominance of Enki over Inanna
or of Gilgamesh over Ishtar; nevertheless, Egypt too is deciding
that the process of individuation and civilization expresses a
breaking away from the feminine to the masculine.
    But if we only interpret the myth in the sociological terms of the
shift from mother-right to father-right, from Neolithic village with
its suppression of the individual to the collective, we miss the other
voices of the polyphonic fugue. When Isis releases Seth she is
expressing the higher feminine wisdom that Seth and Osiris are
not enemies but polarities; they are the twin polarities of the
manifest universe. Horus could not exist as a consciousness in a
physical body if Seth had not originally trapped Osiris in the
coffin. Like the opposition of Christ and Lucifer in esoteric
Christianity, or the opposition of Quetzalcoatl and Tezcatlipoca in
Mexican mythology, Seth and Osiris are twin poles of the
Demiurge who is the artificer of the manifest universe. Isis, in
refraining from killing Seth, knows that Seth can never be killed
until the entire physical universe is consumed. It is for this reason
that, in other versions of the myth, Seth is given the task of being
the boat on the Nile that must carry the bier of Osiris, or being the

prow of the boat of the sun god, Ra. If Horus becomes not merely definitely incarnate but filled with passion, limitation, and ignorance, then the danger is that the ego will repress the esoteric, and that civilization will eliminate all knowledge of the history of the soul. To prevent that collapse, Thoth replaces the crown on Isis, but this time the crown is the most ancient crown of all, a reminder of the old Paleolithic religion of the Great Goddess.

The new balance struck in favor of individuation and civilization is a delicate one, and the slightest shift in emphasis can ruin it. The evolution from matriarchy to patriarchy is a movement from blood revenge and the pressure of the clan to the rule of law and the freedom of the city. But if the feminine is totally repressed and blood, nature, and the esoteric dimension of the heavens totally wiped out, then a terrible situation is created which will necessitate the appearance of another avatar of evolution, a Lilith of transformation through destruction. But that is to rush ahead in the story from Egyptian civilization to our own.

In the liberation of the son from his dependency on the Great Mother is a celebration of the process of individuation. In the rise of Osiris as Lord of the Dead, or guardian deity or tutelary spirit of the astral plane, is the liberation of humanity from the Fall and the establishment of an opening of the astral plane through which humanity can make its way, as individuated souls, to the Great Liberation. As lord of the astral plane, Osiris supervises the interaction of sun and earth which enables all things to grow, but he is also the savior who, through the mysteries expressed in the Egyptian *Book of the Dead,* offers the way out of the intermediate realms of the disincarnate spirits. Lest one think that I am projecting a Buddhist religious vision onto ancient Egypt, it is worthwhile to consider the Egyptologist Rundle Clark's analysis of a painting inside an Egyptian coffin.

So far this coffin has been described as a series of separate and unrelated mythological pictures. If, however, they are interpreted from the bottom upwards, we are given a scheme of the salvation of the soul. In the tomb the soul lies together with its body in the darkness of the mummy-case. It is immobile and helpless, without the distinction of a head, and has to be protected by the serpent and its attendant demons. Nevertheless it is a potentiality, for out of it rises the beetle, the sign for "form" and "coming into being." In the next, the Osirian stage, the night sun penetrates to the Underworld and its rays fall upon the soul in its new form as the body of Osiris. As in the life of nature, where Osiris is the potential life in the earth and the solar rays call forth the vegetation, so the soul can say:

> "I am the plant of life which grows
> through the ribs of Osiris."

But in the next scene the Osirian fate is transcended. The symbol of the rising soul has now become the sun as it mounts above the eastern horizon, adored by the morning stars. Then in Nut and Hikê diagrams we have the breaking of light into the world and the sailing of the sun in its true day-form as Rê. Finally, in the top picture of all, the sun is Universal God, persisting through all his forms, whether by day or night, cosmic and universal.[31]

Through the triumph of Horus, that definite, individuated being, the king of the world, Osiris is raised up to open a way out through the astral plane. With Horus as master of the physical plane, and Osiris as master of the astral plane, humanity is no longer imprisoned by matter. The Fall is reversed in the ascent. Manifestation becomes the vehicle for the resurrection, but in this mystery it is the total quaternity of Isis and Osiris, Seth and Horus that is required to express the nature of the evolution of the human soul. Seth creates the coffin, and then it floats upon his back; the movement from Seth as creator of the coffin to Seth as the bearer of Osiris is the basic enantiodromia in which the Fall becomes the Resurrection. Seth is not a being to be destroyed, for he is the principle of limitation, of measurement into form. For all his terrifying nature, Seth is the necessary archangel of human evolution.

The whole myth is an explanation of the mystery of incarnation. One form of intercourse between Isis and Osiris generates the divine child and king of this world, Horus, but another form of intercourse generates Harpocrates. As I would interpret the myth, when Isis releases Osiris from the tree, she has intercourse with him in her epiphany as a bird and conceives the falcon-god, Horus. When, after the dismemberment of the corpse by Seth (its restriction to the astral plane), she cannot find the phallus of Osiris, so she has intercourse with the wooden phallus and conceives Harpocrates. The union of the spiritual with the shifting and illusory psychic realm of the astral does not generate an illuminated and liberated being, for Harpocrates is born prematurely with an undeveloped physical body, and his limbs are so weak that he cannot stand upon the hard and definite matter of earth. That there is wisdom in this little vignette which Plutarch tacks on in the final clause of the last sentence would be recognized by any abbot of a contemplative school. Those meditators who become absorbed in a psychic rapture or become fascinated with gazing at auras, mind reading, visions, and out-of-the-body travel do not become illuminated beings. They simply become hedonists of the astral realm, just as their fellows in the outside world are hedonists of the physical realm. In the wisdom of Zen Buddhism, the initiates are put to work to ground their meditation, for the last stage of Buddhist enlightenment, as expressed in the famous ox-herding pictures, is not to remain absorbed in *samadhi* but to return to the city "with bliss-bestowing hands." One returns to where one started, but not at the same level of the spiral, for the Resurrection of the Body means that one is able to carry to the heavenly realm the wisdom of the Fall into time. In the return of the prodigal son to the father, the son is taken back and honored almost above the loyal son who never fell. The angels remain with God the Father and do not fall into an animal body in physical time and space, but when a human being is able to liberate his consciousness from that physical entrapment and reascend to the heavenly realms, he is honored almost above the angels. And so it is that the time light bodies took to fall becomes the time falling bodies take to light.

PART FOUR

The Myth Beyond History

The Time Falling Bodies
Take to Light

MYTH IS THE HISTORY of the soul. The history of the ego, with its succession of kings and empires, technologies and wars, is what we are all taught in school. As the lie commonly agreed upon, history becomes the apology for whatever class is in power or wishes to come to power. In our age a class of behavioral and political scientists hopes to wield power over nature and culture, and through genetic engineering and sociobiology to alter the natural selection of the body and the artificial selection of culture to create a perfect, scientific society—rationally planned and rationally managed. Myth and religion, as the old ancestral heritage from the dark ages before the rise of the Technological Society, stand in the way, and so the social scientists have rewritten history to bring it under their control. The history of the soul is obliterated, the universe is shut out, and on the walls of Plato's cave the experts in the casting of shadows tell the story of *Man's* rise from ignorance to science through the power of technology. From the raising of children through the techniques of behavioral modification in the elementary schools to the philosophical indoctrination of students in graduate schools, a class of behavioral scientists has positioned itself at the strategic places of power in our secular society. As psychologists, they are our Thought Police; as professors, they are our Cultural Police; as consultants to government, they are the legislators who empower the Police. Small wonder that when these social scientists write history, they write only a history of economics and technology.

The re*vision*ing of history is, therefore, a revolutionary act. It challenges the legitimacy of a description of reality, and the class of scribes who write that description. If this sounds Marxist it is because I have kept the form of Marx's sociology of knowledge but turned the old man on his head, for in that position he can better converse with the Hegel he himself turned upside down. In challenging the narrative of human origins given to me by the sociobiologists, I am also challenging their narrative of the future of human civilization. At one edge of history or the other, I would prefer to show that the history of their construction is a Hollywood stage set; at either end of the street the ancient stars can be found marking the time the civilization has left before its two-dimensional vanities collapse.

The revisioning of history is, therefore, also an act of prophecy—not prophecy in the sense of making predictions, for the universe is too free and open-ended for the manipulations of a religious egotism—but prophecy in the sense of seeing history in the light of myth. Technological Man has consciously excluded myth from his consciousness; this has brought him back under the sway of the collective *un*conscious. He feels a strong motivation to travel in space, to escape the confinement of mother earth, to rebuild his own version of nature and culture in the imagined total freedom of a space colony. In his utopian fantasy of technology, he creates a mirror-image of the utopian who hopes to find total freedom by escaping society and returning to nature. But in the jungle of Guyana with Reverend Jim Jones, or in the space colonies of NASA, "man" will painfully discover that wherever he goes, he brings his evil along with him.

In the classical era the person who saw history in the light of myth was the prophet, an Isaiah or Jeremiah; in the modern era the person who saw history in the light of myth was the artist, a Blake or a Yeats. But now in our postmodern era the artists have become a degenerate priesthood; they have become not spirits of liberation, but the interior decorators of Plato's cave. We cannot look to them for revolutionary deliverance. If history becomes the medium of our imprisonment, then history must become the medium of our liberation; (to rise, we must push against the ground to which we have fallen). For this radical task, the boundaries of both art and science must be redrawn. *Wissenschaft* must become *Wissenkunst*.

What I am talking about is the resacralization of culture and, in particular, the resacralization of scholarship. I am talking about a movement from ratio to Logos. Under the sway of ratio, a unit is uniform and capable of measurement and mass production; in the light of Logos, each being is unique and yet capable of universal expression. In *Wissenschaft* you train a neutral observer to read a meter with objectivity; all observers everywhere should see the same event and describe it in the same way. In *Wissenkunst* the historian, like the musical composer, creates a unique narrative of time, and in this unique narrative the reader recognizes the universal truth of events. The art of *Wissenkunst* comes from research, for the historian is not free to make up characters and events any more than Aeschylus was free to invent Agamemnon and the Trojan War. In such a narrative, history loses the characteristic absolutism of science and religion; the reader is under no cultural compulsion to *believe in* what he reads, for what he reads is offered in the freedom of imaginative reception that characterizes artistic expression. As in the fictional histories of Jorgé Luis Borges or Stanislaw Lem, the boundaries between truth and fiction are intentionally blurred for the best of artistic and epistemological reasons.

A leader of a cult, whether the cult is religious, political, or scientific, says: "I have the Truth; follow me!" But the *Wissenkunstler* knows that no one can monopolize the Truth. The Truth cannot be expressed in an ideology, for the Truth is that power which overlights the conflict of opposed ideologies. And so the *Wissenkunstler* does not seek to turn his narrative into an apology for a new cult or the propaganda for an aspiring class of priests in a new theocracy. As a revolutionary act of prophecy in an age of political science, *Wissenkunst* is a unique and anarchic expression of freedom, and not a new and aspiring system of indoctrination. If *Wissenkunst* is itself turned into political apologetics, then the fabulous plumed serpent is turned into a monster, a basilisk.

To study myth one must go to a different kind of school from our universities, but the ancient schools are long since gone. Vibrating in another ether, the mystery schools are made out of music, not matter. To go there to study myth, one has to be drawn out of the body in sympathetic resonance with what it is. If one has never floated out of the body in meditation or sleep, then one should be disqualified from writing explanations of Egyptian religion with its Khat, Ba, Ka, Sahu, and Khu. We have built up a materialistic civilization that is concerned almost exclusively with technology, power, and wealth, but the ancient Egyptians built up an entire civilization concerned, almost exclusively, with the psychic and the evolution of the human body as a vehicle for Illumination. The states of consciousness and the psychic experiences which are marginal for us were central for them. What we repress or ignore as a distraction from our proper attention on the physical, or as a possible seductive diversion from our central task of the conquest and domination of nature, or as a path to madness and schizophrenia, was to the ancient Egyptians the *donnée* of human consciousness that had to be dealt with if humanity was to understand its place in the cosmos. Cultures, like artists, focus on different subject matters and media of expression; some develop mastery over the subtle bodies, others choose to build rockets and walk in space suits on the moon. Each culture casts its own shadow, a shadow which is a perfect description of its own form and nature.

The shadow which our technological civilization casts is that of Lilith, "the Maid of Desolation" who dances in the ruins of cities. Now that we have made a single polluted city of the entire world, she is preparing to dance in the ruins of our planetary megalopolis. When man will not deal with Isis, through the path of initiation, he must deal with Lilith. The coming years of the nineteen eighties will be an explanation of this ancient myth.

When we have moved beyond the desolation of all our male vanities, from the stock market to the stock pile of rockets, we will be more open and receptive. Open and bleeding like that archaic wound, the vulva, we will be prepared to receive the conception of a new civilization. Perhaps if we are blessed by the old gods in the next civilization that will follow after this one has played itself out we will come to appreciate "the ancient and forgotten wisdom." In the temple schools of Egypt, evolution was lifted up into a conscious process. The architecture of the central nervous system and the architecture of the temple were so related that the initiate could turn on the spiral to face back from whence he had come, in order to better understand the direction in which he had to go. The temple school was another kind of vehicle for traveling in space and time. The rocket creates all hell below to hurl itself into an abstract and vacuous heaven, but the Egyptian knew that he had to turn to face the instinctive, to lift it up so that masculine transcendence and feminine immanence could become one. He knew that without such internal transmutation he only created his own external destruction.

Lilith has returned. To effect a reconciliation with her, man must not seek to rape the feminine and keep it down under him. If he seeks to continue his domination of nature through genetic engineering and the repression of the spiritual, he will ensure that the only release from his delusions can come from destruction. Lilith will then dance in the ruins of Western civilization. But if man can accept initiation to see that Lilith is his long-lost primordial wife, then the energies of destruction can be transmuted and taken up into the creative destructuring of the old civilization, the industrial civilization that humanity has already outgrown.

Myth, as a history of the soul, is still a history, and each stage of the evolution of consciousness generates its appropriate story. As the spiral of history turns, one archetypal story becomes the recapitulation of the old, the performance of the new, and the overture to what is to come. As a story, the myth of Isis and Osiris is a recapitulation of the myth of the Neolithic Mother Goddess and the dying adolescent son-lover, but in the case of Isis and Osiris, where the lovers are brother and sister, the relationship between the feminine and the masculine is becoming more equal. In the early stages of evolution, nature dominates the human being, the planet dwarfs the tiny human species, but as civilization emerges, the masculine grows to a new level, and so the feminine responds to meet it on that level. The Great Goddess becomes Isis. The story grows from Lascaux to Çatal Hüyük to Abydos, but it does not end there.

The story of Isis and Osiris is an overture to the story of Mary and Jesus. The dead son in the arms of his mother pictured in the famous *Piéta* of Michelangelo is a recapitulation of the ancient theme of the dying male god and the Paleolithic Goddess. But the finishing of a story is also its consummation. In giving his mother away to John while he is dying on the cross, Jesus is preparing to effect his own resurrection. This time it is not the Goddess Isis who raises up the phallus of the dead Osiris to conceive the divine child; the resurrection is not merely the god becoming the Lord of the Dead on the astral plane. This time an integral being incarnates on the physical plane, takes on the entire mystery of death in the mortal physical body, and rises from the dead on the physical plane. Osiris expresses initiatic mastery of the astral plane, but Jesus expresses initiatic mystery of the physical plane through the mystery of a conscious death.

Mary Magdalen is the first to see the resurrected body of Jesus, and in that coupled image of the avatar and the whore is the overture to what is to come in the next world-epoch. As the whore, Mary Magdalen expresses the presence and consummation of the archaic feminine heritage and its transmutation into the archetypal androgyne of the future. Peter, the orthodox and conventional Jew, would exclude Mary Magdalen from the mysteries, but Jesus sees sexuality in a totally different light.

> Simon Peter said to them, "Let Mary leave us, for women are not worthy of Life."
>
> Jesus said, "I myself shall lead her in order to make her male, so that she too may become a living spirit resembling you males. For every woman who will make herself male will enter the Kingdom of Heaven.[1]

Jesus does not mean that women should become like men but that, in the process of initiation, each sex must take on the character of the opposite, before wholeness can be achieved.

> Jesus said to them, "When you make the two one, and when you make the inside like the outside, and the outside like the inside, and the above like the below, and when you make the male and the female one and the same, so that the male be not male nor the female female; and when you fashion eyes in place of an eye, and a hand in place of a hand, and a foot in place of a foot, and a likeness in place of a likeness, then will you enter [the Kingdom].[2]

Mary Magdalen, the surviving form of the ancient temple prostitute, becomes the initiate of Jesus. This radical vision of Jesus is troublesome for the orthodox Peter, and equally troublesome for the orthodox Paul—so much so that Paul will revert to conventional Judaism in his vision of women.[3] But John is not the conventional orthodox Jew, and it is John and Mary Magdalen who stand at the foot of the cross, and it is Mary Magdalen who first sees the resurrected Jesus, and it is John whose understanding can outrace Peter's to see the meaning of the empty tomb.[4] John and Mary Magdalen stand at the foot of the cross, for in the next turn of the spiral their story is to become the historical performance of the eternal myth.

> Those who neither see nor name the place of stillness will much less see the Lord. The uniform throng round the cross signifies the lower nature. And if those whom thou seest by the cross have as yet no single form, then all the parts of him who descended have not been gathered together.[5]

Here, in the apocryphal Acts of John, Jesus alludes to the old mystery of the gathering of the pieces of Osiris at the same time that he announces the doctrine of the Mystical Body of Christ and looks forward to the next world-epoch, the next Platonic Month.

> But when the nature of mankind has been taken up and a generation of men moved by my voice comes close to me, thou [John], who hearest me now, wilt have become the same and that which is will no longer be.[6]

Isis and Osiris are the avatars of one Platonic Month, Jesus and Mary of another. In the Gospel of John, Jesus tells Peter that John is to tarry until he comes again. That is, John is to join the tradition of Melchizedeck, Enoch, and Elijah, of men who do not die but are taken up into Heaven. The Apocryphal Acts of John expresses the Gnostic and docetist heresy of distinguishing the Cosmic Christ from Jesus the Christ. What Jesus is saying to John in this heretical vision is that at the end of our world-epoch, John will be raised to the level of avatar to become what Jesus was in his Platonic Month of two thousand years.

If in the practice of Tantric yoga, one looks into the collective unconscious now, one will see a triptych, something like the Grünewald's Isenheim altarpiece, vibrating in the ether of the astral plane. In one panel we see a painting of the feminine lamenting the fall of the masculine into time; it is a painting of Isis crying above the coffin of Osiris. In the second panel we see the dead masculine in the arms of the feminine, Jesus in the arms of Mary. In the third panel we see neither the Fall nor the Crucifixion but the sacred copulation (*hieros gamos*) of the reunited young lovers. Once it was physical death and crucifixion which nailed consciousness down into matter; then it was a sacrament of Thanatos; but in the world-epoch about to begin it is a sacrament of Eros, a physical sexuality in which the lovers of eternity give birth to the world on the physical plane. The avatars of the New Age, as the Irish mystic A. E. realized in a vision fifty years ago,[7] will not be the solitary male, but the male and the female together.

Myth is the history of the soul. Lest we think that Isis and Osiris, or Jesus and Mary, are only stories from the past, we should look around us to see that a new chapter is being written in our own time. Whatever names these two lovers take, when they come together it will be like the touch of matter and antimatter, the passing and the consuming passion of our world. In the origins of civilization is the overture to its end.

NOTES

Prologue: The Time Light Bodies Took to Fall

1. See Stockhausen, *Sirius* and the author's discussion of the composer's *Jahreslauf* in *Lindisfarne Letter* 10 (West Stockbridge, Mass., Spring 1980).
2. *The New Science of Giambattista Vico*, ed. T. G. Bergin and M. H. Fisch (Ithaca, N.Y., Cornell University Press, 1970), p. 27.
3. See Doris Lessing, *Shikasta* (New York, Knopf, 1979); Jonathan Cott, *Stockhausen: Conversations with the Composer* (New York, Simon & Schuster, 1973); and David Spangler, *Revelation: The Birth of a New Age* (San Francisco, Rainbow Bridge, 1974).
4. See Carlos Castaneda, *A Separate Reality* (New York, Simon & Schuster, 1971), p. 131.
5. See Claude Lévi-Strauss, *The Savage Mind* (University of Chicago Press, 1966), p. 237.
6. Claude Lévi-Strauss, "The Structural Study of Myth," in *Structural Anthropology* (New York, Basic Books, 1958), p. 58.
7. See Gershom B. Scholem, "The Relationship Between Gnostic and Jewish Sources," in *Jewish Gnosticism, Merkabah, Mysticism and Talmudic Tradition* (New York, Jewish Theological Seminary, 1965), p. 74.
8. *The Collected Poems of W. B. Yeats* (New York, Macmillan, 1957), p. 211.
9. Claude Lévi-Strauss, "The Structural Study of Myth," op. cit., p. 58.
10. Edmund Leach, *Genesis as Myth* (London, Jonathan Cape, 1969), p. 7.

11. Robert Graves and Raphael Patai, *Hebrew Myths: The Book of Genesis* (New York, McGraw-Hill, 1966), p. 12.
12. Ibid., p. 82.
13. A. N. Whitehead, *Process and Reality* (New York, Macmillan, 1929), p. 135.
14. Paul D. Maclean, "New Findings Relevant to the Evolution of Psychosexual Functions of the Brain," *Journal of Nervous and Mental Disease,* Oct. 1962, pp. 295, 296.
15. Norman O. Brown, *Love's Body* (New York, Vintage, 1968), p. 136.
16. Some yogis describe this feeling as if the semen literally went up the spinal column, but I feel that notion expresses "misplaced concreteness." However, readers may wish to compare Gopi Krishna, *Kundalini: The Evolutionary Energy in Man* (Berkeley, Shambala, 1971) with Muktunanda, *Guru* (New York, Harper & Row, 1972), p. 85.
17. Raphael Patai, *The Hebrew Goddess* (New York, Avon, 1978), p. 184.
18. See Penelope Shuttle and Peter Redgrove, *The Wise Wound:Menstruation and Everywoman* (London, Victor Gollancz, 1978).
19. John Updike, *Couples* (New York, Knopf, 1968), p. 435.
20. Marija Gimbutas, *The Gods and Goddesses of Old Europe* (London, Thames & Hudson, 1974), p. 152.
21. Frank Waters and White Bear Fredericks, *Book of the Hopi* (New York, Ballantine, 1969), p. 8.
22. Delia Goetz, Sylvanus Morley, and Adrian Recinos, *The Popul Vuh: The Sacred Book of the Quiche Maya* (Norman, University of Oklahoma Press, 1950), p. 86.
23. G.R.S. Mead, *Fragments of a Faith Forgotten* (New York, University Books, 1960), p. 188.
24. Elaine Pagels, *The Gnostic Gospels* (New York, Random House, 1979), p. xxvi.
25. See Jess Stearn, *The Sleeping Prophet* (New York, Doubleday, 1967).
26. H. C. Randall-Stevens, *Atlantis to the Latter Days* (London, Camelot Press, 1966), p. 123.
27. Hans Jonas, *The Gnostic Religion* (Boston, Beacon, 1963), p. 122.
28. Rudolph Steiner, *Cosmic Memory: Prehistory of Earth and Man* (Steiner Publications, West Nyack, N.Y., 1961), pp. 88–93.
29. Marija Gimbutas, op. cit., p. 152.
30. Isaiah 40:3. For an analysis of Exodus as an allegory of initiation, see the author's *Prophecy and Revolution: Five Lectures on the Old Testament* (Lindisfarne Tapes, West Stockbridge, Mass., 1977).
31. Zenna Henderson, *Pilgrimage: The Book of the People* (New York, Avon, 1961).
32. As quoted in Werner Heisenberg, *Physics and Beyond* (New York, Harper & Row, 1971), p. 102.

Chapter One: Hominization

1. E. O. Wilson, *Sociobiology: The New Synthesis* (Cambridge, Harvard University Press, 1975), pp. 4, 547, 562, 563.
2. Ibid., p. 315.
3. H. C. Randall-Stevens, *Atlantis to the Latter Days* (London, Camelot Press, 1966), pp. 117, 118.
4. See, for example, David Clark, "Our Inconstant Sun," *New Scientist,* January 18, 1979, 168–170; also David Clark, Gary Hunt, and William McCrea, "Celestial Chaos and Terrestrial Catastrophes," *New Scientist,* Dec. 14, 1978, pp. 861–863.
5. Barbara Tuchman, *A Distant Mirror: The Calamitous Fourteenth Century* (New York, Knopf, 1979); and Doris Lessing, *Shikasta* (New York, Knopf, 1979).
6. Claude Lévi-Strauss, *The Savage Mind* (Chicago, University of Chicago Press, 1966), p. 11.
7. J. Maynard Smith, *The Evolution of Sex* (Cambridge, Cambridge University Press, 1978), p. 7.
8. See "Sociobiology Is a Political Issue" by Joseph Alber, Jon Beckwith, and Lawrence G. Miller in *The Sociobiology Debate,* ed. Arthur L. Caplan (New York, Harper & Row, 1978), pp. 476–487.
9. E. O. Wilson, op. cit., p. 315.
10. For a sociobiological discussion of the preeminence of female reproductive strategies, see Fred Hapgood, *Why Males Exist: An Inquiry into the Evolution of Sex* (New York, William Morrow, 1979).
11. Gregory Bateson, *Steps to an Ecology of Mind* (New York, Ballantine, 1972), p. 410.
12. E. O. Wilson, op. cit., p. 314.
13. D. H. Lawrence, *Twilight in Italy* (New York, Viking, 1962), pp. 73, 74.
14. Fred Hapgood, op. cit., p. 38.
15. Sarah Blaffer-Hrdy, *The Langurs of Abu: Female and Male Strategies of Reproduction* (Cambridge, Harvard University Press, 1977), pp. 304, 308.
16. Ibid., p. 109.
17. James H. Barkow, "Culture and Sociobiology," *American Anthropologist,* Vol. 80, No. 1 (March 1978), p. 8.
18. Francisco Varela, *Principles of Biological Autonomy* (New York, Elsevier-North Holland, 1979), p. 39.
19. Werner Heisenberg, *Physics and Philosophy* (New York, Harper & Row, 1958), p. 58.
20. Sarah Blaffer-Hrdy, op. cit., p. 278.
21. Gregory Bateson, "The Thing of It Is" in *Earth's Answer* (New York, Lindisfarne/Harper & Row, 1977), p. 147.
22. E. O. Wilson, op. cit., p. 562.
23. Ibid., p. 554, 555.

24. Carl Sagan, *The Dragons of Eden* (New York, Random House, 1977), p. 138.
25. E. O. Wilson, p. 316.
26. Jane van Lawick-Goodall, *In the Shadow of Man* (New York, Dell, 1971), p. 66. See also her "Cultural Elements in a Chimpanzee Community" in *Precultural Primate Behavior*, ed. E. W. Meazil (S. Karger, Basel, 1973).
27. Ibid., p. 94.
28. "Animal Behaviorist Finds Chimpanzees Take Others' Lives," *The New York Times*, April 20, 1978, p. A19.
29. Lawick-Goodall, op. cit., p. 208.
30. Ibid., p. 192.
31. Frederick Engels, *Origins of the Family, Private Property and the State* in *The Selected Works of Karl Marx and Frederick Engels* (Moscow, Progress Publishers, 1968), pp. 468–593.
32. Charles F. Hockett and Robert Ascher, "The Human Revolution" in *Man and Adaptation: The Biosocial Background* (Chicago, Aldine, 1968), pp. 215–228.
33. Richard E. Leakey and Roger Lewin, *Origins* (New York, Dutton, 1977), p. 68.
34. Lawick-Goodall, op. cit., pp. 135, 136.
35. E. O. Wilson, op. cit., p. 569.
36. See Edmund Leach, *The Structural Study of Myth and Totemism* (London, Tavistock, 1967); also his *Genesis as Myth* (London, Jonathan Cape, 1969).
37. Robin Fox, "Totem and Taboo Reconsidered" in *The Structural Study of Myth and Totemism* (London, Tavistock, 1967), p. 161.
38. Elaine Morgan, *The Descent of Woman* (New York, Bantam, 1973).
39. E. O. Wilson, op. cit., pp. 28, 29.
40. Robert Ardery, *African Genesis* (New York, Dell, 1961).
41. C. D. Darlington, *The Evolution of Man and Society* (New York, Simon & Schuster, 1969), p. 49.
42. Glynn Isaacs, "The Food-Sharing Behavior of Proto-Human Hominids," *Scientific American*, April 1978, Vol. 238, No. 4, pp. 90–108.
43. Lionel Tiger, *Men in Groups* (New York, Vintage, 1970), p. 62.
44. Norman O. Brown, *Love's Body* (New York, Vintage, 1968), p. 136.
45. See *The Complete Book of Erotic Art*, ed. Drs. Phyllis and Eberhard Kronhausen (New York, Dell, 1978).

Chapter Two: Symbolization

1. For a scientific and nontheological description of the creation of the universe, see Steven Weinberg, *The First Three Minutes: A Modern View of the Origin of the Universe* (New York, Basic Books, 1977).

2. See Gregory Bateson, *Mind and Nature: A Necessary Unity* (New York, E. P. Dutton, 1979).

3. See the description of a swami's visit to the saint in *Autobiography of a Yogi*, Paramahansa Yogananda (Los Angeles, Self Realization Fellowship, 1968), p. 368.

4. A. N. Whitehead, *Science and the Modern World* (New York, Free Press, 1967), p. 79.

5. Michael Faraday, *Experimental Researches in Electricity* (London, 1844), as quoted in Owen Barfield's *History, Guilt, and Habit* (Middleton, Conn., Wesleyan University Press, 1979), p. 90.

6. *The Apocryphal New Testament*, trans. M. R. James (London, Oxford University Press, 1924), p. 258.

7. I will elaborate on the esoteric dimensions of the Gilgamesh epic in Chapter Four.

8. Noam Chomsky, *Language and Mind* (New York, Harcourt Brace, 1968), p. 59.

9. For a sympathetic discussion of the behaviorist's position, with lengthy reports on the work of R. and B. Gardner and David Premack, see Eugene Linden, *Apes, Men, and Language* (New York, Penguin, 1976). For a discussion of the linguistic approach to the battle between British Empiricism and Continental Rationalism, see Noam Chomsky, *Cartesian Linguistics: A Chapter in the History of Rationalist Thought* (New York, Harper & Row, 1966). See also Noam Chomsky, "A Review of B. F. Skinner's *Verbal Behavior*" in *The Structure of Language*, ed. J. A. Fodor and J. J. Katz (Englewood Cliffs, N.J., Prentice-Hall, 1964), pp. 547–579. For recent comments on the debate concerning language ability in primates, see H. S. Terrace, L. A. Petito, R. J. Sanders, T. G. Bever, "Can an Ape Create a Sentence?" *Science*, November 23, 1979, Vol. 206, No. 4421, pp. 891–902. See also Martin Gardner's review, "Monkey Business" in *The New York Review of Books*, March 20, 1980, Vol. XXVII, No. 4, pp. 3–6.

10. Charles F. Hockett and Robert Ascher, "The Human Revolution" in *Man in Adaptation: The Biosocial Background*, ed. Yehudi Cohen (Chicago, Aldine, 1968), p. 225.

11. As quoted in Ernst Fischer, *The Necessity of Art* (London, Pelican, 1963), p. 26.

12. As quoted in Loren Eisely, *The Immense Journey* (New York, Vintage, 1957), p. 83.

13. Richard Leakey with Roger Lewin, *Origins* (New York, Dutton, 1977), p. 136.

14. *Origins and Evolution of Language*, ed. Harnand, Steklis, and Lancaster, New York Academy of Sciences, 1976, Vol. 280.

15. Julian Jaynes, "The Evolution of Language in the Late Pleistocene," in Harnand, Steklis, and Lancaster, op. cit., pp. 312–325.

16. *The Amazing Newborn*, Health Sciences Communications Center, Case Western Reserve University, Cleveland, Ohio.

17. See Eric H. Lenneberg, "The Capacity for Language Acquisition," in *The Structure of Language*, ed. J. A. Fodor and J. J. Katz (Englewood Cliffs, N.J., Prentice-Hall, 1964), pp. 579–604.

18. As quoted in Ernst Fischer, *The Necessity of Art* (London, Pelican, 1963), p. 26.

19. Ashley Montagu, "Toolmaking, Hunting, and the Origin of Language" in Harnand, Steklis, and Lancaster, op. cit., p. 266.

20. Glynn Isaacs, "Stages of Cultural Elaboration in the Pleistocene: Possible Archaeological Indicators of the Development of Language Capabilities" in *Origins and Evolution of Language*, op. cit., p. 283.

21. Noam Chomsky, *Language and Mind* (New York, Harcourt Brace, 1968), p. 83.

22. Alexander Marshack, "Some Implications of the Paleolithic Symbolic Evidence for the Origin of Language" in Harnand, Steklis, and Lancaster, op. cit., p. 309.

23. *The Teachings of Rumi*, trans. and abridged by E. H. Whinfield (New York, Dutton, 1975), pp. 216, 217.

24. *Darwin: A Norton Critical Edition*, ed. Philip Appleman (New York, Norton, 1970), p. 78.

25. See W. B. Yeats, *A Vision* (New York, Macmillan, 1961); see also Henry Corbin, *Spiritual Body and Celestial Earth* (New York, Bollingen, 1977), p. 229.

26. See Marshack, loc. cit., also François Bordes, *A Tale of Two Caves* (New York, Harper & Row, 1972).

27. Rachel Levy, *Gate of Horn* (London, Pelican, 1948).

28. T. S. Kuhn, *The Structure of Scientific Revolutions* (Chicago, University of Chicago Press, 1962), p. 111.

29. Alexander Marshack, *The Roots of Civilization* (New York, McGraw-Hill, 1972), p. 90. See also his "Upper Paleolithic Symbol Systems of the Russian Plain," *Current Anthropology*, Vol. 20. No. 2, June, 1979, 271–309.

30. Martha K. McClintock, "Menstrual Synchrony and Suppression," *Nature*, January 22, 1971, Vol. 229, pp. 171–179.

31. Elise Boulding, *The Underside of History: A View of Women through Time* (Boulder, Col., Westview Press, 1976), p. 106.

32. Robert Briffault, *The Mothers* (New York, Atheneum, 1977), p. 252. See also Penelope Shuttle and Peter Redgrove, *The Wise Wound: Menstruation and Everywoman* (London, Gollancz, 1978).

33. Elise Boulding, op. cit., p. 106.

34. Alexander Marshack, *The Roots of Civilization*, p. 336.

35. Robert Ardrey, *African Genesis* (New York, Delta, 1961), p. 9. In terms of the sociology of knowledge, one can say that one's vision of the origins of human culture affects one's political behavior in contemporary culture. If one believes that weapons and killing are

the foundation of human culture, then one is inclined to accept a split in which technologically superior cultures move "forward," while "inferior" cultures are helped on their way toward extinction. Through tirage a new global scientific elite determines who will survive, and through sociobiology, who should be chosen to survive. If, on the other hand, one believes with Glynn Isaacs that food sharing is the primordial act which made us human, then the global crisis would generate a vision of compassion and sharing. Ardrey's vision becomes the philosophical foundation and justification for a new authoritarian and technologically managed society; Isaacs's vision becomes the basis for a totally different world culture of compassion, as the Buddhists say, "for the suffering of all sentient beings." All of which is to say that we are what we think and that our vision of the origin of human culture is simply another description of our perception of the present condition.

36. Alexander Marshack, op. cit., p. 337.
37. Ibid., p. 217.
38. Robert Bly, "I Came out of My Mother Naked," in *Sleepers Joining Hands* (New York, Harper & Row, 1973), p. 31.
39. W. B. Yeats, *A Vision* (New York, Macmillan, 1961); see also Robert Graves, *The White Goddess* (New York, Farrar Strauss & Giroux, 1975).
40. Alexander Marshack, op. cit., p. 132.
41. Robert Briffault, op. cit., p. 248.
42. *Proceedings of the American Philosophical Society Held at Philadelphia,* Samuel Noah Kramer, 506, obv., col. 11, pp. 5–33.
43. André Leroi-Gourhan, *Treasures of Prehistoric Art* (New York, Abrams, 1967), p. 174.
44. The English edition is entitled *Treasures of Prehistoric Art* (See above, note 43). See also André Leroi-Gourhan, *Les Religions de la Prehistoire* (Paris, Presses Univeritaires de France, 1964).
45. André Leroi-Gourhan, *Treasures of Prehistoric Art*, pp. 173, 174.
46. Ibid., p. 174.
47. Ibid., p. 511.
48. Annette Laming, *Lascaux* (London, Pelican, 1959), p. 94.
49. For a description of the role of a power vision in the life of a shaman, see *Black Elk Speaks*, ed. John G. Neihardt (Lincoln, Neb., University of Nebraska Press, 1961), p. 20.
50. See Paul D. MacLean, M.D., "Man and His Animal Brains" in *Modern Medicine*, Feb. 3, 1964, 95–106; also his *A Triune Concept of the Brain and Behaviour* (Toronto, University of Toronto Press, 1973).
51. Swami Muktunanda, *Guru* (New York, Harper & Row, 1972), pp. 77, 92.
52. Marija Gimbutas, *The Gods and Goddesses of Old Europe: 7000–3500 B.C.* (London, Thames & Hudson, 1974), p. 144.

53. Ibid., pp. 112, 135.
54. Professor Michael Coe, Chairman of the Department of Archaeology, Yale University, personal communication, 1971. Professor Coe indicated that in his view the *Ur-kultur* was that of the Ice Age hunters.
55. See the author's *At the Edge of History*, (New York, Harper & Row, 1971), ch. 7.; also see John Michell, *The View over Atlantis* (London, Sago Press, 1969).
56. Erich Neumann, *The Great Mother* (Princeton, N.J., Princeton University Press, 1972), p. 90.
57. For an attempt to relate exoteric prehistory to the esoteric traditions of Atlantis, see Lewis Spence, *The History of Atlantis* (New York, University Books, 1968).

Chapter Three: Agriculturalization

1. Gail Kennedy, "The Emergency of Modern Man," *Nature*, Vol. 284, March 6, 1980, p. 11.
2. David Clark, "Our Inconstant Sun," *New Scientist*, January 18, 1979, pp. 168–170.
3. Marshall Sahlins, *Stone Age Economics* (Chicago, Aldine, 1972).
4. Kent V. Flannery, "Origins and Effects of Early Domestication in the Near East and Iran" in *Prehistoric Agriculture*, ed. Stuart Struever (New York, Doubleday, 1971), p. 53.
5. Grahame Clark, *Stone Age Hunters* (New York, McGraw-Hill, 1967), p. 94.
6. See Erich Neumann, *The Great Mother* (Princeton, N.J., Princeton University Press, 1963), p. 114.
7. Erich Isaac, "On the Domestication of Cattle" in *Prehistoric Agriculture*, ed. Stuart Struever (New York, Doubleday, 1971), p. 459.
8. Ibid., p. 462.
9. Laurette Sejourné, *Burning Water: Thought and Religion in Ancient Mexico* (New York, Vanguard, 1956).
10. Ashley Montagu, *Coming into Being Among the Australian Aborigines* (London, Routledge, Kegan Paul, 1974), p. 366.
11. Alexander Marshack, *The Roots of Civilization* (New York, McGraw-Hill, 1972), p. 333.
12. Hertha von Dechend and Giorgio de Santillana, *Hamlet's Mill: An Essay on Myth and the Frame of Time* (Boston, Gambit, 1969), pp. 281, 414.
13. Alexander Marshack, op. cit., p. 332.
14. Kathleen Freeman, *Ancilla to the Pre-Socratics* (Cambridge, Mass., Harvard University Press, 1962), p. 19.
15. Erich Neumann, op. cit., p. 276.

16. Alice O. Howell in a discussion of the author's lecture on Çatal Hüyük at Lindisfarne, Southampton, N.Y., 1975.

17. Negative feedback is a response, as with a thermostat, in which a change signals a stopping mechanism, e.g., the shutting off of a boiler; positive feedback is where the system receives no inhibitory signal. See Kent V. Flannery, "Archaeological Systems Theory and Early Mesoamerica," in Struever, op. cit., pp. 81–100.

18. J. Thomas Meyer, "The Origins of Agriculture: an Evaluation of Three Hypotheses" in Struever, op. cit., pp. 101–122. Professor Fred Wendorf at the 1978 meetings in Houston of the American Association for the Advancement of Science claimed to have found evidence of agriculture in Egypt 17,000 years ago. The size of these agricultural communities seems to have been on the scale of a hunting and gathering band, or about twenty people. Professor Wendorf's finds have yet to be corroborated, but if he is correct in his interpretations, then some communities had extended gathering into gardening about 8,000 years earlier than is now thought to be the case. If true, this would contradict Jane Jacobs's thesis that cities came before agriculture. As Wendorf says: "There must have been some other factor that later inspired the change from small communities to larger settlements." See *New Scientist,* January 11, 1979, p. 90.

19. Erich Neumann, "The Central Symbolism of the Feminine," in *The Great Mother,* op. cit.; see also Marija Gimbutas, *Gods and Goddesses of Old Europe* (London, Thames and Hudson, 1974), p. 136.

20. V. Gordon Childe, *Man Makes Himself* (London, Collins, 1966).

21. Marvin Harris, *Cannibals and Kings: The Origins of Cultures* (New York, Random House, 1977).

22. Jane Jacobs, *The Economy of Cities* (New York, Vintage, 1970).

23. For an explanation of this point of view, see the author's "Planetary Mythologies" in *Passages about Earth* (New York, Harper & Row, 1974), pp. 119–149 and "The Return of the Past" in *Darkness and Scattered Light* (New York, Doubleday, 1978), pp. 107–141.

24. Dragoslav Srejovic, *New Discoveries at Lepenski Vir* (London, Thames & Hudson, 1972), p. 129.

25. Julian Jaynes, *The Origins of Consciousness in the Breakdown of the Bicameral Mind* (Boston, Houghton Mifflin, 1976).

26. Dexter Perkins, Jr. and Patricia Daly, "The Beginning of Food Production in the Near East," in *The Old World: Early Man to the Development of Agriculture,* ed. Robert Stigler (New York, St. Martin's, 1974), p. 90.

27. V. Gordon Childe, op. cit., p. 82.

28. James Mellaart, *Çatal Hüyük* (London, Thames & Hudson, 1967), p. 22.

29. Ibid., p. 226.

30. J. J. Bachoven, *Myth, Religion, and Mother Right* (Princeton, N.J.,

Princeton University Press, 1967), p. 196. Although the
anthropologist Marvin Harris regards the theory of Bachoven to be
a corpse exhumed from the nineteenth century by the twentieth-
century feminists, the liveliness of Bachoven's insights concerning
the relationships between architecture and the female body can be
seen if one compares the earliest forms of humanly created sacred
space. Colin Renfrew has called the megalithic structures on Malta
"The World's First Stone Temples." (See his *Before Civilization*, New
York, Knopf, 1973, p. 147.) If we look at Figure 21 below, we see
that the Maltese temple is an outline of the old Paleolithic obese
Great Goddess. Small clay figurines of the Goddess in her obese
form have been found in Malta. Now, a similar form is also found
in the case of the West Kennet long barrow in England (Figure 22),
and an equally feminine form is found on the island of Skara Brae
(Figure 23). If we also compare the Medamud from ancient Egypt
(Figure 24) with Bryn Celli Ddu in Wales (Figure 25), we can see
that the tomb is the womb, and that in death and ritual all things
return to the body of the Great Mother. Before the rise of
charismatic military chieftans and kings, with their monuments to
the individuated ego, all burial was collective in Megalithic Western
Europe, for all beings are equally the children of the Great Mother.
Now if we stop to consider the vision of the Great Mother in Çatal
Hüyük, with the animals emerging from her womb, and see the

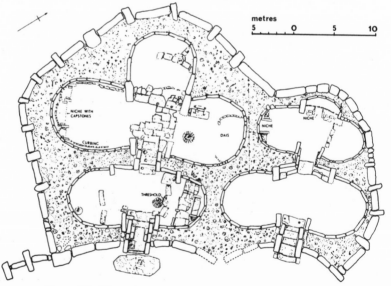

Figure 21. Plan of two stone temples, the Ggantija, from Malta.

0   15ft

*Figure 22. The
West Kennet long
barrow, England.*

Figure 23. House from Skara Brae.

other doorways to the womb in Egypt, Malta, Wales, and the
Hebrides, we can see local approaches to the universal religion of
the Great Goddess. However, archaeologists refuse to see this, for
their form of handling data tends to encourage a peculiar form of
academic aphasia. If one of these archaeologists were to compare a
wooden Quaker meeting house from New England and a suburban
drive-in Baptist church from Texas with a Gothic cathedral, he
would refuse to accept the fact that they were all expressions of the
single universal religion of Christianity.

Archaeologists today separate Çatal Hüyük from Malta, Malta
from Egypt, and all of them from Britain. If one wishes to gain a
more comprehensive understanding, one has to pass over the work
of the narrow specialists to study the works of the art historians like
Keith Critchlow (see his *Time Stands Still: New Light on Megalithic
Science,* London, Gordon Fraser, 1979) and Michael Dames's *The
Silbury Treasure* and *The Avebury Cycle* (London, Thames & Hudson,
1976 and 1977).

The reader should be warned that as he crosses into the field of
the prehistory of Megalithic Western Europe, he is likely to get
caught in the cross-fire of a civil war raging between the
Establishment in the university departments of archaeology and the
challengers outside the specializations. On the side of the
Establishment are Glyn Daniel, R.J.C. Atkinson, and Aubrey Burl;
on the side of the challengers are Alexander Thom, Keith
Critchlow, Michael Dames, and John Michell.

Once again, the sociology of knowledge approach can help us to
see the unconscious assumptions of the combatants in a new light.

VIRGIN SOIL

Figure 24. The Medamud Temple, Egypt.

The Establishment assumes that all civilized people live in cities, and that savages do not, and that if there is any evidence of culture at a high level, it has to come from the cities of the Near East. They make fun of Thom's "Einstein in sheepskin" and see the life of ancient Avebury in a Hobbsian way as "nasty, brutish, and short." They forget that ancient Ireland transformed the emergence of Western Europe in the Dark Ages, and that ancient Ireland did not store knowledge in cities, but in rural monasteries. Something like this pattern of nonurban culture may have existed in the mystery schools of the prehistoric astronomers of the megaliths. By contrast, Thom, Dames, Critchlow, and Michell can appreciate the transmission of knowledge in other ways than of Sumer or Egypt.

Figure 25. Bryn Celli Ddu, Wales.

Critchlow has shown the existence of the Platonic solids a millennium before Plato's *Timaeus*, and Thom has shown the Pythagorean theorem a millennium before Pythagoras, but there is simply no way the orthodox archaeologists can deal with such a scientific revolution. Once again, as T. S. Kuhn has shown, the challengers outside a field are the ones who create the scientific revolutions. The challengers can conceive of an advanced, sacred, decentralized, steady-state culture in the past, perhaps because it is their hoped-for culture of the future. Thus, we can see that the battle over the past is, once again, a battle over the future of human culture.

If one wishes to understand how the universal religion of the Great Goddess survived in Western Europe, and how it did not seem to take the turn experienced by ancient Sumer, then one would be well advised to consider the work of Dames and Critchlow. It would seem that in Avebury, Stonehenge, and Malta the mystery cult of menstruation/mensuration reached its most consummate development.

31. James Mellaart, *Earliest Civilizations of the Near East* (New York, McGraw-Hill, 1965), p. 101.
32. Charles F. Hockett and Robert Ascher, "The Human Revolution" in *Man in Adaptation*, ed. Yehudi Cohen (Chicago, Aldine, 1968), p. 222.
33. James Mellaart, *Çatal Hüyük*, p. 184. For a critique of Mellaart, see Ian Todd, *Çatal Hüyük in Perspective* (Menlo Park, Calif., Cummings Publishers, 1976).
34. Marvin Harris, op. cit., p. 58.
35. Elizabeth Davis, *The First Sex* (New York, Putnam, 1971), p. 86.
36. J. M. Synge, *The Aran Islands and Other Writings* (New York, Vintage, 1962), p. 61.
37. A.F.C. Wallace, "Revitalization Movements," *American Anthropologist*, LVIII (April 1956), pp. 264–81.
38. For a beautiful description of the religious mystique of the hunt, see William Faulkner, "The Bear" in *Go Down Moses* (New York, Modern Library, 1940).
39. Leon Festinger et al., *When Prophecy Fails* (New York, Harper & Row, 1964).
40. Robert Redfield, *The Primitive World and Its Transformations* (Ithaca, N.Y., Cornell University Press, 1956).
41. Elise Boulding, *The Underside of History: A View of Women through Time* (Boulder, Col., Westview Press, 1976), p. 146.
42. James Mellaart, *Earliest Civilizations of the Near East*, p. 112.
43. Jane Jacobs, op. cit., p. 38.
44. George Thomson, *Aeschylus and Athens* (London, Lawrence and Wishart, 1973), p. 29; see also his "Matriarchy" in *The Prehistoric*

Aegean: Studies in Ancient Greek Society (London, Lawrence and Wishart, 1978), pp. 149–294.

45. C. S. Lewis, *Surprised by Joy* (London, Fontana, 1959), p. 13.

Chapter Four: Civilization and Alienation in Ancient Sumer

1. James Mellaart, "The Late Chalcolithic Period" in *The Cambridge Ancient History*, Vol. I. *Prolegomena and Prehistory* (Cambridge, Cambridge University Press, 1970), p. 325.
2. James Mellaart, "The Halaf Culture," op. cit., p. 281. See also his *The Neolithic of the Near East* (New York, Scribners, 1975), p. 126.
3. James Mellaart, "The Earliest Settlements in Western Asia from the Ninth Millennium to the End of the Fifth Millennium B.C." in *The Cambridge Ancient History*, Vol. I., Part I, p. 289.
4. Samuel Noah Kramer, *The Sumerians, Their History, Culture, and Character* (Chicago, University of Chicago Press, 1963), p. 179.
5. Thorkild Jacobsen, *The Treasures of Darkness: A History of Mesopotamian Religion* (New Haven, Yale University Press, 1976), p. 112.
6. Samuel Noah Kramer, *The Sumerians*, p. 180.
7. Ibid., p. 182.
8. Ibid.
9. Ibid., p. 183.
10. Thorkild Jacobsen, op. cit., p. 36.
11. Samuel Noah Kramer, *Proceedings of the Philosophical Association of Philadelphia*, 506, obv., col. ii, pp. 5–33. See also Thorkild Jacobsen, op. cit., p. 45.
12. Thorkild Jacobsen, op. cit., p. 38.
13. Samuel Noah Kramer, *Proceedings of the Philosophical Association of Philadelphia*, pp. 508–509, 1–11.
14. Samuel Noah Kramer, op. cit., *Paps*, 507, obv., col. iii, 9–36.
15. Thorkild Jacobsen, op. cit., p. 62.
16. Ibid., p. 62.
17. "Plato could still speak the language of archaic myth. He made myth consonant with his thought, as he built the first modern philosophy. He could speak it, because he was a Pythagorean, and myth was their technical language." As quoted in Hertha von Dechend's syllabus for her course in "Ancient Cosmology" given at the Massachusetts Institute of Technology, 1966–67. At that time, I was a colleague of Professor von Dechend in the Department of Humanities and had occasion to discuss her theories with her.
18. Hertha von Dechend and Giorgio de Santillana, *Hamlet's Mill: An Essay on Myth and the Frame of Time* (Boston, Gambit, 1969), p. 290. Professor de Santillana worked on editing von Dechend when he was sick and near death, and so this book is not the best expression

of their theories. Encyclopedic, but rambling, it is often as chaotic as it is cranky. This weakness, however, should not mislead the reader. The work is very important in seeking to recover the astronomical and cosmological dimensions of mythic narratives.

19. G. S. Kirk, *Myth, Its Meaning and Functions in Ancient and Other Cultures* (Berkeley, University of California Press, 1970), p. 111.
20. Samuel Noah Kramer, *The Sumerians*, p. 153.
21. Ibid.
22. See Footnote 22 in the Prologue.
23. From "Two Songs from a Play," in *The Collected Poems of W. B. Yeats* (New York, Macmillan, 1957), p. 210.
24. Samuel Noah Kramer, *The Sumerians*, p. 197.
25. Thorkild Jacobsen, op. cit., p. 212.
26. Samuel Noah Kramer, *The Sumerians*, p. 200.
27. Ibid., p. 203.
28. Thorkild Jacobsen, op. cit., p. 195.
29. Alexander Heidel, *The Gilgamesh Epic and Old Testament Parallels*, (Chicago, University of Chicago Press, 1963), p. 16. For a version aimed at the general reader, see N. K. Sandars, *The Epic of Gilgamesh* (London, Penguin, 1960).
30. "The Dating of Travertine from the Bilzingsleben Archaeological Site," R. S. Harmon, J. Glazek, K. Nowak, *Nature*, Vol. 284, March 13, 1980, p. 134.
31. Claude Lévi-Strauss, *The Raw and the Cooked* (New York, Harper & Row, 1969).
32. Alexander Heidel; see note 29.
33. In order to maintain his theory that consciousness arose in the sixth century B.C., Prof. Julian Jaynes has to change the date of the origin of the Gilgamesh epic: "There is certainly no warrant to suppose, as have some popularizers of the epic, that the seventh century B.C. rendering of the story of Gilgamesh goes back to the Old Babylonian era." See Julian Jaynes, *The Origin of Consciousness in the Breakdown of the Bicameral Mind* (Boston, Houghton Mifflin, 1976), p. 252. Professor Jaynes begins his study with an interesting analysis of memory and introspection and notices that when we remember ourselves swimming in the sea we have a mental image of ourselves in the sea that we never saw. If Professor Jaynes had extended his studies of introspection into zazen or yogic forms of meditation, he would understand that the ego is just such a construction that is extended over the gaps in time from moment to moment. In fact, Professor Jaynes confuses the ego with consciousness. There is a relationship between the rise of the ego and the rise of civilization, but consciousness decidedly does not begin in the sixth century B.C. The reductionist tendencies and impulses of Jaynes's approach tend to turn history into a Procrustean Bed; the body is mangled to fit the theory.

34. Robert Graves and Raphael Patai, *Hebrew Myths: The Book of Genesis* (New York, McGraw-Hill, 1966), p. 113.
35. St. Augustine interpreted the square ark of Noah as a symbol of Christ and his church; see *The City of God* (Baltimore, Penguin, 1972), p. 643. Thus we can see that through gematria and Biblical exegesis of traditional materials, the esoteric vision of the ark survived into classical times.
36. "Lamentation for the Destruction of Ur" as quoted in Thorkild Jacobsen, pp. 89, 90.
37. R. A. Crossland, "Immigrants from the North" in *The Cambridge Ancient History*, Vol. I, Part 2, (Cambridge, Cambridge University Press, 1971), pp. 861, 874.
38. Erich Neumann, *The Origins and History of Consciousness* (Princeton, N.J., Princeton University Press, 1970).
39. Helmut Wilhelm, *Eight Lectures on the I Ching* (New York, Harper & Row, 1964), p. 16.

Chapter Five: Civilization and Initiation in Ancient Egypt

1. R. T. Rundle Clark, *Myth and Symbol in Ancient Egypt* (London, Thames & Hudson, 1978), p. 98.
2. Eberhard Otto, *Ancient Egyptian Art: The Cults of Osiris and Amon* (New York, Abrams, n.d.), p. 60. For the complete text and Plutarch's commentary, see "On Isis and Osiris" in *Plutarch's Morals*, Trans. C. W. King (London, Bell, 1908), pp. 1–71.
3. E. A. Wallis Budge, *Osiris and the Egyptian Resurrection* (New York, Dover Reprints, 1973), p. 384.
4. For an esoteric interpretation of the Isis and Osiris myth, one that will make mine seem quite exoteric, see Rudolph Steiner's *Egyptian Myths and Mysteries* (New York, Anthroposophic Press, 1971).
5. Hertha von Dechend, syllabus for a course in ancient cosmology, Massachusetts Institute of Technology, Spring 1966, pp. 38, 40.
6. Henri Frankfort et. al., *Before Philosophy* (Chicago, University of Chicago Press, 1946). F. M. Cornford, *From Religion to Philosophy* (New York, Harper & Row, 1957).
7. There is a group in London called Research into Lost Knowledge Organization. Scholars like Anne Macauley, John Michell, and Keith Critchlow have written and lectured about the Pythagorean tradition. A list of publications is available from the society at 36 College Court, Hammersmith, London, W6, England. In New York Professor Ernest Maclain has worked to reconstruct the Pythagorean tradition in his two books, *The Myth of Invariance* (New York, Nicholas Hays, 1977) and *The Pythagorean Plato* (New York, Nicholas Hays, 1978).

8. See the author's essay on the return of hieroglyphic thought, "The Future of Knowledge" in *Darkness and Scattered Light* (New York, Doubleday, 1978), p. 174.
9. In R. T. Rundle Clark, op. cit., p. 266.
10. All the following quotations from Plutarch are from Eberhard Otto's translation in *Egyptian Art: The Cults of Osiris and Amon* (New York, Abrams, n.d.), p. 62.
11. The significance of the number seventy-two was pointed out to me by my colleague at Lindisfarne, Christopher Bamford. Mr. Bamford also notes that in the Irish *Book of Invasions* the number of languages created after the fall of the tower of Babel is said to be seventy-two. In some of the Cabbalistic material, seventy-two is also said to be the numbers of the names of God. Mr. Bamford is currently at work on a book on the Western esoteric tradition.
12. See Erich Neumann, *The Origins and History of Consciousness* (Princeton, N.J., Princeton University Press, 1954), p. 220.
13. E. A. Wallis Budge, *Osiris and the Egyptian Resurrection* (New York, Dover Reprints, 1973), Vol. II., p. 134.
14. Henri Frankfort, *Kingship and the Gods* (Chicago, University of Chicago Press, 1948), p. 61.
15. In a sad and tragic battle both sides are wrong; to get a sense of the crankiness on both sides of the battle lines of Egyptian archaeology, see John Anthony West's popularization of the work of R. A. Schwaller de Lubicz, *The Serpent in the Sky* (New York, Harper & Row, 1979), and Peter Green's attack on all the new books on ancient Egypt, "Tut-Tut-Tut" in *The New York Review of Books*, Vol. XXVI, No. 15, October 11, 1979, pp. 19–32.
16. For a description of a modern artist's sensitivity about this ancient knowledge, see W. B. Yeats, *A Vision* (New York, Macmillan, 1956), p. 219.
17. E. A. Wallis Budge, *Osiris and the Egyptian Resurrection*, Vol. I., pp. 48, 52.
18. For a discussion of how esoteric physiology relates to the architecture of the central nervous system and the architecture of the Egyptian temple, see R. A. Schwaller de Lubicz, *The Temple in Man*, trans. D. and R. Lawlor (Boston, Autumn Press, 1977).
19. R. T. Rundle Clark, op. cit., p. 167.
20. See Gopi Krishna, *Kundalini: The Evolutionary Energy in Man* (Berkeley, Shambala, 1971); also his *The Secret of Yoga* (New York, Harper & Row, 1972).
21. See Robert Thurman, "The Politics of Enlightenment," *Lindisfarne Letter 8*, Winter 1979, pp. 20–33.
22. For a scholarly discussion of landscape angels in the Islamic tradition, see Henry Corbin's "Visionary Geography" and "Geosophy and the Feminine Angels of Earth" in *Spiritual Body and Celestial Earth* (Princeton, N.J., Princeton University Press, 1977).

23. See Figure 18, p. 214 in Henri Frankfort, *Kingship and the Gods* (Chicago, University of Chicago Press, 1948).
24. R. T. Rundle Clark, op. cit., p. 106.
25. Ibid., p. 122.
26. Alexander Marshack, *The Roots of Civilization* (New York, McGraw-Hill, 1971), pp. 330, 332.
27. Erich Neumann, *The Great Mother* (Princeton, N.J., Princeton University Press, 1955), p. 276.
28. R. T. Rundle Clark, op. cit., p. 122.
29. Erich Neumann, *The Origins and History of Consciousness* (Princeton, N.J., Princeton University Press, 1954), p. 67.
30. R. T. Rundle Clark, op. cit., p. 199.
31. Ibid., p. 255.

Epilogue: The Time Falling Bodies Take to Light

1. "The Gospel of Thomas," trans. T. O. Lambdin, in *The Nag Hammadi in English*, ed. James Robinson (New York, Harper & Row, 1977), p. 130.
2. Ibid., p. 121.
3. St. Paul, Corinthians, I, 7:9.
4. Peter sees the empty tomb in the physical sense of "looking," but John sees the tomb in the sense of "knowing." *Theorein* is the verb used for Peter, *idein* for John in verse 8. See Raymond Brown's *The Gospel of John, Anchor Bible*, Vol. 29A (New York, Doubleday, 1970), p. 986.
5. See "Jesus' Round Dance and Crucifixion" by Max Pulver in *The Mysteries, Papers from the Eranos Yearbooks* (New York, Bollingen Books, 1955), p. 181.
6. Ibid., p. 181.
7. A. E. (George William Russell), *The Avatars* (London, Macmillan, 1929).

INDEX

Page numbers in italics refer to material in illustrations.